Ǫ da gaho dę:s

McGill-Queen's Indigenous and Northern Studies
(In memory of Bruce G. Trigger)
JOHN BORROWS, SARAH CARTER, AND ARTHUR J. RAY, EDITORS

The McGill-Queen's Indigenous and Northern Studies series publishes books about Indigenous peoples in all parts of the northern world. It includes original scholarship on their histories, archaeology, laws, cultures, governance, and traditions. Works in the series also explore the history and geography of the North, where travel, the natural environment, and the relationship to land continue to shape life in particular and important ways. Its mandate is to advance understanding of the political, legal, and social relations between Indigenous and non-Indigenous peoples, of the contemporary issues that Indigenous peoples face as a result of environmental and economic change, and of social justice, including the work of reconciliation in Canada. To provide a global perspective, the series welcomes books on regions and communities from across the Arctic and Subarctic circumpolar zones.

1 When the Whalers Were Up North
Inuit Memories from the Eastern Arctic
Dorothy Harley Eber

2 The Challenge of Arctic Shipping
Science, Environmental Assessment, and Human Values
Edited by David L. VanderZwaag and Cynthia Lamson

3 Lost Harvests
Prairie Indian Reserve Farmers and Government Policy
Sarah Carter

4 Native Liberty, Crown Sovereignty
The Existing Aboriginal Right of Self-Government in Canada
Bruce Clark

5 Unravelling the Franklin Mystery
Inuit Testimony
David C. Woodman

6 Otter Skins, Boston Ships, and China Goods
The Maritime Fur Trade of the Northwest Coast, 1785–1841
James R. Gibson

7 From Wooden Ploughs to Welfare
The Story of the Western Reserves
Helen Buckley

8 In Business for Ourselves
Northern Entrepreneurs
Wanda A. Wuttunee

9 For an Amerindian Autohistory
An Essay on the Foundations of a Social Ethic
Georges E. Sioui

10 Strangers Among Us
David Woodman

11 When the North Was Red
Aboriginal Education in Soviet Siberia
Dennis A. Bartels and Alice L. Bartels

12 From Talking Chiefs to a Native Corporate Elite
The Birth of Class and Nationalism among Canadian Inuit
Marybelle Mitchell

13 Cold Comfort
My Love Affair with the Arctic
Graham W. Rowley

14 The True Spirit and Original Intent of Treaty 7
Treaty 7 Elders and Tribal Council with Walter Hildebrandt, Dorothy First Rider, and Sarah Carter

15 This Distant and Unsurveyed Country
A Woman's Winter at Baffin Island, 1857–1858
W. Gillies Ross

16 Images of Justice
Dorothy Harley Eber

17 Capturing Women
The Manipulation of Cultural Imagery in Canada's Prairie West
Sarah Carter

18 Social and Environmental Impacts of the James Bay Hydroelectric Project
Edited by James F. Hornig

19 Saqiyuq
Stories from the Lives of Three Inuit Women
Nancy Wachowich in collaboration with Apphia Agalakti Awa, Rhoda Kaukjak Katsak, and Sandra Pikujak Katsak

20 Justice in Paradise
Bruce Clark

21 Aboriginal Rights and Self-Government
The Canadian and Mexican Experience in North American Perspective
Edited by Curtis Cook and Juan D. Lindau

22 Harvest of Souls
The Jesuit Missions and Colonialism in North America, 1632–1650
Carole Blackburn

23 Bounty and Benevolence
A History of Saskatchewan Treaties
Arthur J. Ray, Jim Miller, and Frank Tough

24 The People of Denendeh
Ethnohistory of the Indians of Canada's Northwest Territories
June Helm

25 The *Marshall* Decision and Native Rights
Ken Coates

26 The Flying Tiger
Women Shamans and Storytellers of the Amur
Kira Van Deusen

27 Alone in Silence
European Women in the Canadian North before 1940
Barbara E. Kelcey

28 The Arctic Voyages of Martin Frobisher
An Elizabethan Adventure
Robert McGhee

29 Northern Experience and the Myths of Canadian Culture
Renée Hulan

30 The White Man's Gonna Getcha
The Colonial Challenge to the Crees in Quebec

31 Toby Morantz
The Heavens Are Changing
Nineteenth-Century Protestant Missions and Tsimshian Christianity
Susan Neylan

32 Arctic Migrants/Arctic Villagers
The Transformation of Inuit Settlement in the Central Arctic
David Damas

33 Arctic Justice
On Trial for Murder – Pond Inlet, 1923
Shelagh D. Grant

34 The American Empire and the Fourth World
Anthony J. Hall

35 Eighteenth-Century Naturalists of Hudson Bay
Stuart Houston, Tim Ball, and Mary Houston

36 Uqalurait
An Oral History of Nunavut
Compiled and edited by John Bennett and Susan Rowley

37 Living Rhythms
Lessons in Aboriginal Economic Resilience and Vision
Wanda Wuttunee

38 The Making of an Explorer
George Hubert Wilkins and the Canadian Arctic Expedition, 1913–1916
Stuart E. Jenness

39 Chee Chee
A Study of Aboriginal Suicide
Alvin Evans

40 Strange Things Done
Murder in Yukon History
Ken S. Coates and William R. Morrison

41 Healing through Art
Ritualized Space and Cree Identity
Nadia Ferrara

42 Coyote and Raven Go Canoeing
Coming Home to the Village
Peter Cole

43 Something New in the Air
The Story of First Peoples Television Broadcasting in Canada
Lorna Roth

44 Listening to Old Woman Speak
Natives and Alternatives in Canadian Literature
Laura Smyth Groening

45 Robert and Francis Flaherty
A Documentary Life, 1883–1922
Robert J. Christopher

46 Talking in Context
Language and Identity in Kwakwaka'wakw Society
Anne Marie Goodfellow

47 Tecumseh's Bones
Guy St-Denis

48 Constructing Colonial Discourse
Captain Cook at Nootka Sound
Noel Elizabeth Currie

49 The Hollow Tree
Fighting Addiction with Traditional Healing
Herb Nabigon

50 The Return of Caribou to Ungava
A.T. Bergerud, Stuart Luttich, and Lodewijk Camps

51 Firekeepers of the Twenty-First Century
First Nations Women Chiefs
Cora J. Voyageur

52 Isuma
Inuit Video Art
Michael Robert Evans

53 Outside Looking In
Viewing First Nations Peoples in Canadian Dramatic Television Series
Mary Jane Miller

54 Kiviuq
An Inuit Hero and His Siberian Cousins
Kira Van Deusen

55 Native Peoples and Water Rights
Irrigation, Dams, and the Law in Western Canada
Kenichi Matsui

56 The Rediscovered Self
Indigenous Identity and Cultural Justice
Ronald Niezen

57 As affecting the fate of my absent husband
Selected Letters of Lady Franklin Concerning the Search for the Lost Franklin Expedition, 1848–1860
Edited by Erika Behrisch Elce

58 The Language of the Inuit
Syntax, Semantics, and Society in the Arctic
Louis-Jacques Dorais

59 Inuit Shamanism and Christianity
Transitions and Transformations in the Twentieth Century
Frédéric B. Laugrand and Jarich G. Oosten

60 No Place for Fairness
Indigenous Land Rights and Policy in the Bear Island Case and Beyond
David T. McNab

61 Aleut Identities
Tradition and Modernity in an Indigenous Fishery
Katherine L. Reedy-Maschner

62 Earth into Property
Aboriginal History and the Making of Global Capitalism
Anthony J. Hall

63 Collections and Objections
Aboriginal Material Culture in Southern Ontario, 1791–1914
Michelle A. Hamilton

64 These Mysterious People
Shaping History and Archaeology in a Northwest Coast Community, Second Edition
Susan Roy

65 Telling It to the Judge
Taking Native History to Court
Arthur J. Ray

66 Aboriginal Music in Contemporary Canada
Echoes and Exchanges
Edited by Anna Hoefnagels and Beverley Diamond

67 In Twilight and in Dawn
A Biography of Diamond Jenness
Barnett Richling

68 Women's Work, Women's Art
Nineteenth-Century Northern Athapaskan Clothing
Judy Thompson

69 Warriors of the Plains
The Arts of Plains Indian Warfare
Max Carocci

70 Reclaiming Indigenous Planning
Edited by Ryan Walker, Ted Jojola, and David Natcher

71 Setting All the Captives Free
Capture, Adjustment, and Recollection in Allegheny Country
Ian K. Steele

72 Before Ontario
The Archaeology of a Province
Edited by Marit K. Munson and Susan M. Jamieson

73 Becoming Inummarik
Men's Lives in an Inuit Community
Peter Collings

74 Ancient Pathways, Ancestral Knowledge
Ethnobotany and Ecological Wisdom of Indigenous Peoples of Northwestern North America
Nancy J. Turner

75 Our Ice Is Vanishing/Sikuvut Nunguliqtuq
A History of Inuit, Newcomers, and Climate Change
Shelley Wright

76 Maps and Memes
Redrawing Culture, Place, and Identity in Indigenous Communities
Gwilym Lucas Eades

77 Encounters
An Anthropological History of Southeastern Labrador
John C. Kennedy

78 Keeping Promises
The Royal Proclamation of 1763, Aboriginal Rights, and Treaties in Canada
Edited by Terry Fenge and Jim Aldridge

79 Together We Survive
Ethnographic Intuitions, Friendships, and Conversations
Edited by John S. Long and Jennifer S.H. Brown

80 Canada's Residential Schools: The History, Part 1, Origins to 1939
The Final Report of the Truth and Reconciliation Commission of Canada, Volume 1

81 Canada's Residential Schools: The History, Part 2, 1939 to 2000
The Final Report of the Truth and Reconciliation Commission of Canada, Volume 1

82 Canada's Residential Schools: The Inuit and Northern Experience
The Final Report of the Truth and Reconciliation Commission of Canada, Volume 2

83 Canada's Residential Schools: The Métis Experience
The Final Report of the Truth and Reconciliation Commission of Canada, Volume 3

84 Canada's Residential Schools: Missing Children and Unmarked Burials
The Final Report of the Truth and Reconciliation Commission of Canada, Volume 4

85 Canada's Residential Schools: The Legacy
The Final Report of the Truth and Reconciliation Commission of Canada, Volume 5

86 Canada's Residential Schools: Reconciliation
The Final Report of the Truth and Reconciliation Commission of Canada, Volume 6

87 Aboriginal Rights Claims and the Making and Remaking of History
Arthur J. Ray

88 Abenaki Daring
The Life and Writings of Noel Annance, 1792–1869
Jean Barman

89 Trickster Chases the Tale of Education
Sylvia Moore

90 Secwepemc People, Land, and Laws
Yerí7 re Stsqeys-kucw
Marianne Ignace and Ronald E. Ignace

91 Travellers through Empire
Indigenous Voyages from Early Canada
Cecilia Morgan

92 Studying Arctic Fields
Cultures, Practices, and Environmental Sciences
Richard C. Powell

93 Iroquois in the West
Jean Barman

94 Leading from Between
Indigenous Participation and Leadership in the Public Service
Catherine Althaus and Ciaran O'Faircheallaigh

95 Against the Current and Into the Light
Performing History and Land in Coast Salish Territories and Vancouver's Stanley Park
Selena Couture

96 Plants, People, and Places
The Roles of Ethnobotany and Ethnoecology in Indigenous Peoples' Land Rights in Canada and Beyond
Edited by Nancy J. Turner

97 Fighting for a Hand to Hold
Confronting Medical Colonialism against Indigenous Children in Canada
Samir Shaheen-Hussain

98 Forty Narratives in the Wyandot Language
John L. Steckley

99 Uumajursiutik unaatuinnamut / Hunter with Harpoon / Chasseur au harpon
Markoosie Patsauq
Edited and translated by Valerie Henitiuk and Marc-Antoine Mahieu

100 Language, Citizenship, and Sámi Education in the Nordic North, 1900–1940
Otso Kortekangas

101 Daughters of Aataentsic
Life Stories from Seven Generations
Kathryn Magee Labelle in collaboration with the We^{n}dat/Wa^{n}dat Women's Advisory Council

102 Aki-wayn-zih
A Person as Worthy as the Earth
Eli Baxter

103 Atiqput
Inuit Oral History and Project Naming
Edited by Carol Payne, Beth Greenhorn, Deborah Kigjugalik Webster, and Christina Williamson

104 Ǫ da gaho dę:s
Reflecting on Our Journeys
Gae Ho Hwako (Norma Jacobs) and the Circles of Ǫ da gaho dę:s
Edited by Timothy B. Leduc

Ǫ da gaho dę̱:s
Reflecting on Our Journeys

Gae Ho Hwako (Norma Jacobs)

and the

Circles of Ǫ da gaho dę̱:s

Edited by

TIMOTHY B. LEDUC

McGill-Queen's University Press
Montreal & Kingston • London • Chicago

ISBN 978-0-2280-1197-2 (cloth)
ISBN 978-0-2280-2141-4 (paper)
ISBN 978-0-2280-1294-8 (ePDF)
ISBN 978-0-2280-1295-5 (ePUB)

Legal deposit third quarter 2022
Bibliothèque nationale du Québec
Reprinted 2023
First paperback edition 2024

Printed in Canada on acid-free paper that is 100% ancient forest free (100% post-consumer recycled), processed chlorine free

This book has been published with the help of a grant from the Canadian Federation for the Humanities and Social Sciences, through the Awards to Scholarly Publications Program, using funds provided by the Social Sciences and Humanities Research Council of Canada.

Funded by the Government of Canada | Financé par le gouvernement du Canada | Canada | Canada Council for the Arts | Conseil des arts du Canada

We acknowledge the support of the Canada Council for the Arts.
Nous remercions le Conseil des arts du Canada de son soutien.

McGill-Queen's University Press in Montreal is on land which long served as a site of meeting and exchange amongst Indigenous Peoples, including the Haudenosaunee and Anishinabeg nations. In Kingston it is situated on the territory of the Haudenosaunee and Anishinaabek. We acknowledge and thank the diverse Indigenous Peoples whose footsteps have marked these territories on which peoples of the world now gather.

Library and Archives Canada Cataloguing in Publication

Title: Ǫ da gaho de:s : reflecting on our journeys / Gae Ho Hwako (Norma Jacobs) and the Circles of Ǫ da gaho de:s ; edited by Timothy B. Leduc.
Other titles: Reflecting on our journeys
Names: Gae Ho Hwako, author. | Leduc, Timothy B., 1970- editor.
Series: McGill-Queen's indigenous and northern series ; 104.
Description: Series statement: McGill-Queen's Indigenous and Northern studies ; 104 | Not all diacritics in title could be transcribed. | Includes bibliographical references and index.
Identifiers: Canadiana 20230567231 | ISBN 9780228021414 (softcover)
Subjects: CSH: First Nations. | CSH: First Nations—Social life and customs. | CSH: First Nations—Social life and customs—Study and teaching. | LCSH: Canada—Ethnic relations. | LCSH: Canada—Ethnic relations—Study and teaching. | LCSH: Reconciliation—Canada. | LCSH: Knowledge, Theory of. | CSH: First Nations Elders.
Classification: LCC E78.C2 G32 2024 | DDC 305.897/071—dc23

Contents

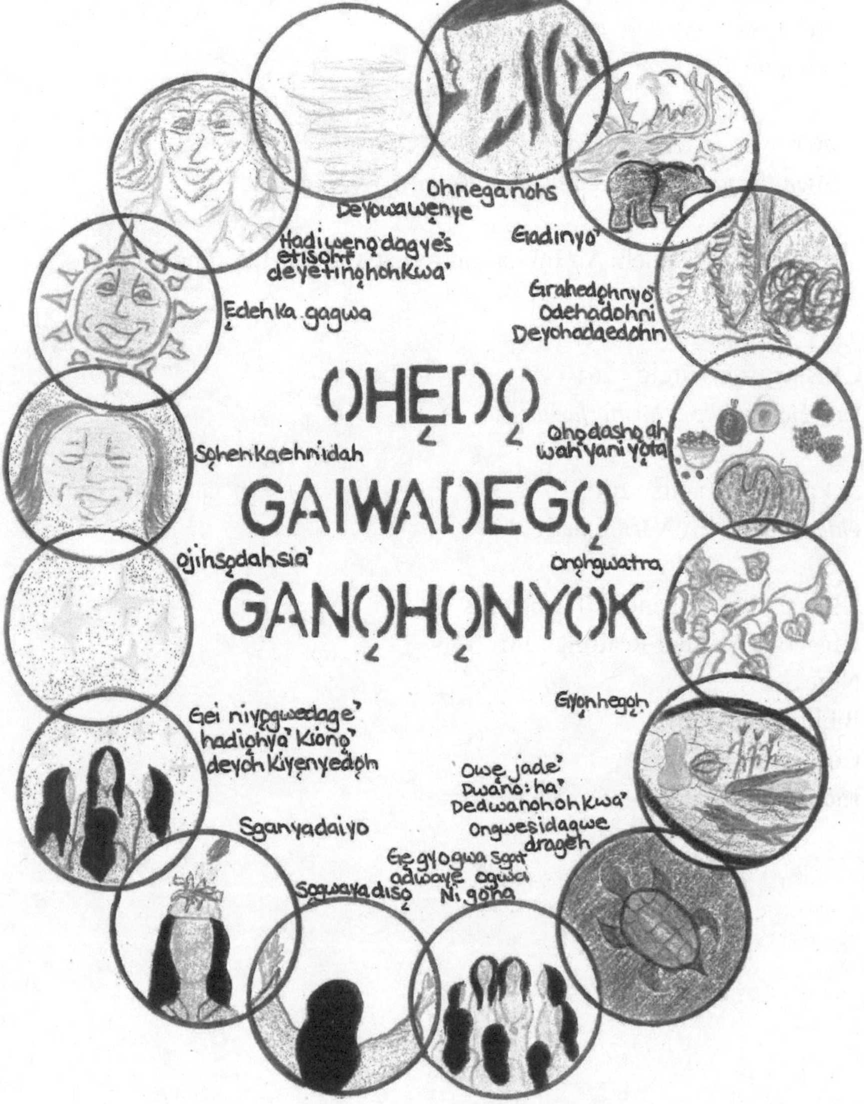

The Ganǫhǫnyǫhk (Thanksgiving Address) in the Cayuga Language.
Drawing by Gae Ho Hwako (Norma Jacobs).

Ganǫhǫnyǫhk (Thanksgiving Address, or "Words before All Else")

Gae Ho Hwako (Norma Jacobs)

Ge' gyo kwa (The People)

We the people give thanks for our existence and for the people whom we pass on the paths of our journey. We need each other for our well-being as we share conversation, knowledge, laughter, and love. By sharing our dreams, thoughts, and visions, we honour and acknowledge the gifts that we each bring, as they are important to the development of ourselves, our families, our clans, our nations, our communities, and the wholeness of life. The prayers that we share are for our health and well-being. We remember our journeys, stories, and songs, and we recognize that we are those sacred spiritual beings who descended from the Sky World to work on this spiritual journey with E tinoha ongwesidage'dra gwe' (our Mother Earth). We say *nya weh* (thank you) for the great visioning of our Creator. Let it be that way in our minds!

E tinoha ongwesidage'dra gwe' (Our Mother Earth)

She is a life giver, as all life begins with her! She teaches us about values, boundaries, forgiveness, encouragement, patience, love, laughter, strength, and *awehaode'* (soft, kind, embracing words). Her *awehaode'* embrace us with those winds that keep us strong in ourselves, ever supporting us with provisions of comfort. She is our foundation; we walk upon her body every day, ever so gently massaging her so that she can provide us with the luxuries of life. E tinoha ongwesidage'dra gwe' connects all the roots of the plants, trees, flowers, and medicines. All the roots are interwoven so that they can supply their energy to everything. We never go without the nurturance of her love, which is our very existence. We say *nya weh* to our Mother Earth for all that she provides. Let it be that way in our minds!

Onohgwatrah so:a (Our Medicines)

Each element that is mentioned in this address carries responsibilities and leadership roles. The leader of our medicines is the *oye'gwa oawe* (our sacred tobacco). The medicines that grow in our environment are plentiful, with many different varieties. During pregnancy, we have lots of medicines that we can take for cleaning out our system and making our organs, bones, and muscles more flexible so that we will have an easier time when giving birth. We are surrounded by medicines and are given opportunities to seek them out through ceremony and in our personal dedication to honouring their gifts of healing by greeting, acknowledging, and thanking them. We say *nya weh* to the medicines. Let it be that way in our minds!

Wayaniyohnta (The Hanging Fruits)

It is great that we look forward to celebrating the annual return of the hanging fruits, first greeting their leader, known as the *jihso'dak* (wild strawberry)! We layer our soft words to her so that she will again bring into our presence her medicine and sustenance. She reminds us of where we come from and our responsibilities, not only to ourselves but also to all involved with the continuance of life. She brings her families to build relationships with everyone, and it is our responsibility to go and meet her in that sacred space so as to honour one another. It is fun searching for the ripe berries and seeing all the humps in the field as the people bend over or squat to pick the berries. The *jihso'dak* begins a cycle of growth, as she provides a pathway for the other hanging fruits to journey this way and to receive the benefits of meeting us pitiful humans. We say *nya weh*. Let it be that way in our minds!

Gakwa sho:a (Our Sustenance)

We give thanks for our foods, the corn, beans, and squash, which we call the Three Sisters. They are our sacred staple foods and are meant to enhance and support our bodily functions, offering us the essential nutrients that assist in the development of our minds so that we can make the best decisions. They are like family who offer support by sharing their energy; that is their special duty. We say *nya weh* to our sustenance. Let it be that way in our minds!

Odehadonih (The Forests)

We give thanks to the many variety of trees, with the leader in our lands being the maple. The maple brings medicine in the form of sap to cleanse our bodies of the many illnesses that have accumulated through the winter months. We are reminded of the importance of cleansing as the nutrients of the sap renew our bodies and minds. The trees also bring gifts of wood for fashioning many things, like our lacrosse sticks, which enhance our hand-eye coordination, speed, and discipline when we play with them. Trees tell us about the importance of communication and about our connection to E tinoha ongwesidage'dra gwe' (our Mother Earth). We learn all of this from the trees that surround us with their leaves and medicines. We give thanks to the *odehadonih* for their lessons. Let it be that way in our minds!

Ga di nyo (The Game Animals)

The deer is the leader in our forests. They have antlers that are like antennae, and they inform the animals when someone is approaching in their home environment. We are so fortunate that we still have the opportunity to have encounters with the beauty of the animals who wander in and out of the *odehadonih*. Their presence reminds us to be humble and thankful that we are still able to fell game animals in order to feed the bodies and minds of our families. We give thanks to the animals for their unlimited care in nourishing us, and we say *nya weh*. Let it be that way in our minds!

Ojihde so:a (The Birds)

The leader of the birds is the eagle, he flies the highest and has the greatest vision. There are many birds, and they each have a special time and place in the cycles of nature. They help us to deal with loss or mental health issues like depression through their beautiful songs, which lift up our minds and return us to a state of wellness. We give thanks to the birds, *nya weh*. Let it be that way in our minds!

Onekdangyogwe (The Waters)

We are so grateful for the waters, which come in many forms and sizes, like the oceans, lakes, rivers, streams, and wells. Water is a female energy that surrounds us and gives life. We are carried in water for nine months and are birthed through water. It quenches our thirst. We need water to survive, and it is a medicine that heals and cleanses. We give thanks to the water, *nya weh*. Let it be that way in our minds!

Se deyowawe'nyeh (The Winds)

We are so fortunate for the changing winds that warm and cool the earth and work to accommodate the changing seasons. They come and wrap around us like a blanket, holding us strong and giving us comfort. We are fortunate that we have not experienced the horrendous destructions of tornados or other strong forces of wind in our lands, although we have been forewarned that these things will happen when we fail to ensure our responsibilities of thankfulness, respect, and humble recognition of the limits assigned to us by the Creator. We say *nya weh* to the winds for being with us through our journey of life. Let it be that way in our minds!

E'dehka gakwa se dwa ja (Our Eldest Brother the Sun)

This great orb of light brings us daylight and warmth! People would freeze to death without his energy. We need the light to see and to appreciate what has been provided for us. We need our Eldest Brother the Sun to warm the earth so that we may plant our crops and so that the other plants, which support us, can grow as well. We acknowledge our Eldest Brother and say *nya weh*. Let it be that way in our minds!

Etisoht sohekawhnidat (Our Grandmother the Moon)

Our Grandmother the Moon's monthly changes are the calendar for the cycles of women. She monitors the birth of our children and guides us with her wisdom, which is like the moon's subtle glow. She controls the tides of the water and reminds us of the importance of self-care. We say *nya weh* to our Grandmother the Moon for always reminding us of our responsibilities. Let it be that way in our minds!

O jihso'dasha (The Stars)

Although we have forgotten the names of the stars, they still assist our Grandmother the Moon in whatever way they can. They remind us of our aunties and our ancestors who have gone before us, and we give thanks for their unconditional love and guidance. We say *nya weh*. Let it be that way in our minds!

Our Teachers

We have been gifted with many teachers who continue to bring messages from the Creator about how to live according to the instructions of our ceremonies, songs, and speeches. Our ancestors teach us about the importance of boundaries, values, discipline, and honouring oneself. We are fortunate to have so many young ones emerge from the earth who take our culture seriously. Our stories and songs guide us to stay in balance, and if we stray, the Creator does not judge us but understands that we are on this difficult human journey. We say *nya weh* for our teachers. Let it be that way in our minds.

Geihnyenoh de yo ki ye'nya dohn (Our Spiritual Helpers)

These spiritual beings guide and support our journeys, keeping us aware of our attitudes and behaviours so that we may be safe. When we leave our places of shelter and travel away from our families, our helpers keep us safe. And when we return home, they offer a web of safety so that we might arrive at our places of shelter. We say *nya weh* to those spiritual beings. Let it be that way in our minds!

Shogwaeyadisho' (The One Who Created Our Bodies)

We acknowledge the great visioning for our human journey. Our original instructions for relating with each other were handed down to us by Shogwaeyadisho' (the Creator). Everything was provided for our health and well-being on this human journey, and all that is expected of us is that we give thanks for all that is! So we send our greatest greetings to Shogwaeyadisho', who carries our best interests in health and wellness. We say *nya weh*. Let it be that way in our minds!

Daneto n'agahtgwe nih. (That is all for now.)[1]

Ǫ da gaho dę̃:s

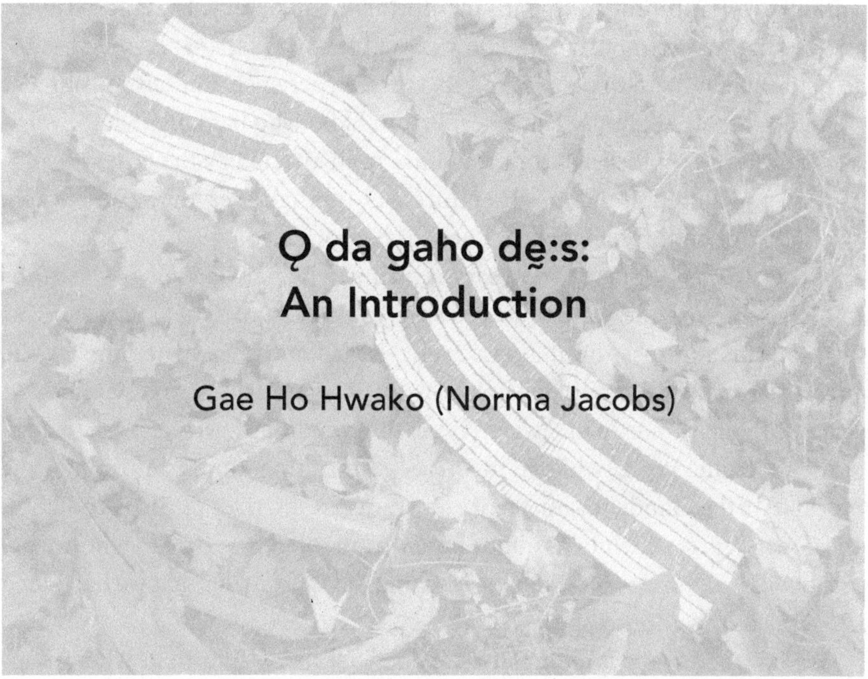

Ǫ da gaho dę̰:s: An Introduction

Gae Ho Hwako (Norma Jacobs)

The Kaswen:ta (Two Row) Wampum is a treaty belt whose beginnings are between two nations of people, depicted as the Haudenosaunee canoe and the European ship as they go down the river of life. At the time of this treaty, *which stretches back four centuries*, we discussed and agreed on what it meant to maintain our identities and not to interfere in each other's ways of living. Its original instruction was for the people of the ship to remain on their vessel and for us to stay in our canoe. Everything that we needed to live a good life was in our canoe, our Longhouse. We had our council, government, culture, and way of life, as reflected in our ceremonies, language, and teachings, all of which were meant for us. The ship brought its own culture, values, and principles. We did not need to get into this other vessel because we already had a canoe that was filled with knowledge for guiding and directing our people.

Gae Ho Hwako is my Ongwehowe name. It means "ancestral females holding the canoe before me," and it positions me in an ancestral line of great women of the Wolf Clan in the Cayuga Nation of the Great Haudenosaunee Confederacy. I am given the responsibilities in our canoe of empowering myself, my family, my community, the nation, and the Confederacy. I was told by my mother that it was important to know my cultural ways so that I would be able to help explain them to people, and it is these experiences and responsibilities that I hold as a Longhouse Faith Keeper and Elder who has taught at universities, colleges, and other institutions. I have been affected by the onset of colonialism and all that it did to our culture, but through everything, I have held strong to our culture, language, values, and beliefs.

I have worked for over forty years at trying to help my people of the canoe and those across the waters on the ship to understand that the Two Row Wampum is not just about a past event. It also carries instructions for the present, for how we should try to live every day, so that we can discipline our ways of living rather than always trying to develop more and more, to consume more and more, while in the process spreading more confusion in the world. For the Haudenosaunee, our position on the river of life is rooted in the Great Peace, which talks about how we are to remain true to who we are as a people, to those values, stories, teachings, and protocols that we had when we came to meet those on the ship.

We have many teachings that are beneficial for us and that, when practised, can block the impact of everything that the ship brought across those salt waters, which had been our protection. I have been taught not to participate in ideas or programs that the ship brought to engage our people, as they can subtly change our thoughts and beliefs. During my time as Elder-in-Residence at Wilfrid Laurier University, it was my intention to stay in my canoe. I would not behave as lesser than but rather as an equal, just as was originally agreed to in the Two Row treaty! For I am not the son or daughter of those on the ship, they are not my parents, and I have thoughts on how to proceed with the interests of Indigenous peoples at heart. I am not here to change anyone but rather to empower those I meet to rise to their highest potential. I am trying to become a clear and powerful person by shedding the impacts of colonialism that make us rigid and unfeeling.

From the beginning of our relations with the ship, we tried to prevent its interference by meeting with the new arrivals and agreeing to the Two Row positioning of our cultures on the river of life. Colonialism impacted us in many ways, as everything looked so good and easy on the ship compared to the life that we had, but our ways of living were meant to teach us about discipline, being respectful, and taking pride in who we were. This was done by working with the land, gathering the berries, reciting the Great Law, and offering those first words of the Ganǫhǫnyǫhk (Thanksgiving Address) to all the beings we depended upon.

When I look around, I see the many gifts that surround and nurture us – all of life in its many forms, from plants and medicines to trees and animals. This great abundance of energy and love that is this great Turtle Island, North America, came from E tinoha ongwesidage'dra gwe' (our Mother Earth). Women are the foundation of life, as it is they who carry life into this world. Wherever one comes from, it is a woman who gave us life! That cannot be changed. It is a natural law of our human existence. We can see that we are one with nature by how our bodies work with the land that is the body of our Mother Earth.

E tinoha ongwesidage'dra gwe', this great woman, has forgiven us time and time again for forgetting our place upon her. She becomes agitated when we ruffle her beautiful dress of many colours, which she has worked ever so diligently and honourably to prepare. Her dress is decorated with the relations of nature, which change through all her seasons. She is a wonder woman who shows us how to uplift our spirits with medicines, colourful dress, songs, and ceremony. When she speaks, her family listens, and she encourages them to come forward and share their beauty. She asks us to teach about shelter and healing, the strength of diverse relationships, good boundaries, character, and purpose. Her roots show us how to be supportive of one another and how to embrace one another with love. These are her gifts, which bring us into life's balance.

The Two Row Wampum is active in all our relations. It is not just something that we hold up when having a council meeting or when trying to revitalize and relearn what the wampum is about. It is a part of our everyday lives and every relationship that we have. Our travels into the experiences of this world are a sacred journey. Being here, we need to utilize the tools and gifts that we have received to further our development in the ways of respect and sacredness. Our relationship with all things should be sacred. Each morning, we need to give acknowledgment and thanksgiving, as it is daylight again and we all have life. At night time, we honour the day for our experience and for the people we had conversations with – when we laughed, shared stories, and came to a better understanding of who we are in this relationship with all things. We are always giving thanks and honouring those who have come into our lives, while trying to strengthen and enhance these relations by being who we are on these waters.

Everything was given to us for our sustenance. We had to work for it by going out into the bush or field to search for those things that were filled with good vitamins and nutrients. We understood our relationship with them and how they flourished following the arrival of the first fruit, the *jihso'dak* (wild strawberry). It was followed by all the different kinds of fruits, from those in the low bushes all the way up to those in the tall trees. The ceremony of thanking the food not only honours what we eat by speaking to it but also asks that nothing bad come into our bodies. The food that enters your body is not going to harm you because through prayer you have asked its spirit to give you what it can. These ceremonies were given to our people to help us in all our relationships, whether it be with food or water. Negativity always has the potential to come into our lives and destroy the sacredness of our relations, and in that interference, we can get lost; we can fall into negativity and not know where or who we are. It is always possible to take in unhealthy food, drink water that is polluted, or trust people who have not come into our lives in a good way, so healing ceremonies are applicable in many different ways.

With all this sustenance and with these ceremonies to remind us of our responsibility to give thanks, we were a healthy people who had a way of life in the canoe that was complete for us. So when the ship came and brought all those things that changed our way of life and belief, from the Bible to residential schools to the Indian Act to the punishment of jail to alcohol, it caused much pain and suffering. This outcome was not beneficial for us, and it did not happen by chance. The changing of our minds was done subtly through trade that brought barrels of alcohol to our communities because they said that it was good for us and that it was valuable. It may have been good and precious to those on the ship, but it was not good for us, as it was a toxin to our bodies, communities, culture, and spirit.

The Two Row Wampum teaches us to maintain what we have in our canoe so that each of us can live by what has been given to us. If the ship has some kind of conflict from its past that is impacting its values and our relationship, then those on board need to go into their depths to understand the root of what happened. That is what I was taught to do as one who grew up in the Haudenosaunee culture. In times of trouble, we go back to our beginnings in the creation story and to other teachings, like those of the Peacemaker and

Ayenwatha, and we follow them into the present to understand what happened to make us this way. We are always in motion, always active in getting clarity by looking back and recognizing that we are a reflection of what is in the Sky World – of its sacred purity.

We have forgotten about *ǫ da gaho dę:s* (the sacred meeting space) between the ship and the canoe, where we originally agreed on the Two Row and to which we must return today if we are to talk about the impacts that we have experienced because of its violation. It is always about finding a way to that sacred space where we can do ceremony to acknowledge, validate, and really understand what came into our lives when we met Western culture. We now suffer from the consequences of those relations – from the diet that we have to soil that cannot grow food the way that it once did to polluted waters whose fish are no longer good to eat. Our way of life has been disrupted. We no longer go hunting or fishing; we cannot do many things because the power of our culture was taken away by the ship. We have come to believe in something that was not of our teaching because of the impact of residential schools, the Indian Act, and many other actions that interfered with our ways of being and thus violated the Two Row.

If we spend time with the Two Row, it can help us to consider where we have come from to reach our present moment and thus can guide our future actions. It can teach us the value of keeping our cultural ways of living separate and independent, while also recognizing that when we walk side by side in a spirit of respect for each other, it is possible to connect and learn. We can maintain a friendship so as to travel on these waters together, but we should stay on our *row* by affirming its concepts and philosophy of life. I think about this interaction in terms of our diverse human relationships as males with females, females with females, males with males, parents with children, and adults with Elders. It is always about nurturing *ǫ da gaho dę:s* between us so that we can communicate with one another and be really clear about who we are in these relationships. We each need to discuss and understand what the other is saying by asking ourselves, "Do I really understand what you mean and where you are coming from?" As our conversation evolves, we can come to a real understanding of what the other means. This is what we refer to as *ganigǫhi:yo* (a good mind), and it is needed to come to *ǫ da gaho dę:s*.

Ceremony is important to all our Two Row relations, as it is a way of knocking at the door of another with a good intention to be respectful and caring. This knock is an act of acknowledging that those on the ship are approaching someone's home and thus are asking to come in with respect, with clarity, and in a way that honours those whose home is being entered. What happened following our Two Row agreement was something very different. Those from the ship knocked at the door, came in, and then started changing things in our home because they did not like the furniture. They began asking why we coloured it this way and not another. They questioned everything instead of offering compliments and honouring the invitation to come into relationship with the protocols of that home. I could not walk into the home of others and demand that they change, disregarding the ceremonies and ways of their home. It was disrespectful and went against our original understanding of who we were and how we would work together to create a balance, not only within ourselves but with all our relations on the river of life.

Every place is sacred, and we need to ask permission in order to respectfully come into it. Being respectful to what is already there is beneficial for those who are in that environment, and thus it is a way of being that is really important in building relationships between people and creation. We can help everything to come alive and flourish through respect, and a long time ago when the diverse peoples of the canoe were fluent in their languages and cultures, they understood this practice with clarity. They had the kind of relationship where they could talk with one another in a spirit of respect. Our Haudenosaunee culture teaches us how to honour one another and all beings of creation, but many today do not have the language and understanding to connect deeply with these teachings of our ancestors. Because of the ship's interference and impacts on us, we no longer have a wholistic sense of how we originally arrived at this place of respectful relations. Many in the canoe have forgotten how important those laws were in managing our lives, families, and nations.

Having the Two Row Wampum's nation-to-nation way of understanding our relationship is important, as we can follow it throughout our lives, recognizing where we have come from and where we need to go. It reminds us of the importance of discipline and communication, such as talking about what was done, being able to say that I do not appreciate what happened, as it was not respectful, and asking others whether they are going to change. The Two Row is a reminder that we once tried to talk with each other about our common understanding that people have feelings and that we can hurt them by saying certain things, not listening, or behaving in ways that interfere and are not beneficial for everyone.

As such, the wampum asks us whether we are going to sort out our relationship across the waters and within ourselves. Each of us has an internal relationship between our minds, behaviour, emotions, and spirit as we try to create a balanced conversation so that we can understand what is going on within and then bring that into our relationships. It is like counselling: you share and validate your story just as you would with a counsellor when in need. This helping relationship makes me think of the Peacemaker and Ayenwatha in the Great Law story of the Haudenosaunee.

The message of the Peacemaker is the Gayensra'go:wa (Great Law). It is a message of the good mind – a message of peace, power, and righteousness. The Peacemaker was a prophet of the Confederacy, a fatherless child sent by Shogwaeyadisho' (the Creator) to convey the message of peace to the nations of the Haudenosaunee who were at war with each other. The Peacemaker came to remind the people of the kind of life that was intended for us and to demonstrate how people of healthy mind, body, and spirit naturally seek harmony, balance, and peace. His message was simple, powerful, and direct, and it was sent to restore the good mind to the People of the Longhouse.

The Peacemaker did that first with Ayenwatha, who was grieving at the forest's edge for the loss of his daughters in all the violence. Coming out of the woods, the Peacemaker asked Ayenwatha what was wrong, but he was in such great distress that he could not respond. He was trying to make sense of all the violence and loss, and so he began placing strings of wampum over a sumac branch that he had fashioned. As he was doing that, the Peacemaker overheard and approached him from the bushes. The Peacemaker used the wampum in the same way and repeated the words that he heard, and in this way Ayenwatha knew that he was being heard. This man, the Peacemaker, really did care and wanted to know about his life, and so they began to communicate in a way that made Ayenwatha feel better. After that, they carried the message of the good mind to the five warring nations, whose people accepted the Gayensra'go:wa and buried their weapons beneath a Great Tree of Peace.

Originally recited in our communities every two years, the Gayensra'go:wa is one of the philosophies that has kept our culture and traditions strong and intact throughout the centuries of colonial conflict. It tells of a time when

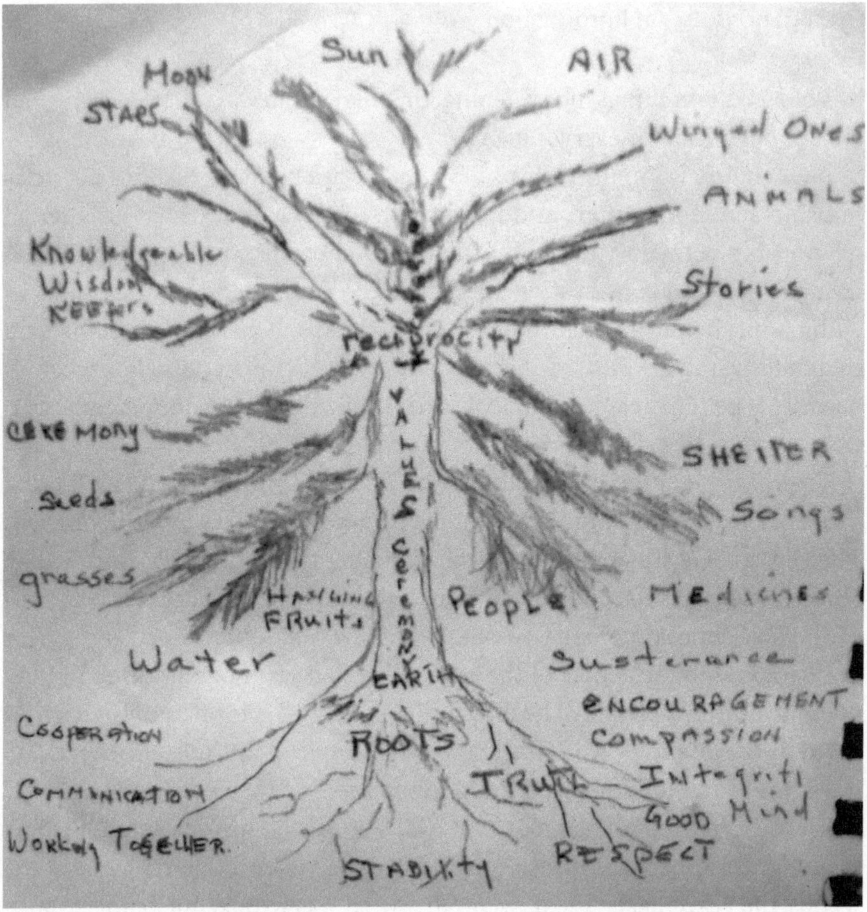

The Tree of Peace and Values. Drawing by Gae Ho Hwako (Norma Jacobs).

our people were confused and warring, both within themselves and with outside nations, having forgotten the path that the Creator had intended for us and the kind of life that we should be living. We are told that the Creator replaced those buried weapons with the good mind and that the Peacemaker's philosophy remains in our collective conscience. We are told that *righteousness* occurs when people's minds and emotions are in harmony with the intentions of the Creator and when their actions promote *peace*. The natural product of unified people of the good mind is the *power* to enact true *peace*.

In our ceremonies, we have speakers who take opposite sides, mirroring the relation between Ayenwatha and the Peacemaker. The younger and older brother counsel and reflect each other, saying, "This is what I heard you say.

Am I hearing correctly?" So they respond back and forth until they are really clear about the nature of the conversation and what issue is in need of fixing. There has to be this kind of clarity before the canoe and the ship once again can start travelling side by side down the river of life. We need this complete understanding in order to become friends again by creating a relationship based on trust, especially after so much interference.

If people from outside the Confederacy agreed to discipline their minds to align with the Tree of Peace, the Gayensra'go:wa, then they would be welcomed under its spreading branches. To do that, we need to reflect on our roots and to bring our reflection into relationship with this vision of peace for ourselves and all our relations. We are spreading this peace within and without. The progression of this inclusive vision was halted with contact and the turbulence of our Two Row relations.

What is good about the truth and reconciliation process is that it asks all of us to look at ourselves and to examine thoroughly our minds and hearts. What needs to be cleared up within ourselves and our relations? It asks each of us to reflect back so as to clear up those things by regurgitating them and asking, "Was this real?" Reconciling with ourselves is an original law of the Haudenosaunee that can be seen in the story of the Peacemaker and Ayenwatha, and it is not something that we made up. It is a spiritual law of this creation, of E tinoha ongwesidage'dra gwe', that has been instilled in our Longhouse, and it is this that we brought into relation with the people of the ship.

There is a dark and bright side to E tinoha ongwesidage'dra gwe', and it is the actions of her family that keep her in balance. When her children are being violated, she expresses her hurt and pain through the voice of our Grandfathers the Thunder Storms. The raindrops are her tears, crying for the broken promises and disruptions of peace. As with any mother who can feel the heartache of her children, she shows herself in the form of cleansing and renewal as she washes the abused and polluted lands with the tears of rain. They are given as words of encouragement to refresh the body and soul. The children tug at her skirt, asking for support and acknowledgment of the unjust abuse of her sacred family. The lesson of disciplining ourselves has not been learned, and so the violations continue in the form of broken and disrespected boundaries. Her family has suffered!

Our true mother is becoming the storm that can be seen all around us today! There are always consequences, and we humans are beginning to feel her anger. E tinoha ongwesidage'dra gwe' has given us the tools to work with when there is an energetic disruption of our peace. Her sacred territory needs and wants to be respected, and so she requests that we visit her places of pristine bountiful meadows and view the fine stitches of the decorative lace that adorns her dress. She asks us to take time to appreciate the stories sewn into every knoll and rolling hill as she dances and celebrates in honour of those who continue to hold up the responsibilities of her family.

My mom used to always say *ęsęhsgwaowhaneh*, meaning that you need to expand the teaching or story beyond what you hear and see; it is about clarity, questioning, and seeking answers. What does this mean to you? How do we use that in our life? How do we understand that? We always seek clarity as we explain the teachings to our family, children, and community. It is a process for understanding our relationships, like that between a man and a woman, who should understand their values so as to discipline their minds and bodies before they create another life. Those shared values that direct our relationships are important, and that is what the Two Row Wampum is about. We need to value what other people have and how they have been brought up in ways that do not interfere, although we can always learn from each other through conversation.

Now, I want to say *sgeno* to each of you who is coming into these circles of *ǫ da gaho dę:s* to reflect on your place in this journey of life. When you greet someone with the word *sgeno*, my mom would say that you are saying hello and that are you well. You are asking, "Are you in the good mind? Do you carry the Great Peace brought to us by the Peacemaker and Ayenwatha? Do you carry that peace found on the river of life? Do we each have the ability to travel back to the very beginnings of creation when we left the Sky World to start this human journey? We have come into these relations to reflect on all that and to say yes to what was given to us, for that is how we are supposed to be living our life.

Kentyohkwa, Sewatahonhsi:yohst! (A Call to Listen Closely!)

Kawennakon (Bonnie Whitlow)

I am grateful to Gae Ho Hwako (Norma Jacobs) for starting us off "in a good way"[1] with the Ganǫhǫnyǫhk (Thanksgiving Address). Recognizing that her terminology reflects her nation, I will use my language – Kanyen'keha, the Mohawk language – to refer to the same practice, which we call the Ohén:ton Karihwatéhkwen.

I first worked with Gae Ho Hwako and Winnie Thomas-kenha – *kenha* indicating deceased – at Awehaode Communication in the mid-1990s. At that time, more than 50 per cent of their work was about teaching people what is said when a speaker recites a full, Longhouse version of the Ohén:ton Karihwatéhkwen. The appropriateness of this particular introduction to our original teachings is not lost on me. The only place to start is at the very beginning. In true Haudenosaunee fashion, they began their teachings with creation.

I am always aware that I answer to my community first. I am perpetually conscious that I may lack the cultural fluency to speak with any authority at all – that I may have misunderstood, that I may be mistaken, or that my cultural translations may be wrong. Those not from one of our communities may be unaware of the additional community protocols and demands that we are expected to follow. I answer to hundreds of people from my own community and thousands from the rest of our territories. Even while living or working off-reserve, I am aware that there is a mutual responsibility: I to them and they to me.

I am grateful to have been in the right place at the right time and to have been afforded the opportunity to learn from our Faith Keepers in such a profoundly reconnective, life-transforming way as I entered adulthood. Here, I would note the tension of sharing our traditional teachings in a manner that honours our cultural norms while writing a word-processed document designed for proper writing practices in a colonial language. The program itself is compelled to underscore, call out, and urge me to reject (and "correct") the passive voice. The passive voice is a conscious choice that aligns with Haudenosaunee principles, which dictate that one is simply a vessel – a hollow bone – through which the ancestors speak to others.

In this particular instance, I recognize that the universal energies have placed upon my path these doors of opportunity to work with Gae Ho Hwako and others. I was afforded the choice to open these doors and walk through them or to leave them closed and walk past. I am glad that I opened the doors, behind which was access to a plethora of grounded cultural teachings and teachers who would change my entire life. When I was ready, my teachers did indeed appear before me and guide me along a path of cultural and language revitalization that will continue for the rest of my life. Thus I did not "take" these opportunities; they were offered. Acknowledging our style or choice of voice matters in a way that can be seen in Gae Ho Hwako's teachings and in the unique ways that each person responds to them in this book.

What follows in my words is an amalgamation of thirty years of traditional Haudenosaunee teachings from Gae Ho Hwako, her family, and countless others. I must also acknowledge the many Onkwehón:we (lit. "original beings") from communities across Turtle Island who shared their time, energy, and so much of themselves and their ancestral practices. Although I cannot always name or recall when and where I heard or learned various teachings – my memory is imperfect – I can recall the essence of the conversation. I have been fortunate that so many Faith Keepers, traditionalists, and medicine men and women were willing to share their time with me.

In countless presentations, Gae Ho Hwako has shared her mother's words with all of us, and I feel obligated to repeat them here, particularly the understanding that although it was important for us to go and listen to the speeches, it was everyone's responsibility to *skowanaht* – or *ęsęhsgwaowhaneh* (expand the teaching) – by taking that information and growing it in order to take it further. I have kept this idea close to my heart. In some cases, I am still discovering layers of meaning from teachings that I heard thirty years ago. Every time I think that I know something, I encounter another teacher who shares a deeper teaching and who adds another layer of meaning. This practice is endless.

I can only hope that these words help and that they do our teachings some justice. I hope all who read these words know that I am thankful for their patience, their love, and their trust. If I make a mistake, I hope that you can make it right in your minds and that together we can all evolve toward a higher consciousness.

The Ohén:ton Karihwatéhkwen is a reminder to think back on our origins. It tells us about the creation of the world and reminds us of where the Onkwehón:we came from. We think back to the beginnings of the earth and acknowledge the full extent of the work that the natural world performs. Here, I must draw a parallel to an oft-repeated refrain in feminist writing as we recognize that which others have forgotten. With the Ohén:ton Karihwatéhkwen, the Haudenosaunee publicly uplift and acknowledge the "invisible work" of the nonhuman world.[2] We remind our neighbours that every grain of sand, blade of grass, and drop of water has a soul, a spirit, a name, likes and dislikes, a responsibility to uphold, and functions to perform so that the world may continue.

We share the Ohén:ton Karihwatéhkwen so that others might more easily understand the simple wisdom in a daily expression of our thanks. We explain the speeches to remind ourselves, and those who may not speak our languages, that even when *we* forget, those entities continue to do their work and remember their duties. Faithfully, they honour that original contract with Shonkwaya'tihson (the Creator, lit. "he finished our bodies"). That contract between themselves and the Creator was accepted during the creation of the earth, and they continue their work to uphold and nurture the human being.

In English, people frequently refer to the Ohén:ton Karihwatéhkwen as the Haudenosaunee Thanksgiving Address. Although the English term "thanksgiving" accurately captures the purpose or intention of the recital, the phrase itself is not a careful translation that reflects the cultural context of the Kanyen'keha words. Literal translations such as "the leading order of business" and "the matters before all else" are more precise. These phrases allude to our creation story. As a protocol, the Ohén:ton Karihwatéhkwen is an excellent example of a modern practice deeply rooted in antiquity. It is a heartfelt tradition, a blanket meant to wrap around us, the intellectual and philosophical fabric of our ancestors. It not only suggests who we are as Haudenosaunee but also carefully reminds us of where we come from, where we will go, and how we can get there while preserving our cultural legacy. We continue to echo and reaffirm our ancestors' gratefulness today so that our children (and their children) might also experience the call of an ancient, powerful identity that binds them to their past and present – and to our collective future.

Whenever three or more people assemble, we take that first moment to renew our relationship to the natural world. We humbly observe our complete dependence on every other element in creation as our cohabitants on the earth. We pay homage to the knowledge that human beings are the weakest link. Without every other element on earth functioning fully to maintain this delicate balance, we (the human being) would perish. We recognize that the opposite is also true. Without human interference, everything else in the natural world would seek a natural balance so that all could flourish equally. Putting through the words of the Ohén:ton Karihwatéhkwen is a requickening of an ancient contract. It hearkens back to *tsi tyotáhsawe tsi yonhwentsiá:te* (when the earth began) – to the moment when Sky Woman seeded this planet with life and the twins created everything upon the earth. From that moment, the Onkwehón:we agreed to remember to honour all of creation and to be thankful. Unlike the Europeans, we do not view humankind above or superior to creation but as part of it. We acknowledge our deep human vulnerabilities.

In practice, and when delivered in our language, the Ohén:ton Karihwatéhkwen confirms an everlasting kinship with the land and the environment. Using familial terms such as "our Mother Earth," "our Eldest Brother the Sun," "our Grandmother the Moon," "the Three Sisters," "our Grandfathers the Thunder Storms," and "our ancestors," we recognize each member of the natural world as kin. We have an innate responsibility to support, nurture, and love these other beings as family and to recognize that they care for us in the same way. When we recite their names, we call out to all beings who have walked, lived, and died upon the earth since time immemorial and whose genetic imprint still resides within the land, air, and water of this planet. We remind ourselves that our mother, the earth, sustains everything that sustains us. When we recite the name of each element, we also speak of all the work that each one does so that human life may continue.

Through the Ohén:ton Karihwatéhkwen, we recognize the entirety of the natural world as sentient beings, with minds, bodies, and spirits. It is hoped that each of those entities might hear our words and know that we, the Onkwehón:we of today, will remember to fulfill our human duty by continually leaving before them a gift – our thanks.

I am thankful that we, the Haudenosaunee, still speak our languages, practise our original ways of being, sing our original songs, and dance our original dances. It is a miracle that our practices have been sustained across countless millennia, from creation until now. I am keenly aware that through centuries of a violent relationship with colonial peoples, many original nations on Turtle Island were completely annihilated – dispossessed of their land, language, and cultural heritage. Many Onkwehón:we nations in North America can glimpse remnants of their looted cultural legacy only through glass cases, or hoarded in museum archives, or referenced in historical texts, where they are conceptualized through a European gaze and framed by colonial language and thought. I extend my gratitude to all our *yethihsot'okón:'a* (grandparents and ancestors) who resisted so that today we might be able to speak *onkwawenna* (our original languages) and to practise *onkwehonwe'néha* (the ways of being of the original people), which refers to the convergence of Indigenous ontology, epistemology, axiology, and theory.

The Ohén:ton Karihwatéhkwen reveals the strength and power of our Haudenosaunee cultural heritage – a heritage that would compel all those who preceded us to resist the relentless attempts to colonize our lands, bodies, and minds. It is our ancestral teachings that will help us to successfully navigate our way through this time of transition, as those with "hearts of honey"[3] help us to bridge the time between worlds. We bid good riddance to the unsustainable misdeeds of an imperialistic, patriarchal, and capitalistic Western culture.

For now, I have done my best to explain some of my thoughts about what I have learned about the basic premises of the Ohén:ton Karihwatéhkwen. It may or may not be the way that I think about these same ideas tomorrow.

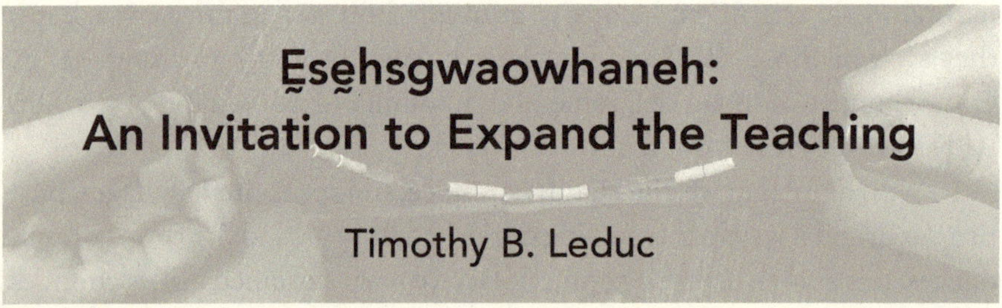

Ę̰sę̰hsgwaowhaneh: An Invitation to Expand the Teaching

Timothy B. Leduc

It is an honour to follow Kawennakon's (Bonnie Whitlow's) "call to listen closely" to Gae Ho Hwako's (Norma Jacobs's) opening Ganǫhǫnyǫhk (Thanksgiving Address) and to really feel into the gratitude for all that we have been given in this life. As I write these words, a heavy July rain has just tempered two weeks of hot summer sun by bringing refreshment to the parched ground. Feeling the cool rain fall upon my face, the spirit of thanksgiving arises from within me like the mist that now hangs above the ground, vegetation, and roads around my house. The renewal of rainwater, the warmth of sun, the droplet-speckled leaves of so many plants, so much medicine, the moist soil of E tinoha ongwesidage'dra gwe' (Mother Earth), which supports life, and the ancestors and spirits, who are like the mist, all remind me of our first human responsibility to express thanks for this great mystery given by Shogwaeyadisho' (the Creator).[1]

To feel and write of gratitude at this time when the Covid-19 global pandemic has taken many lives can seem misplaced, almost disrespectful, yet if I look closely into the storm of uncertainty, I can sense the relational spirit of the Ganǫhǫnyǫhk. It has raised our awareness of global interconnectivity, as well as an attentiveness to localized ways of relating that can submerge our lives into a hotspot. Social distancing to keep healthy boundaries and contact tracing to see how an infection travels have opened us to a world of once invisible relations. As fear takes over those who thought that they were in control and as systemic injustices make the vulnerable more vulnerable, the pandemic also haunts us with the continued presence of colonial abuses against Indigenous and Black peoples, against women of colour and their children, and against E tinoha ongwesidage'dra gwe'.

There is a deep interconnectivity to this life, and that is what the Ganǫhǫnyǫhk is meant to bring us into alignment with. When we do not have a way to wisely attend all our relations, we may fall into the kind of difficult learning that now afflicts our lives. I cannot help but recall the environmental sense of interconnectivity that began to arise on the ship in the 1960s not out of gratitude but due to a growing awareness of how chemical and nuclear pollutants were accumulating through all the relations of the planet. For Gae Ho Hwako, the environmental and social issues that intensify with each passing year are most fundamentally rooted in the ways of societies whose people have forgotten to express gratitude for all that we have been given.

We have started *Ǫ da gaho dę:s: Reflecting on Our Journeys* in the spirit of gratitude that guided the contributors of this book through a series of reflective circles with Gae Ho Hwako. I recall the hope, joy, and tears of our first gathering like it was yesterday. The circle began with the Ganǫhǫnyǫhk, for as Kawennakon says, we start with these words anytime more than three come together. With that spirit brought into the room, Gae Ho Hwako then gifted each of us a wampum bead to express her thanks for our presence and for our commitment to bringing this book into creation. In taking these sculpted pieces of quahog shell into our left hands, the hand closest to our heart, we were agreeing to reflect on our stories as they come into relation with the teachings of the Kaswen:ta (Two Row) Wampum.

With this gift of wampum, the first of three in-person circles began to unfold our writing of a book that also came to be guided by the inclusive spirit of a circle. As we shared intentions and listened to each other, we envisioned what might be possible in a book structure informed by Indigenous Elder knowledge. In time, the book slowly took the form of three sharing circles guided by Gae Ho Hwako's teachings on the spirit of the Ganǫhǫnyǫhk and the Two Row Wampum. We begin with *ge' gyo kwa* (the people) of the Two Row, continue with the creation of E tinoha ongwesidage'dra gwe' (Mother

Earth), and conclude with the spirit of peace and friendship given by *geih-nyenoh de yo ki ye'nya dohn* (ancestral/spiritual helpers) and by Shog-waeyadisho' (the Creator).

Our reflections can be seen as a stringing together of wampum that renews our understanding so that we may hand the string to others in "a pledge of truthfulness and sincerity."[2] As the late Cayuga chief Jacob Thomas wrote, this Haudenosaunee practice stretches back to the Great Law of Peace, when each chief delivered "a string of wampum, one span of the hand in length, to the Peacemaker." This act affirmed that his people "would discipline their minds and spirits to obey and honour the wishes of the Council" and thus would "be made welcome to take shelter under the branches of this tree."[3] There is a similar discipline to these circles, each forming a connective string that expands our understanding of what is needed to renew peace in this time of a pandemic, climate change, protests, and the National Inquiry into Missing and Murdered Indigenous Women and Girls (MMIWG) – a time when truth and reconciliation are called for by all the relations of E tinoha ongwesidage'dra gwe'.

The Two Row Wampum is important for thinking with, as it carries knowledge that can help us to reflect on where we have come from to reach our present moment of change. As Gae Ho Hwako highlights, this wampum belt is more than just a "treaty," as this translation into European languages tends to reduce our understanding to a political and economic focus. Those dimensions are part of a more inclusive circle that strings together family, community, nation, culture, land, spirit, and our place in all the relations of the Ganǫhǫnyǫhk. The ship's approach to the Two Row and other agreements has been fundamentally different from the beginning. In the words of Canada's Truth and Reconciliation Commission (TRC), "Government officials have viewed the Treaties as legal mechanisms by which Aboriginal people ceded and surrendered their lands to the Crown. In contrast, First Nations, Inuit, and Métis peoples understand Treaties as a sacred obligation that commits both parties to maintain respectful relationships and share lands."[4]

One of the central teachings offered by Gae Ho Hwako in this book reverberates: "We have forgotten about *ǫ da gaho dę:s* (the sacred meeting space) between the ship and the canoe, where we originally agreed on the Two Row and to which we must return today if we are to talk about the impacts that we have experienced because of its violation." At other times, I have heard her describe this space as a small vessel where the ship and the canoe met centuries ago and attempted to share the understandings that informed their unique ways to achieve the Two Row's promise of peace, friendship, and truth. In the words of Thomas, "There is a bridge for all people to cross, a common belief to bring us together. There is only one Creator."[5] *Ǫ da gaho dę:s:* is a sacred place where we are asked to honour our responsibilities by slowing down to reflect on the "truth" of colonial violence, which can be seen without and within.

I was first brought to meet Gae Ho Hwako by what seemed like a faint call when I heard her name spoken by students and others and then when I saw her speak in a short YouTube video. Sitting on a lawn chair outside at an event, she said to the interviewer that perhaps we needed to share some of our teachings and that maybe some from the ship were ready to hear them. Over the past six years, trust and respect have grown between us as we have co-taught courses on wholistic healing, truth, and reconciliation at Wilfrid Laurier University. Often, we cycle back to her teaching on *ǫ da gaho dę:s* and the importance of reflecting on the Two Row Wampum in a way that is "a part of our everyday lives and every relationship that we have."

I originally approached Gae Ho Hwako to co-teach a social work course called "Indigenous Wholistic Healing," as she could offer a culturally rooted understanding to the students that was beyond my Two Row positioning. My ancestors have lived for centuries along the great river Kaniatarowanenneh – known to most by its colonial name, the Saint Lawrence. I am French Canadien on my mother's side and French Canadien with unclear Mohawk and Wendat relations on my father's side. We are French Canadiens who cannot speak the language, and I am an English-speaking Canadian with no British ancestry. As I recount in more detail later in this book, I have a matrilineal root to the ship and do not claim to be Mohawk, Wendat, or Métis. In other words, I cannot teach or write from an Indigenous grounding, so I focus on the ship's (French Canadien, social work, and environmentalist) relations with the Indigenous canoe. We took a Two Row approach to our teaching, and I tried to model for our settler social work students a different quality of relation.

Yet as I taught alongside Gae Ho Hwako and engaged with her Haudenosaunee teachings, the uncertainties of the world came to make more sense – just as they did for our students. Many of my reflections crystallized as I spent time with a fallen white pine whose roots reached twenty feet into the air. Although I began visiting this tree about twenty years ago when it was still standing, Gae Ho Hwako counselled me to spend more time with it after its fall in 2018. Coming in a spirit of thanksgiving, I often reflected on her teachings about the white pine located where the Peacemaker and Ayenwatha guided "the five warring nations, which accepted the Gayensra'go:wa (Great Law) and buried their weapons beneath a Great Tree of Peace." Although this story would arise during my time with the fallen pine, it is more often invoked for me by the Two Row Wampum's call for peaceful relations and by the ship's failure to attend to its responsibilities – its sacred obligations.

As I followed Gae Ho Hwako's guidance, this pine began teaching me a different approach to knowledge that came to inform how I approached this book. Initially, I had asked Gae Ho Hwako whether she was interested in being interviewed for a research project on a Two Row approach to the role of Elder knowledge at the university, an institution of the ship. After an ethics approval, we started talking about that, but it did not take long before we agreed that an academic approach to qualitative research was too constraining for such a discussion. Gae Ho Hwako's knowledge in this venture was more important than my "willful" academic ideas and ways, so we began re-envisioning a book with her as the primary author and with me as a supportive editor.

Descending the white pine's root mound and entering the hole where this great teacher stood, I came face-to-face with a system of roots that continue to hold the soil that once gave it nourishment and grounding. Here, I cannot help but reflect on those colonial machinations that have long interfered with the cultural roots of the canoe and the life-giving gifts of the river of life, from a legacy of religious missions that stretch back to the 1639 building of Sainte-Marie-au-pays-des-Hurons on the shores of Lake Huron, to Canada's first residential school on the Grand River – the Mohawk Institute, built in 1831 – to the Sixties Scoop, in which social workers charged with placing Indigenous children in foster care took over the project of Indigenous assimilation as the schools closed, to today's overrepresentation and underfunding of Indigenous children in child welfare. Rather than engage the possibility of a sacred meeting, the institutions of the ship continue to shape-shift so that its isolating hull can violently convert those in the canoe and create dependencies.

Making the connection across what are often seen as distinct issues, the TRC asserts that Canada "pursued this policy of cultural genocide because it wished to divest itself of its legal and financial obligations to Aboriginal people and gain control over their land and resources."[6] This dynamic continues to undermine a nation that took global leadership on the 2016 Paris Climate Accords and nationally affirmed the TRC's "Calls to Action" but has done so while touting developments like the Trans Mountain Pipeline and pipelines in Wetshuwetsen territory that will impact land, water, climate, and people. From the perspective of Gae Ho Hwako's teaching, the ongoing storms that we are experiencing today are not simply phenomena out in the world but are relational responses of all the beings in the Ganǫhǫnyǫhk to a cultural imbalance on the ship that has many systemic tendrils, including the way that knowledge is conceived in academic spaces.

The university is a place of learning where it has long been assumed that all stories can be brought into a cohesive uni- (one) verse (story). As the container of myriad branches of knowledge, it wants to say that everything fits into its neatly carved up disciplines, which are part of the ship's hull. It is in these depths that "resources" have long been shipped, that peoples have been converted or enslaved, that the assumptions of racial superiority and universality that fuelled the Doctrine of Discovery have been modernized within a melting pot culture, and that our academic ways of researching knowledge about living in this world have been constrained. Offering a complementary environmental view on our stormy waters, Michael M'Gonigle and Justine Starke ask, "What does it mean when an institution 'churns out students whose entire training is rooted in an assumption of unending economic growth' and then across campus environmental researchers highlight the unsustainable nature of such growth?"[7] Such division of knowledge is a systemic tool for maintaining the shape-shifting forms of colonial violence.

In fostering knowledge that supports this consumptive way, the university has become an artificial tree of knowledge that is planted nowhere. It is not to be found on the river of life, and thus it extends the colonizing trajectory even as it creates space for Indigenous Knowledge Keepers, truth and reconciliation, and Indigenizing. As Mi'kmaw scholar Marie Battiste writes,

"Indigenous peoples throughout the world are feeling the tensions created by a Eurocentric education system that has taught them to distrust their Indigenous knowledge systems, their elder wisdom, and their own inner learning spirit."[8] This is what Gae Ho Hwako sees so clearly from her canoe when she says, "I would not behave as lesser than but rather as an equal, just as was originally agreed to in the Two Row treaty!" To learn what is required if we are to enact truth and reconciliation, the university needs to prune its systems, curricula, and assumptions, while nurturing sovereign, autonomous spaces from within which Indigenous Knowledge Keepers can stand and teach in ways that respect their cultural integrity.

An Elder is an individual who over a lifetime has come to deeply internalize and embody the teachings, ceremonies, practices, and histories of Indigenous culture(s) and thus is recognized by the community and the nation as a respected Knowledge Keeper and teacher. Attaining such knowledge and wisdom requires effort, time, and what Gae Ho Hwako describes as a "discipline" for respecting ways of living that equals and often surpasses the ways of living promoted by an academic trained in any of the university's diverse disciplines. For those in the canoe who have suffered uprooting violence, there is a great need for this wholistic knowledge warmed by the heart of living relations.

But, as Thomas taught based on his cultural knowledge and experience as an Elder at Trent University, there is something of value in it for the ship: "Wisdom is meant to be shared, and society is in great need. Now is the time to listen to our elders. Many non-native people are coming to me these days and they are saying that they are Christian but that what they hear from me is what they are looking for. Many young people are pulling away from the church to seek a clearer vision. This is what we are talking about. It does not matter what colour we are, we need to come together. Mother Earth has suffered so much abuse."[9]

In approaching the sharing spirit of *ǫ da gaho dę:s*, it becomes clear that the living Indigenous cultural teachings carried in the Ganǫhǫnyǫhk and the Two Row Wampum cannot be constrained by the boxes of colonialism. It may seem that Gae Ho Hwako, like Thomas before her, is working on the ship, given that she has taught at the university as an Elder for periods of time. But the reality is that she is in her canoe. Her work is directed toward enhancing her community and culture by revitalizing spaces for others to reconnect with these teachings, but she is also working across the river of life for the benefit of all relations. She comes onto the ship and tells us of the Indigenous land where this teaching is really being offered, and she asks us to come back into relation with our position on the Two Row – to take up our sacred place on Turtle Island, rather than all space, as a central discipline for approaching *ǫ da gaho dę:s.*

❁ ❁

The circles of this book embody what Gae Ho Hwako describes as "*ęsęhsgwaowhaneh*, meaning that you need to expand the teaching or story beyond what you hear and see; it is about clarity, questioning, and seeking answers." Each of her three sets of teachings are followed by reflective responses from four of the circle participants, who write from their Haudenosaunee, Anishinaabe, Métis, mixed, or in my case, French Canadien relational positions. Some of us are scholars who work in the university, others are authors, and some are community activists, but we all have attempted to bring our experience and knowledge into reflective relation with the teachings. That is what I have begun to introduce here through this account of my relation with Gae Ho Hwako's opening teaching, a fallen white pine, and the nature of this book. Through such a cycling process, we each try to *ęsęhsgwaowhaneh* (expand the teaching).

If we can truly renew the spiritual obligations of the Two Row Wampum, we can transform how we nurture and share relational knowledge. As I discuss in the first and third circles, my experience with the white pine and the river of life is not merely a metaphorical understanding from which, as an academic, I have attached researched knowledge. Rather, these living relations offer ways to transform what and how I know. The writing of Kawennakon on the challenge of Indigenous storytelling in the first circle is similarly indicative: "It felt like I could hear/see someone (who was not me) just inside my left ear and behind my left eye. He/she/they were telling and showing me story images to share. I also know that they were demanding. There was a story that I tried to avoid that they wanted shared."

The way that she feels her way into the stories that need to be shared has a connection to Indigenous language that resonates with how Thomas talked about "thinking in Indian" before translating "into English." The reason for the difficulty, he explained, is that the translation process transcends a simple search for word equivalents, especially in a context of "possibly incommensurable" cultural and linguistic differences between English and Indigenous languages. In his words, "When you say something, it actually comes out from your heart."[10] I cannot help but think of various chapters that have this felt quality, particularly the contribution by Barbara-Helen Hill, who in the concluding circle talks about knowledge that is warmed by the heart through friendship with a sheltering tree.

It seems that "thinking in Indian" is meant to ensure that English opens to the relational understandings of Indigenous languages and teachings. In a sense, this book partakes of the approach offered by Thomas, as we collectively story our relations with the nature of this sacred space known as *ǫ da gaho dę̱:s* – a living word whose translation into English takes a whole book composed of many voices and stories. All the contributors also reflect on their own experiential relation to the violence of colonialism in unique ways that are responsive to elements of Gae Ho Hwako's teaching. In response to the first set of teachings on *ge' gyo kwa* (the people) of the Longhouse and the Two Row Wampum, Shelly Hachey shares with us her experiences of the child welfare system as a mixed-race child and how these experiences have informed her journey toward Indigenous wholistic healing. Within the next circle, focused on E tinoha ongwesidage'dra gwe' (Mother Earth), Kitty Lynn Lickers reflects on the struggles of Indigenous women like herself who are "in between" various worlds because of ongoing colonial violence, and she considers the kind of ceremonial storytelling that is needed for a sustainable future.

Then there is Giselle Dias, in the final circle, who talks of an abusive prison system built on the body of a living creation but does so while lifting "up two-spirit and queer Indigenous writers who give voice to identities and sexualities that exist outside binaries." It is an approach supported by others, like Lianne C. Leddy, who draws upon Anishinaabe knowledge to critically hold in check patriarchal assumptions embedded in the English language and its institutions. In her words, "Raising my daughter has been the most empowering and transformative experience of my life, and I have taken to heart the works of Indigenous women scholars who see the possibility of resurgence through our teachings for the next generation." The chorus of reflections within and across our circles makes it clear that the Canadian nation is at a moment of choice, as highlighted in the intersection of global environmental issues, the pandemic, MMIWG, uprooted children and families, bodies unearthed in graves around residential schools, and a general political malaise in the face of the extensive changes that are needed today.

We are always trying to find our way to that sacred space where, Gae Ho Hwako says, we can "do ceremony to acknowledge, validate, and really understand what came into our lives when we [in the canoe] met Western culture." All the contributors were drawn in their own way to these circles, but this spirit of *ęsęhsgwaowhaneh* does not end with us. Near the end of each circle, a space of invitation is given to you, the reader, to come into this ceremony by handing you a string of wampum. If you decide to take it, we ask you to "expand the teaching" by reflecting on your experiences, stories, knowledge, gifts, and responsibilities. What part of Gae Ho Hwako's teachings or subsequent reflections reverberate in the spirit of your being? What stories from your own experience do they raise for you? Where in your life can you work toward truth, healing, and transformation?

We come to *ǫ da gaho dę:s* as people with diverse origins but a common interest in the use of writing, education, community work, and sharing to change the destructive direction that we are headed. At the back of the book, you will find a "Glossary of Indigenous Terms" that is meant to support your reflective journey through these teachings, which are deeply grounded in language.

To clarify the common Indigenous roots of our approach, we close this introduction and each of the circles that follow with a short prayer of reflection that draws on the distinct, yet complementary, Anishinaabe teachings of Elder Awnjibenayseekwe (Banakonda Kennedy-Kish Bell). Although the Anishinaabe share the Grand River lands where we conducted these circles with Gae Ho Hwako's Haudenosaunee nation, Awnjibenayseekwe's words arise from Lake Superior, where she was born. She is a cultural teacher, an Elder in Wilfrid Laurier University's Faculty of Social Work, and a traditional practitioner who has served Indigenous communities for over forty years. In fact, the form of this book is partially inspired by the way that her teachings are encircled in the seventh edition of the book *Case Critical: Social Services and Social Justice in Canada* (2017), which she co-authored. With that, I hand the closing of our introduction to Awnjibenayseekwe so that she can guide us into the spirit of our first circle.

Maamoyaawendamow (Gratitude)

Awnjibenayseekwe (Banakonda Kennedy-Kish Bell)

The Ganǫhǫnyǫhk (Thanksgiving Address), the Haudenosaunee greeting to the natural world, always engages me in deep reverence, awe, and respect. I have been inspired, found shelter, experienced reciprocity and gratitude within these words again and again.

I am grateful for my memories of Ernie Benedict's kind honest voice lifting up the Ganǫhǫnyǫhk's words at our day's beginning, with the smoke of smudge. As a Mohawk Elder, Ernie lived his Original Instructions, stood up for the people, and lifted up Indigenous knowledge with great humility and friendship. I am grateful for the many years of work we shared.

I am grateful to Gae Ho Hwako (Norma Jacobs) for lifting up the first words of the Ganǫhǫnyǫhk in our work together. In her words, "When I look around, I see the many gifts that surround and nurture us – all of life in its many forms, from plants and medicines to trees and animals. This great abundance of energy and love that is this great Turtle Island, North America, came from E tinoha ongwesidage'dra gwe' (our Mother Earth)." Her Cayuga teachings fill me with *maamoyaawendamow* (gratitude).

I am grateful for the words of Onaubinisay (James Dumont), Elder, Knowledge Carrier, and Chief of the Eastern Door Midewiwin Lodge. Through his translations of our Anishinaabe teachings and relentless work in our communities, myself and many others were able to access and be informed by the depth of those teachings.

The teachings and stories of our Lodge bring me to address the spirit of *maamoyaawendamow*, as does the Haudenosaunee Ganǫhǫnyǫhk. Having heard Onaubinisay say "the universe cares. Our First Mother cares for all her offspring"[1] fills me with gratitude again and again. Gratitude is essential in striving for balance, harmony, and good relations, and it is central to what we call Mino-Bimaadiziwin (the Good Life). I remember Onaubinisay hearing the Ganǫhǫnyǫhk spoken by Haudenosaunee children; he was brought to tears by their beauty and told all those gathered that he knew the future was in good hands.

In the times we live in, we wrestle with forces in society that defy kind humility and the honest holding up of the truth of our relational place within creation. Gratitude is essential to engaging reciprocity. Gratitude is kinship, is relational, as is Kindness. The concept itself cannot exist outside relationship. We are accountable to our First Mother, the Earth – Shkaakamigokwe in Anishinaabe and E tinoha ongwesidage'dra gwe' in Haudenosaunee.

Gae Ho Hwako and I share the awareness and value that we are the children of our First Mother. In her words, "We can see that we are one with nature by how our bodies work with the land that is the body of our Mother Earth. E tinoha ongwesidage'dra gwe', this great woman, has forgiven us time and time again for forgetting our place upon her." There is urgency in the vision of this work that a growing number of us share. We are committed to remembering the importance of our place upon the body of our First Mother, our place in the Ganǫhǫnyǫhk. In the Sharing circles of *ǫ da gaho dę:s* (the sacred meeting space), we sit with this truth again and again.

In the words of Onaubinsay, "We are all relatives because we have the same mother."[2] In my territory, we speak to our relations with regard, as in the Ganǫhǫnyǫhk, giving thanks to the swimmers, crawlers, plants, trees, four-legged, two-legged, flyers, and unseen ones, to the forces of the four directions and the winds, to the great and small waters, the sky, and the star realm, to our Mother Earth, Grandfather Sun, and Grandmother Moon, and to the Great and Forever Mystery. These words, too, fill me with gratitude. They cause me to realize that we have responsibilities to each other, to our First Mother, and to all her offspring.

In lifting up our first words each day, let them be filled with gratitude. *Megwetch* (thank you) for all of creation and for our place in creation. I am full of gratitude to all my relations, for they continue to follow their Original Instructions.

At sunrise in my daybreak prayer, I find myself asking Gitchi Manidoo (the Creator) for help in following my own Original Instructions, help in staying on my own path, so that I can do the work I came here to do. I ask for help in coming to know the nature of my work during the stage of life that I am in now. Each stage has sight and insight – a way of engaging, experiencing, and expressing an intelligence that becomes a way of behaving and being. The Good Life for me is in the coming to the place, the stage I am in, wholly present to my responsibilities relationally. May I greet each day with respect and gratitude for all my relations, for life. I ask for support to engage and come to know more fully, for a way to recognize, those ones who are waiting, ready to engage their bundle.

Thanksgiving calls me to reflect on all my relations and on my meaning, purpose, and responsibility. We are connected in such a way that all we do impacts all of life. When we do harm, we harm ourselves. There is grief here, too, for we as humans rarely return that care. In our failure to engage reciprocity, we cause harm. In this way, gratitude and thanksgiving are the desire for, the reaching for, and the making of balance, harmony, and peace. We recognize and give thanks for each sustaining, life-giving force of creation. I give thanks for the people who share with me, care for me. I give thanks for the teachings, for those who held onto those teachings, ceremonies, songs, dances, and for the knowledge that we are truly all related.

In this way of giving thanks, I lift up my teachers, my children, my grandchildren, and my family, both given and chosen. I give thanks to Onaubinisay, Peter O'Chiese, Art Soloman, Ernie Benedict, to my ancestors, and to those who held onto our Midewiwin Lodge. I lift up Laura Mastronardi and Ben Carniol for the creative collaborative Sharing in our work, and in the work they do with all our relations. I lift up those ones I have visited, those ones who have visited me, and those ones who have lifted my spirit, touched me with their beauty: the Sky Realm, Grandmother Moon, and Grandfather Sun, bird life, eagles, those hawks, the blue jays, and chickadees, the deer, fox, and coyote. They fill me with gratitude and wonder.

The Third Fire. Drawing by Awnjibenayseekwe (Banakonda Kennedy-Kish Bell).

I am grateful to Gae Ho Hwako for her courage to speak to and share her teachings, for inspiring me to share from my own place, my own learning. She respects and honours her teachers and continues to follow her Original Instructions. Tim Leduc holds responsibility for tending the fire of this book. He takes up his responsibility to hold us in a sheltered place where we work together in the circles of *ǫ da gaho dę:s*. I am grateful for Gae Ho Hwako's mentorship of Tim, and I am filled again with gratitude and wonder at the reflections caused and experienced in the journey of this book.

Here, we have the opportunity to engage humility, take up responsibility, and approach our place at the Third Fire, or *ǫ da gaho dę:s*; that reciprocity is so necessary in all our relations, that peace and friendship whose flames we desire to fan. At the Third Fire, our place is centred in the spirit that brings us into relation with others. We are reaching to take up our place in this creation, as in the Haudenosaunee sense of *ǫ da gaho dę:s*, where the *maamoyaawendamow* of the Ganǫhǫnyǫhk fans those flames of peace and friendship, reciprocity, cooperation.

Gitchi Manidoo is the centre of all life – to which I address the spirit of this work and give thanks for this circle, this coming together to lift up our voices in Sharing. There is Strength here to nourish, to come to know again and again, to stand up together and condition all that we do with gratitude, with respect.

I lift up Kind Honest Sharing, know the Strength that emerges from these values. Onaubinisay says, "Respect conditions all other values."[3] We share the belief, value, and love of gratitude – how we are meant to come together with Kind Honesty to take up our place in the circle of life. In doing that, we become who we are again and again. This is the potency of those first words and of those closing words that bring us full circle each day.

"Let it be that way in our minds." These words softly say to me we are indeed all related. I believe that *ganigọhi:yo* (a good mind) is informed by spirit, heart, and intelligence, is respectful, inclusive, and cooperative. The conception of coexistence is a spirit-informed, lifelong-affirming pursuit and engagement of peace, balance, and harmony. Surely Mino-Bimaadiziwin is the outcome of respect and gratitude.

In this way, thanksgiving engages us, is central to the nature of the way we take up our place, lift up our voice, experience and express respect for our interdependence, our connectedness, our responsibility for sustainable relations. This can emerge only from a deep and abiding regard for the life that gives life – the energy and force of the source of all life. Yes, "let 'us' be that way in our minds." As Vine Deloria Jr writes, "Western science, following Roger Bacon, believed man could force nature to reveal its secrets; the Sioux simply petitioned nature for friendship."[4]

Maamoyaawendamow nikaaniganaa. (In gratitude for all my relations.)
Maamoyaawendamow Gitchi Manidoo. (In gratitude for the Creator, the Great Mystery, the All Spirit.)

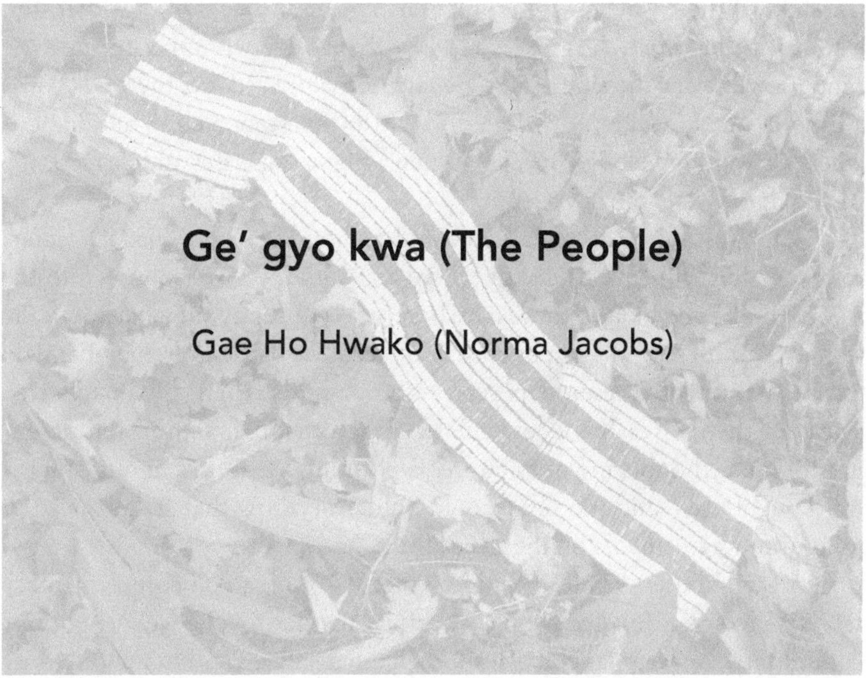

Ge' gyo kwa (The People)

Gae Ho Hwako (Norma Jacobs)

> We the people give thanks for our existence and for the people whom we pass on the paths of our journey. We need each other for our well-being as we share conversation, knowledge, laughter, and love. By sharing our dreams, thoughts, and visions, we honour and acknowledge the gifts that we each bring, as they are important to the development of ourselves, our families, our clans, our nations, our communities, and the wholeness of life. The prayers that we share are for our health and well-being. We remember our journeys, stories, and songs, and we recognize that we are those sacred spiritual beings who descended from the Sky World to work on this spiritual journey with E tinoha ongwesidage'dra gwe' (our Mother Earth). We say *nya weh* (thank you) for the great visioning of our Creator. Let it be that way in our minds!

We have long forgotten about *ǫ da gaho dę:s* (the sacred meeting space) between the rows of the Kaswen:ta (Two Row) Wampum, where we get information and where we communicate, acknowledge, and validate what we each bring into relationship across the river of life. The Two Row instructs us to travel down these waters without interfering with the ways of the other, and it warns us that if we choose to straddle the space between the ship and the canoe, it will bring difficulties. We are taught that if we do so, there will come a time in our life when it will be difficult to maintain a clear mind about where we want to belong, especially when a big storm arises and disturbs the waters that we are journeying upon.

If you have one foot in the canoe and one on the ship, when the waters roughen, you will have to decide where you stand. We are so drawn to the ways of both rows today that we have become confused about where we really want to be, and as the storm intensifies, it becomes harder to remember who we are. In times like these, people can become confused and fall into the river. They lose themselves. It is a powerful teaching about maintaining the sacredness of life by honouring our culture. Everything we need is in our canoe – our Longhouse – and the ship should hold everything that settlers need to honour our agreements on the river of life.

Our Longhouse – Haudenosaunee culture – is based on complementary relationships that involve people working together for the wellness of our community. We were taught to respect all our relations and to uphold those values that form the foundation of our being. The intention to be complementary is what needs to shape our whole behaviour. In our traditional government of chiefs and clan mothers, everybody looked after everybody else. It is so powerful to learn in this way about establishing good boundaries for being who we are and about what relationship is really about. It is important for us to know because it keeps us from being caught in those negative behaviours that can hurt our relations, and if these behaviours do arise, you have a bundle of values and practices for dealing with them.

The building of the longhouse structure is important to us, as it contains the medicine of our life. Our structures are made from the wood of the trees and forests around us, and that is the best medicine because it emanates the energy of the forest into the families who live in these homes. The people receive this medicine and return it when they honour these trees by using them in the structures that they live in. The people and the trees work together, creating relations of protection and honour. From this relationship, we begin to understand and see that we need each other in order to survive and to live in a good way.

Nothing in this world stands alone, as we are always connected to everything else in creation. When we give birth, we cut the cord that attaches us to the baby, and when it dries, we are supposed to bury it. If it is a girl, we bury the cord by the house so that she will be powerful in everything that she does in making her home good for her family. The cord of males is buried out in the woods or in a woodpile. I do not know whether people today know about woodpiles, as it was a long time ago when we burned wood for heat, which meant that we had to cut it and bring it into the house. Men had to go and clean the forest for that wood, and those teachings identified where the responsibility of men was found and what gave them the strength and the endurance to work hard in the woods. Their muscles and strength are different from mine since I am a woman. I know that their strength is different, as there is not a man who would be able to give life because of the pain that women go through.

The trees tell us about the importance of communication; and they tell us about our connection to E tinoha ongwesidage'dra gwe' – our original Mother Earth. We learn all of this from the trees that surround us with their leaves and medicines. The berries, hanging fruits, nuts, flowers, shrubs, great vines, and everything that we bring into the home are given to us by those trees. Everything that we gather is our medicine, which we get from the environment that we work with. We are in that relationship to sustain one another, and so we do a ceremony before we go into the space of the trees. We ask them for protection as we come into their midst. This practice honours them. It is about learning how to be in a good relationship, and it can be related to a structure like our longhouse or to our work.

These are the first things that we consider in learning how to create wellness in this atmosphere. Here, we are reminded of our relationship with the earth – of how these relations are complementary to us and how we are complementary to them. Our Longhouse tradition presents this whole world of excellence to us, so we communicate and share stories of what we learn. Spending time in the woods teaches us about the patience that it takes to nurture relationships like those between a man and a woman. For their relation to be strong, they need to support each other, and that is how relationships are supposed to be. It is not about love, as love is created over time when we share with one another. Love comes from empowering each other and from keeping each other strong. Why not try that? To be supportive and encouraging so as to empower people to be all they can be – that is what the trees in the woods and in the longhouse structures remind us to do.

Look at how old these trees are as they stand in the forest; they have such energy. I went into the woods because I was feeling down about getting older and how I am limited in doing certain things, and then I saw this maple tree that was split. I thought that despite its condition, it still makes sap. So I put some pails on that maple, and the tree gave the most sap – more than the young saplings. I thought to myself, "What a gift." The Elders really are a gift to the people because of what we can offer from our experiences. What we hold makes us strong and gives our community life, but like my relationship with that tree, we need to go into the woods and celebrate who the Elders are. This is what returns us to our Mother Earth and to the medicines that she carries, all of which benefit our mental, emotional, physical, and spiritual health.

We try to take the good ways of being in relationship that our Elders teach about and incorporate them into the structure of our Longhouse. Our culture needs that strong foundation. All the conversations in the home begin to build our attitudes of being grateful and happy for one another, and as we continue to treat each other well, it almost becomes like we can read each other's mind. You become so close to the others, aware of their likes and dislikes, that you can feel the vibration of their energy – of their soul. If this energy can pass between two people, it certainly can also pass between those trees and the people. The trees begin to shape how we behave – how we respect and honour one another. We do not want to do anything to interrupt or hurt this relationship.

Even though we have emotions like anger when we get hurt, something in the values held by the tree asks us to sit down and talk in order to reason things out. We have to use our mind to talk about things so that everything comes into balance again, and then those negative energies will move out of our home. We are always moving with the energies between us, and it takes time to do that. Because these moments that we give to each other are sacred, we put everything aside so that nothing can interrupt or interfere. It is so important in our lives to take time, even if it is just five or ten minutes, to sit with another or with oneself. If someone comes to visit while we are doing so, we say that we are busy right now and thereby establish strong boundaries.

This is our time to sit down and talk about those things that have interrupted our relationship and about why I am angry or forgot to practise self-care.

When I was growing up, my mother always said that you do not go into somebody's house and run through it, going into every room. You are a visitor, so if you want to play, you go outside. You need to respect another's place. So when my grandchildren come to my house, if they look in my drawers and open cupboards, I ask, "What are you doing?" I tell them, "You cannot do that in my home. You can look but do not touch." My daughter gets upset and leaves. But those things are precious to me; every gift from someone has a story behind it. Because they are growing and forming their minds and bodies, the children need to understand another's boundaries. This discipline is being shared all the time, even in our ceremonies that teach us about life, relationships, and communication. They tell us about boundaries with each other and with creation, and each ceremony is different in shaping us to be disciplined.

At the beginning of our Two Row relations, the ship had no foundation for understanding our ways. Those on board had a purpose for coming here and had no time to hear about the Longhouse or to establish strong boundaries and treat us well. The colonial attitude was that the sooner they got us disconnected from our land and culture, the better. Their real focus was on land rather than on good relations. The ship remains focused on the ways of patriarchy. Even when they have women in positions of power, they are still controlled by the colonial systems, institutions, and politics. This is connected to why Indigenous women are also experiencing so much violence, as they are the closest to the land and thus to our foundation in E tinoha ong-wesidage'dra gwe'.

The Two Row Wampum was meant to protect all of us so that we could be who we were and live our lives. From the beginning, we talked about the value of noninterference, but now we cannot help what has happened and must struggle with all the colonial influences. How do we understand and respond in all this confusion that has built up over time? People were treated badly in the residential schools or adopted homes, and from this experience has come a fear that is still present in our community. With all the confusion that came with colonialism as the ship's teachings and ways influenced our Longhouse, as with other lodges of the Indigenous canoe, we forgot our teachings about

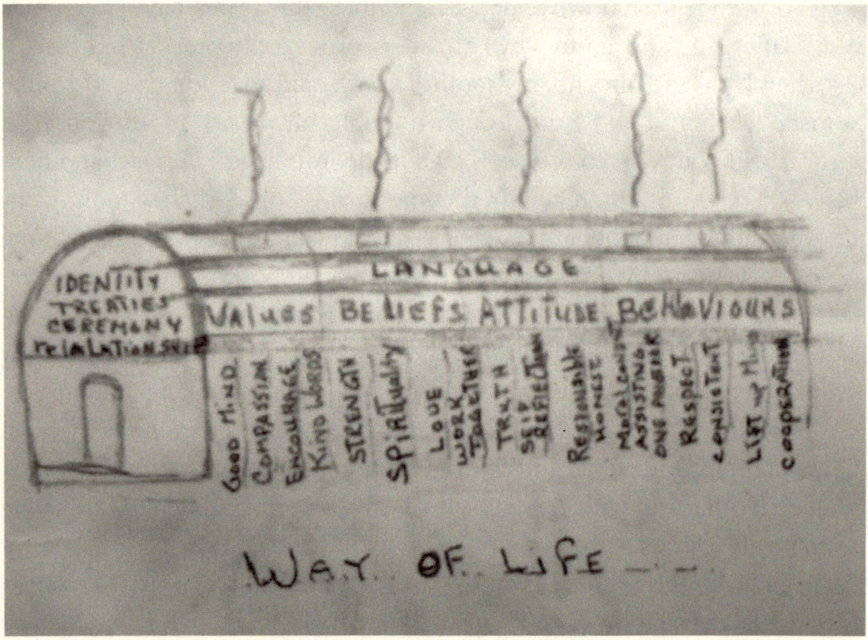

The Haudenosaunee Longhouse Way of Life.
Drawing by Gae Ho Hwako (Norma Jacobs).

having *ganigǫhi:yo* (a good mind) and no longer talked about all that was happening. We forgot about the values and stories of the Longhouse because we were trying to survive rather than live.

From the beginning, the ship thought that our land was rich, and it moved quickly to take the nutrients out of E tinoha ongwesidage'dra gwe' by doing things like forestry, mining, oil drilling, and fracking. Our kids were sent off to residential schools or were adopted out to non-Native families, and certainly these experiences deteriorated the connection of our people to the Longhouse. The adoptive parents often did not talk about our kids' original parents or about the fact that they were Native, and thus they came to believe what was learned in that home. A great many children have been lost through Canadian policies that interfered with our Longhouse. Colonial practices have been a detriment not only to our people but also to all the people of the world, who are suffering from the social and environmental impacts of these ways. When we see everything as a resource, we lose a sense of what is sacred in our everyday lives. We forget the importance of the Ganǫhǫnyǫhk (Thanksgiving Address), and thus uncertainty and confusion grow for future generations.

Over time, the ways of Western culture have seeped into all aspects of our lives, and now many of our people have become confused or ill. Many have come to believe that we are not capable of looking after our own children, even though our teachings give us everything that we need. I can think about these teachings through my many relationships as a grandmother or parent. If children who have done something disrespectful respond to my concerns by saying, "Yeah, I won't do that again," I do not discipline them because they have already said in their own words that they understand. They have responded and said that they will change, so when teaching discipline, we cannot resort to the red willow, which is one of the medicines in the Thanksgiving Address and offers teachings for discipline in our lives. We respect children's promise to behave, and if I step over that line and discipline them anyway, I am in the wrong. I will have overstepped our agreed-upon sacred boundary. This is one Longhouse teaching for taking care of children.

All that children really want is to be listened to, they want to communicate, and they want the safety of a home. They want to have hope, and they want to know that they belong somewhere – that somebody cares about them. These are simple things. They do not want a car unless we bring that into their minds. My mom used to say, "You have a baby and you want the child to have something new because the neighbours bought one, so you buy that for them. Oh, they got a new buggy, so I am going to get that, too. They got a new car, so I am going to get that, too. What is going to happen when your child is sixteen and wants a car?" A balance needs to be created. Some things are necessary, but there are some extras that we can do without. I remember making little scones with my grandchild, and I said, "You do not need a measuring cup. Just pour a little milk in and mix it up, and if it is not pliable enough, then slowly add more liquid." Think about it; you do not need all of those special tools to make a scone or pie. I have no rolling pin, so I flatten the crust out with my hand, and I know that it should be soft enough for me to do that.

We need to use our minds about what we want and need. It is all about conversation. Do we really need that? Do our children need all that plastic stuff? We used to climb trees; they want us to climb them, clutch onto them, and swing from them. These activities connect us to the Longhouse structure, its values, and its ceremonies, and through this connection, we can begin to teach. We need to start with a basic conversation about needs and wants because we can have many wants that we do not really need.

These issues fill our lives today. Everything has to move fast because the institutions and ways of the ship want us to be confused about what they are doing until it is done – until it is too late. We are all busy with jobs that have their mandates and timelines, so we do not get a chance to sit down and really reflect on all these things. But sometimes, I receive a text from someone who has heard me speak, and they say that they miss the stories and teachings. It could be about medicines, how everything that we need to be healthy can be found in our soils. That is true for us in the Longhouse: our medicines and stories come from these soils. There are ceremonies that we can do in order to reflect on and share who we are, but to do so, we have to slow down and listen.

Our ways of the Longhouse do not fit with the Canadian government's policies and with ways of living that do not take the time to look at all of these things. So much is missing from the view of the ship, and that is why we are in this turmoil. All my life, I have been disciplined to stay in the Longhouse, to be who I am, and not to get caught up in the confusion and hardship of straddling the space between the Indigenous canoe and the ship. I know lots of people who struggle with wanting to be in the canoe but are on the ship. It is hard for them to decide where they stand on the river of life because of this confusion. The waters around them are always dark and deep. It is hard to find answers about who they are and how to live because of the interference related to colonialism and to institutions like the residential schools. What can they do? There is so much confusion in those dark in-between waters, and it raises questions about how to retrieve people.

In our Indigenous communities, there have been disputes about Native women who have married non-Native men, and people have been asked to leave the reserve because of the legacy of Canada's Indian Act. We hear of many conflicts these days related to bloodlines. We have a lot of Native women who have brought their non-Native men into our community, and many in our community do not like what happens when those men start businesses under the umbrella of the Native woman so as to not pay taxes. I have also seen a lot of people from the ship who want to be Native, but their bloodline cannot be changed. In our Longhouse, the women carry the ancestral bloodline.

There are so many conflicts and there is so much confusion in these uncertain waters about what our roles and responsibilities are in relation to where we stand in the canoe or on the ship. Do we follow the legacy of Canadian laws? Do we understand what this approach is doing to our children? When I think about this confusion, I reflect on teachings that talk about adding rafters to the Longhouse. The relations in our environment are and were always changing, and this ability to add space to our culture was about being flexible and about being compassionate so that more people could be brought under the Great Tree of Peace. We have always had the ability in our culture to invite people in if they are coming in a spirit of peace and without the intention to change our way of life as Haudenosaunee.

We have ceremonies for adoption, but I do not know whether, after all the interference, our people really understand today what adoption is about. When you adopt others, they become your children, so you need to teach them the way that you would your own child. You need to teach them the values, stories, and songs of our Haudenosaunee culture. They have to feel connected and understood; they have to feel that they have a place of belonging. This is not about changing them but about empowering them to be who they are so that they can bring their gifts into relation. This is the space of *ǫ da gaho dę:s*, where we can broaden our thinking and ways of relating.

It is hard to unfold and straighten all this out because the ship's interference has created such confusion. Some of our people believe that things should be more open, whereas others believe that we need to be more rigid. Both views are often clouded with fear. This fear stops us from practicing Haudenosaunee teachings about forgiveness or even acknowledging the extent of what needs to be forgiven. Many children do not know that they are Native, and then all of a sudden, they find out and want to come home. They often arrive to experience a great wall in the community, a wall that says, "These are the laws about how to relate."

Because of our fear, we have grown rigid in saying that you or your ancestral line should have known better. People had no idea that being connected to the bloodline of a woman who left the community would interrupt their lives and all the generations who followed them. It is not the fault of their descendants that they were adopted out and had no sense of their identity or origins. Many of our people also now work in government, social services, the university, and other institutions of the ship. They have been influenced by their education and do not know much about their own Indigenous cultures.

There are divisions in Haudenosaunee communities because of these circumstances, so when I talk about culture, I am saying that this is what the Longhouse tradition tells us and that this tradition contains protocols about the way that things are supposed to be for us. A return to this tradition is needed if we are going to straighten out all these issues that are related to the colonization experienced through the Indian Act, residential schools, and the fate of Missing and Murdered Indigenous Women and Girls (MMIWG). Every community has been affected by colonialism, but despite this fact, there are still people, Elders, who know the structure and protocols of the culture. I know from experience that outcomes are best when we start with this foundation, with the protocols of the Longhouse.

We need to take time to discuss all this confusion. Our relations with the ship across the river of life have involved a transgression of the spiritual laws regarding noninterference, and this transgression has impacted the protocols in many of our ceremonies. We need to make these complex issues right by returning to the spirit of the teachings so as to root out the impacts of the Canadian government and culture on our identity and ways of living. All these divisions are a legacy of Canadian laws, and thus in this confusion, I return to the Longhouse tradition and bring these issues back to the Two Row Wampum.

It seems improbable that the Two Row could truly be honoured again. We have come this far over the past 500 years, and it will probably take that many years to unravel everything and to get at the real truth again. What does that mean for our everyday lives? How do we hold strong to our values so that we can empower people rather than disempowering them? Many on the ship have the same concern, and I have heard some talk about all the institutions and historic politics that are impacting their ways of living. How long is it going to take for them to unravel where they have come from and why their family is here now? It is a huge journey and task to unravel all that, but we have to say that it is possible if we are of a good mind and come to *ǫ da gaho dę:s* and if we put our hearts into it and discipline our ways of relating on the river of life. We have to start now!

The People in the Ganǫhǫnyǫhk (Thanksgiving Address).
Drawing by Gae Ho Hwako (Norma Jacobs).

Helping people
That's my concern
Willing to share my experience
Willing to learn
About the pain, the hurts, the anger

The strength it takes
To keep it inside
Turn it around, release it
You are strong, let it be known
No need to hide, open your heart to the warmth of the sun

The Creator has given so many gifts
Tears, laughter, anger, and pain
All will relieve the stress and sadness

Use these gifts and you will gain
Tears for cleansing
Laughter for happiness of the heart
Anger to recognize the loss of personal boundaries
Pain to realize humanness

Get on with the Great EXPERIENCE
Of life
Not time to hold grudges
A time to forgive
Love one another
We do not have time to be the judges

Our own lives to live
To find peace and contentment
Means more to me
Then to live with resentment

Yesterday is gone
That belongs in the past
Today is what counts
Live it in loving amounts
Tomorrow we know nothing about
Living today in humility and gratitude
Brings about a better attitude

I hope I have given the most today
For someone who needed
That smile, that shoulder to cry on
That hug, that time to share and be heard
When someone needed it most
For sometime, I know not when
I will turn to you
When I need a friend

Awehaode Communication: Journeying with Norma

Kawennakon (Bonnie Whitlow)

Before we begin, I want to take a moment to recognize the foundational writings of so many of the great scholars among the Onkwehón:we (lit. "original beings") who have successfully quantified and argued the validity of story and storytelling. Storytellers and orators play a distinguished role in our Haudenosaunee communities, as they maintain, transmit, and generate knowledge. Unlike our Western counterparts, an Onkwehón:we audience expects storytelling, not books, to be the primary means used to convey *onkwehonwe'néha* (the ways of being of the original people).

Onkwehón:we storytelling requires orators to evoke in listeners (or readers) a certain level of trust. We invite them to accompany us on a journey without a roadmap or the reassurance of a series of signs that point to a final destination. We do not naturally start with a thesis statement and then build the story or argument with a goal in mind. Instead, we simply start and then see where the conversation wants to go. You can see a reflection of the teachings of Gae Ho Hwako (Norma Jacobs) in the words of John Mohawk:

> It would be an Iroquois way of doing things to tell a story and to refuse to tell the listener what he/she should have learned from the story. The Iroquois pattern would be to tell a story and to ask the listener to use his/her own mind to see what they think the story means. This would

> most likely be done in a group, which would then discuss various elements of the story together, somewhat the same way some teachers do in university classes today. Iroquois teachers of the traditions, in my experience, are willing to accept that different people at different stages of life are able to grasp and learn from different elements of a story at different moments. Their point might be only that the story should be told and discussed among the generations.[1]

The protocols of storytelling allow many messages to manifest at once. This possibility also means that it is not the speaker's or writer's job to prescribe importance or preference to any one element in the story or to define for the audience what should be taken away. Rather, it allows for individuals to hear the messages that they are ready to hear. I reflect on the oral tradition as we weave together a series of stories and experiences that uplift the Haudenosaunee teachings shared by our many Faith Keepers, like Gae Ho Hwako. In writing, I strive to allow the words to flow through in the same way. I am less effective.

When I first started to work with Gae Ho Hwako and Winnie Thomas-kenha – kenha *indicating deceased – at Awehaode Communication (and later with Alfred Keye), they asked me to create materials and activities that would help people to understand what they wanted to teach. We would all sit in our little one-room office space, and they would ask me to listen while they shared teachings with each other. Afterward, I was to create materials (such as writings, pamphlets, etc.) that we could give to the people who attended the workshops or who wanted to learn more. If I did not understand something, they provided the clarity, and we fixed the materials. To this day, I cannot believe that this was a job and that I was paid to do it. It was a nerd's dream come true.* Nyá:wen yethishot'okón:'a *(thank you to the ancestors).*

I think about this experience often – how it was a gift and a responsibility. It was during this time that we created the Circle Wampum and Condolence Workshop. I still use this interactive workshop today, often teasing audiences by suggesting that I am going to make colonization fun. I prefer the activity to the KAIROS *Blanket Exercise because it focusses on the future and does not leave people mired in the traumatic history of colonization and violent relations with Canada. It shows how we survived because of the inherent resilience encoded in* onkwehonwe'néha. *We happily share these teachings and hope that people align with Haudenosaunee tenets of abundance instead of Western assumptions of scarcity. We uplift their mind so that they might flourish and view life from a position of joyfulness and hope.*

Here, we must have an uncomfortable conversation about cultural difference, entitlement, and appropriation. The workshop raises a different question all together when non-Haudenosaunee people enjoy it and then want to take it, use it, and inevitably profit from it. We have to remind people that the Two Row Wampum has three rows of beads between the people on the ship and those of us in the canoe. The Two Row tells us that we must filter our words and communication with others through the three white wampum beads of peace, friendship, and respect. Yet we must defend our boundaries while pointing to a prominent colonial instinct that demands unfettered access to all knowledge that it can consume and eventually commodify. From dreamcatchers to sweat lodges, Onkwehón:we practices are admired, extracted, decontextualized, rebranded, and glorified under the guise of respect and love for our culture – and the pretext that we are being honoured. We must insist on telling our own stories.

We have to contrast colonial thinking with Onkwehón:we practice, which requires that we recognize and honour boundaries. We teach our communities consent by recognizing that some knowledge "is not for you." It is useful here to consider Audra Simpson's work and her stance that we must "make the ethnography itself a refusal" and must resist "a presumptive claim of interpretive ownership; it is a statement of theft."[2] I have fielded many calls and emails from people who were enlightened by our workshop and called to ask for more explanation so that they can use it themselves (including several from the creators of the KAIROS Blanket Exercise). Many ask me to explain condolence and the ending again so that they can show others. Each time, I have become uncomfortable and have not responded. Although I understand the attraction, the foundations of the workshop are not mine to give away, nor will I support or promote the appropriation and theft of our culture.

We know that the workshop is effective because the practice of uplifting the mind was a gift sent by the Creator to our people at a time of great need. This practice united five warring nations and ushered in a time of peace and prosperity for all. Condolence is the foundational premise of our entire

Confederacy. The workshop is an interactive deep dive into Haudenosaunee experience and culture, simplistic yet profound. The power and beauty of our traditions are revealed by spirit, not simply made by people. I can understand the attraction and why people want to take it and show others. But we are protective of the content because one needs to understand the cultural constructs from within. Being told that we will not give them the permission to use the workshop can be a hard pill to swallow for those not accustomed to being told no.

Without any warning, Gae Ho Hwako and Winnie-kenha began to leave fifteen minutes at the end of their presentations for me to speak. I can remember being overwhelmed the first few times that I spoke publicly. I asked myself, "What do I have to offer?" especially following the depth that they demonstrated. After the initial shock wore off, I began to listen more intently and to think about how I could highlight the main points that I had grappled with during our office "lectures." I began to listen for gaps – things that we had discussed privately but that were not voiced during their talk.

One day, when talking about my nervousness to speak on something that I knew nothing about, Gae Ho Hwako told me to get my tobacco out. She told me that tobacco was a gift from the Sky World and that when we hold it in our left hand and ask for help in our languages, then our words and our thoughts go into the tobacco. When we burn that tobacco, the smoke will be able to pierce the space between the earth and the Sky World and will carry our words and thoughts to the ears of Shonkwaya'tihson (the Creator). She gave me a short speech that I could memorize and use when I was asking for help. And, most importantly, she told me that we are like a hollow bone through which our ancestors speak and that if we allow ourselves to be used as their instrument, the words that we need will be there. It certainly could not hurt to try, so I tucked that nugget away and vowed that I would follow her suggestion at the next opportunity.

Shortly afterwards, Gae Ho Hwako had double-booked herself and asked me to fill in for her at the last minute. Only after I agreed did I find out that it was at Trent University's Elder gathering and that the topic was Haudenosaunee concepts of love. The venue and my lack of knowledge on the subject urged me to back out. Gae Ho Hwako insisted. She told me that I had promised to help her when she asked and that this was what she needed. On my doorstep, I grabbed my tobacco, sent my plea for help out into the universe, and made my offering. Then off I went.

I had no money, no car, and no time to prepare. I hustled up a ride and arrived extremely late, just as the opening panel of presenters was finishing. I was ushered onstage and thrown into the spotlight. To this day, I have no idea what I said. I remember that there was a lot of laughter and that my workshops were so full that people were sitting on the ground. I do know that I learned the importance of the practice of being like a hollow bone.

I opened with the Ohén:ton Karihwatéhkwen (Thanksgiving Address), the speech that Gae Ho Hwako had taught me, and then I introduced myself. It is a hard feeling to describe, so bear with me. It felt like I could hear/see someone (who was not me) just inside my left ear and behind my left eye. He/she/they were telling and showing me story images to share. I also know that they were demanding. There was a story that I tried to avoid that they wanted shared. I cannot recall why I tried to refuse telling it. My guess is that my fear of displaying public vulnerability was my struggle. After I sidestepped the story the first two times, it dropped in front of my eyes, and I could see nothing else. It was either tell that story or just stand there confused, staring into space, in front of the entire audience. I had to submit, and when I did, the flow was there. Although I was completely unaware of the passage of time, the helpers were not. With exactly five minutes left, I had just enough time to do a closing, and then the experience was just over.

Looking back, I see that I had not even realized that I was being groomed for anything, and I am equally unsure whether either Gae Ho Hwako or Winnie-kenha were intentionally doing so. This is only how I experienced this teaching, and I share my reflections so that others may discover more about this practice. Years later, another mentor and friend from Akwesashne would tell me that I could simply ask the ancestors to slow down so that I could finish with one story before they shared another. That knowing has been very useful.

If academics are serious about their stated Indigenization and decolonization strategies, they must expand their understanding of the parameters of Onkwehón:we oral tradition. *Onkwehonwe'néha* "systems have always been primarily oral, yet they sustained complex social, cultural, spiritual, and political systems long before the arrival of the Europeans."[3] Having to write endnotes in a document created with a word-processing program in order to explain our literary choices is a great example of how colonial aggressions play out and the subtle forms that oppression can take. A word-processing program is infused with colonial literary norms and expectations that can be absurd, such as its unrelenting "need" to signal "correction" in a sentence that includes the passive voice. Even in the broader academic setting, where individuals may believe themselves to be wholeheartedly creating inclusionary spaces for Indigenous thought, we can highlight a barrage of expectations that consistently signal to Indigenous scholars that our natural, uncolonized, Onkwehón:we rhythms are unacceptable. This situation exemplifies the kinds of emotional labour that we undertake as Onkwehón:we in the academy.

I am a Haudenosaunee storyteller and can rest comfortably knowing that there is a developing recognition of this choice within the academy.[4] I hope my voice joins the chorus of Onkwehón:we scholars as we uplift and defend an ancient Haudenosaunee cultural legacy envisioned in a modern context. I hope that our words convey our passion for revitalization and that they demonstrate our love for our nations and the intention of positive transformation. In the minds of my Haudenosaunee colleagues, family, and friends, it is a universal, self-evident truth – a truth so basic that it does not need to be stated but is simply known and accepted – that *onkwehonwe'néha* has always been the antidote to colonialism. Our ancient practices will help us to safely navigate the troubled waters as we watch the downfall of capitalism and the Western world. I, for one, am happy to know that there are sustainable ways to engage with the natural world and that these practices are veiled and embedded in our cultural legacy. Indeed, this legacy has sustained us across the centuries of violence that followed our apocalyptic first contact with Europeans. We will continue to thrive.

At Six Nations of the Grand River Territory (and throughout the Confederacy), when a person who has learned the ceremonial speeches and had been chosen to speak on behalf of the people recites a story or speaks publicly, there is a common ending that acknowledges a person's humanity. It provides cultural safety and comfort for the orator. I call for a similar understanding in print. Here is a summary of a standard closing that I use at the end of a public recital of the Ganǫhǫnyǫhk (Thanksgiving Address): "I am honoured to stand humbly before the people, the natural world, and the Creator. Today, it is my duty to speak the words of thanks on our behalf. I recognize that I have done the best that I am able. If I have made a mistake or have forgotten something, I ask that those who are gathered here together will make it right in their minds."

A Personal Story of Dispossession and Reconnection

> Real people (among the Haudenosaunee or Iroquois, *onkwehonwe*) have more than an awareness of the relationship of spirit to matter, for they strive to live the Creator's way and that experience of living leads them to a spiritual life. We see manifestations of the Creator's way all around us in the wind, the rocks, the mountains, the rain, and our spirits are often lifted by the incredible beauty of these things.[5]

Understanding the transformational impact of my reintroduction to ancestral teachings shared by Gae Ho Hwako, the entire Jacobs family, Winnie-kenha, and so many others means unravelling a labyrinth of social policies that contributed to my familial dispossession. Taking a cue from Shawn Wilson in *Research Is Ceremony* (2008), I share some of who I am as a Kanyen'kehaka woman and some of what that means to me and how it informs my identity. We come to know each other through relationships, as "relationality requires that you know a lot more about me before you can understand my work."[6]

Now that I have located myself culturally and respected the protocols of my nation, I can introduce myself according to mainstream convention, although my Haudenosaunee patterning remains. My real name is Kawennakon (lit. "it's in her words/language"), and my English name is Bonnie Whitlow. I am a Haudenosaunee (Iroquoian) woman, and by matrilineal bloodline, I was born into the Kanyen'kehaka (Mohawk Nation) and the Yonkwaskare:wake (Bear Clan) of Ohswe:ken (Six Nations of the Grand River Territory). I share a personal, yet commonplace, story of cultural deprivation.

I was raised off-reserve, less than a stone's throw outside of the boundary line and directly across the river. Off-territory meant that we were one of only two Onkwehón:we families whose children attended public school in a small local village. We were the only people of colour in an all-white school and all-white district. For this reason, my schooling was the same as most other Canadians, with little to no reference to Onkwehón:we people, our languages, and our cultures and with zero reference to Indigenous-settler relations. My education imparted a white-washed history that began at European contact, with derisive reference to anything Onkwehón:we.

The early 1980s was the first time that I can recall hearing my mom talk about being a status Indian. Bill C-31 had been passed, and she was able to get her status back. That was cause for celebration and for excitement around our house, which left a huge imprint on my psyche. Until that moment, I did not know that the government had denied us our identity and rights as Onkwehón:we. We were Mohawk, as were all our friends and family, and I had never questioned why we lived off-reserve, whereas all of our cousins lived on the reserve.

I would later learn that the Enfranchisement Act had decreed that my mother needed to give up her status when she married my father. Even though she was full-blooded, my mother was no longer eligible to live on the reserve and could not legally own any of her family land. The same thing happened to my father's mother, my grandma Hazel. Despite being full-blooded, she also lost her status and was kicked off the reserve when she married my grandpa Eddie. My grandpa Eddie was half-blooded but never had status because his mother had been kicked off the reserve when she married a newly landed Irish immigrant. Once married, they also could not live on the reserve or own land there, so Hazel and Eddie bought land across Indian Line – yes, the township still uses that name – and they raised their children, including my father, as close to the reserve as physically possible, a literal stone's throw from the rest of their families. These were circumstances that I had never considered as a child.

Although the government may have been confused about our identity, my mother was not. We were Mohawk of the Bear Clan and were reminded of this often. She was one of those women who knew the genealogy of every single person she ever met. She kept paper clippings of birth and death announcements and she took endless pictures at family gatherings. She knew everyone's family, every distant relative, every marriage, and every divorce. She was an epic genealogist and kept most of this information in her head. I wish that I had listened. I wish that I remembered even half of what she told me. She carried all that familial knowledge for us and tried to get us to pay attention. If I had known that there would come a day when I would help with names and need to know the family lines, I would have paid more attention. I chastise myself often.

Spurred on by the tumultuous spirit of the Oka Crisis in 1990, I began seeking answers in earnest. I questioned what made me a Mohawk woman and how that was different from Joe Canadian, who was a character in a popular beer commercial at the time. Like many before me and many after me, a land occupation shook me awake. The fact that Canada had called in 4,500 troops to bully and threaten Mohawk women and children was mystifying. I could not understand how this self-proclaimed "peaceful and polite" country was using military force and state violence to silence our women. What was going on? The events of 1990 galvanized my soul, and I would spend the rest of my life reconnecting to our traditions, listening to our histories, and revitalizing my language. Since that time, I have dedicated my life to decolonizing my mind, body, and soul. I am not done yet.

Writing this during Covid-19 and amidst the 1492 Land Back Lane occupation, I reflect on these nationwide Onkwehón:we actions. An interesting pattern emerges. Every uprising sparks a new fire of revitalization and rediscovery of our traditional ways. Generally, some sort of state-sanctioned violence against Indigenous people occurs, and the community responds by coming together to publicly defend our boundaries and one another. Together, we fall in love with how being unified feels, and we are compelled to learn more about onkwawenna *(our original languages),* onkwehonwe'néha *(the ways of being of the original people), the Kayanere'kowa (Great Law of Peace), and the Kanonhses (Longhouse).*

It is through Onkwehón:we doctrine that we listen to each other and to the universal energies as we try to understand what is being shown; that our ancestors offer us an opportunity to learn from every experience; and that, if we listen closely and see the signs being laid before us, we can begin to understand our human journey on a deeper level. Sometimes, it can be cloaked by a shroud of hate. But, if you listen closely and are lucky, you can see beyond the ugliness to the beauty being revealed. State violence invokes unity and resurrects a collective community identity by providing poignant reminders of who we are, where we come from, and where we need to go.

In this transitional time between worlds, we are being given an opportunity to pick up the precepts of the Kayanere'kowa and to find our way back to ourselves. When we return to our ancestral practices, we re-enliven the peaceful and joyful existence that the Creator had originally intended. We are told the original instructions that we are to remember, and we are told to be thankful.

Modern Contexts of Onkwehonwe'néha?

I adopted an intense, anti-colonial stance in the early 1990's. I have dedicated my adult life to decolonization by returning to ceremony, studying our traditional history, acquiring technical knowledge of our medicines, and improving my ability to speak my ancestral language. As I enter the field of Onkwehón:we scholarship and research, I intend to co-opt the resources of the institution for the betterment of my community. I reject the imposition of Euro-Canadian frameworks and "inquire in ways that hook up with … intellectual projects in the service of indigenous sovereignty."[7]

There is heated controversy in our territories as to whether it is ethical in Haudenosaunee terms to enter the ship, make space for ourselves, share our teachings and worldview with its inhabitants, and possibly interfere with its direction, either deliberately or unintentionally. The basic tenets of the Tekeni Teyoha:te (Two Row Wampum) are often the philosophical locale for this debate.

The Tekeni Teyoha:te is the oft-quoted foundational treaty between the Haudenosaunee and the Dutch that immediately defines and calls for an intercultural relationship of noninterference between the ship and the canoe. Since contact with Europeans, the Haudenosaunee have maintained distinct principles of sovereignty and self-determination and have agreed to enter negotiations with the immigrant nations based on the three explicitly defined pillars of peace, respect, and friendship. In words similar to Gae Ho Hwako's teachings, the Akwesasne Mohawk Council writes, "Some say that the two rows of purple beads represent two separate vessels traveling parallel to each other down the 'River of Life.' The Haudenosaunee are in their canoes. This symbolizes their culture, laws, traditions, customs and life-ways. The non-Haudenosaunee are said to be in their ship, which symbolizes everything that they carry in their culture, laws, traditions, customs and lifeways. It is said that each nation shall stay in their own vessels, and travel the River of Life side by side. It is further said that neither nation will try to steer the vessel of the other, or interfere [with] or impede the travel of the other."[8]

The Tekeni Teyoha:te also represents a cautionary tale for the Haudenosaunee. It tells us that although we may visit one another, we cannot control the other's vessel and cannot stand astride the two, with a foot in each one. There will be a time when the vessels come upon obstacles or rapids, and those who do not choose one vessel will fall into the waters and perish. Although not always explicitly stated in mixed company, it is simply understood in our communities that the only reasonable choice is the canoe.

The metaphor contends (or assumes) that it is absolutely unethical, in Haudenosaunee terms, to try to interfere with the ship. But I feel drawn to question whether the intrinsic colonial nature of the ship is immutable and sacrosanct? Countless examples of colonial interference with our canoe, which have changed our communities forever, demonstrate that this assertion is fallible and that the inverse is also possible. Further, there are many prominent people who have entered the ship (be it the academy or the electoral system), helped to make instrumental change, and returned home with their ancestral identity intact. I think of our beloved Arthur Manuel and John Mohawk. Such people open the door for questioning the possibility of how we can successfully interrupt the assimilative agenda of the colonial state while working within the confines of the institutions that were designed to erase us completely.

There are historical examples wherein hybridization is the very reason that *onkwehonwe'néha* survived at all. Notably, the Karihwi:yo (Code of Handsome Lake) is a foundational adaptation of practice and tradition that inarguably changed the where and how of ceremonial practice. It was an evolutionary and innovative change that saved the core of who the Haudenosaunee are today. This transformation of our spiritual expression and practice preserved traditionalism amidst the onslaught of colonialism. After we abandoned living in matrilineal, multi-family, longhouse homes and adopted nuclear family dwellings, the Kanonhseshne (denoting both the physical buildings and the Longhouse tradition) became the focal point for traditional practice and intergenerational transmission of language and culture. Can we replicate these results in other colonial spaces like education and the system of elected governance?

Pretendians and Expertise

Because "pretendianism" centres on questioning identity and authenticity, we recognize how quickly tensions arise. This is not a discussion about those dispossessed through various "Indian" removal and assimilation policies, such as enfranchisement, intermarriage, the Sixties Scoop, child welfare removal, foster care, and adoption. For the dispossessed, there is a well-worn pathway that we can take to return to our nations and reclaim our rightful space as we learn and practise culture and tradition within our community circles. In Haudenosaunee terms, we are called to follow the white roots of peace back to the sheltering branches of the Tree of Peace. Many of us are diligently working to restore our familial, community, and national identities. It is not enough for one of us to self-proclaim an ancestral identity. We have to be seen putting in time and work in our communities before the other members will claim us as one of their own. The academy needs to recognize that our identities are not simply individualistic, as they are expected to be in settler society. Ancestral identities are collectively defined by clan, community, and kin. There is some later discussion about who our communities recognize as culturally fluent and how university hiring practices tend to favour individuals with false identities who then reproduce tokenized, colonial stereotypes. Sometimes, people are consciously hired who will go along without creating waves, and sometimes the universities are constrained by legal policies and simply by not knowing how to ask the ancestry questions. When we say that this is an institutional problem, that is because in our community, this is the first question that we ask each other, "So where ya from?" We are triangulating. We need to figure out how we are connected to each other and who we have in common. There is no dance or deflection because we check in afterwards and confirm each other's stories.

This discussion is primarily directed at the prevalent and ongoing practice among non-Natives of creating a completely false claim to Onkwehón:we ancestry and then taking up academic positions of authority on Indigenization and decolonization. There are some high-profile cases, like Andrea Smith and Ward Churchill in academia and Joseph Boyden and Michelle Latimer in the arts. There are hundreds more who are currently being scrutinized in academic institutions in North America and thousands worldwide, as well as thousands more in myriad professional fields. It is a global phenomenon.

The academy is currently under fire to reconcile with itself how its system has repeatedly led to the hiring of non-Onkwehón:we or barely Onkwehón:we, who are often complete frauds, as their in-house "Indigenous" experts. After thirty plus years of articles, several high-profile cases, and a variety of terms to refer to the practice – ethnic identity fraud, wannabe, race-shifter, pretendian, and so on – you can still investigate every institution and find these questionable hires in Indigenous studies departments who are teaching Indigenous classes and proclaiming to design Indigenous curriculum, all while profiting from their water-thin assertions of identity. These hires often succeed because the individuals who make up institutional hiring committees have no way to quantify and/or verify authenticity. In general, systemically racist academic hiring protocols favour inauthenticity, weed out the actual Onkwehón:we whom colonial institutions are designed to attract, reproduce whiteness, and reject diversity. These systemic processes will need to be redesigned and decolonized in order to attract and retain Onkwehón:we academics.

Throughout history, countless Faith Keepers have argued that *onkwehonwe'néha* is not found in a book; you cannot learn to be Onkwehón:we by reading about it. Rather, it is a land-based discipline that happens in concert with your community. It is an ever-growing, always evolving knowledge base that is not meant to be recorded, static, and fixed – caged by text in a colonial language, surrounded with colonial logics and ethics, supported by a colonial epistemology, and limited by the author's perception at the time that the story is written. As Shawn Wilson writes, "A problem with writing down stories is that it makes it very difficult to change them as we gain new learning and insight."[9]

Generally speaking, the academy's definitions of Indigenous authority (via degrees granted) contradict our Onkwehón:we protocols for authenticating Knowledge Keepers and for identifying experts. Senator Murray Sinclair, chair of Canada's Truth and Reconciliation Commission, concisely expressed a similar perspective on Anishinaabe authority, expertise, and academic Elderism. Hiring committees across the nation that are looking to hire Indigenous talent would be well served if they took note of the question asked by Sinclair in the following: "It has been my experience that many so called Traditional Elders don't know the first damn thing about traditional teachings. They just make things up or use what they read in books. I don't trust most of them. Traditional and spiritual people had to be mentored for a long time before they could claim that title. Institutions are at fault for hiring people as Elders who don't deserve the title, but once you have the door with the title on it, your career as an Elder is set. I always need to know the answer to this question: 'Where did you get your teachings?' before I go into ceremony with anyone. You should too."[10]

At Six Nations (and in other pockets of the Confederacy), there is a well-known and often expressed community distaste for academia – particularly for "Iroquoianists" (i.e., non-Haudenosaunee ceremonial researchers and students of Haudenosaunee studies) who challenge the authority of our Haudenosaunee Faith Keepers and their leadership based on something that they read in a book, often written by outsiders. On the reserve, traditional practitioners carry a large responsibility for the rest of us. They plan, coordinate, and preside over ceremonies, feasts, and speeches for both on- and off-reserve community members. They spend their lives "doing" and demonstrating their growing expertise in front of a vast community of fellow traditionalists. They earn their knowledge across decades by listening and watching as they help their mentors and teachers to fulfill their ceremonial duties. In academia, our ceremonialists are erased by practices that require us to cite people who have written things down rather than community experts who have maintained the practices, carried the knowledge across millennia, and transmitted our culture to future generations. From a Haudenosaunee point of view, academic practice is completely backwards.

The confines of the colonial academy and "higher learning" stifle our traditional definitions of how one accrues knowledge. Western literary norms decontextualize our teachings and place them in a small, heavily structured, textual box that constricts the vitality of those messages, not allowing them to live, breathe, or change. We assume that the colonial box nullifies and rejects our cultural blueprints in their entirety. But is it possible that there are facets of the academy that can support and fortify our revitalization efforts? In the words of Devon Mihesuah and Angela Wilson, there is much that "we can do to Indigenize the academy; to carve a space where Indigenous values and knowledge are respected; to create an environment that supports research and methodologies that are useful to Indigenous nation building; to support one another as institutional foundations are shaken; and to compel institutional responsiveness to Indigenous issues, concerns, and communities."[11]

In her book *In Divided Unity: Haudenosaunee Reclamation at Grand River* (2016), Theresa McCarthy deconstructs the white supremacist foundations of Iroquoian studies and how institutions usurp control and authority in cultural spaces. She sheds light on the absurdity of an accredited university program about everything Haudenosaunee that was designed by colonial peoples for colonial peoples inside the walls of a colonial institution. She unravels the web of entitlement and the assumed authority across all academic disciplines that together establish a "tradition of non-Indigenous 'expertise' on Haudenosaunee tradition." As she writes, "Whether challenged by detractors or yearned for by supporters, the authenticity of Haudenosaunee traditions has become something that seemingly anyone can evaluate. This sense of entitlement is connected to many other forms of settler entitlement that shape Indigenous lives. The many forms of external authority over Indigenous peoples – authority created and reinforced by laws, legislation, policies, and academic research – have given rise to a profoundly normalized culture of 'folks who think they know better' when it comes to Indians. How else can we explain the tendency for settlers to feel completely entitled to tell us how to be?"[12]

Along with the rejection of colonial definitions of authority, we must highlight a community definition of expertise, expressed in terms of cultural fluency and, by contrast, cultural illiteracy. When you combine this definition with the assertion that *onkwehonwe'néha* does not reside in books, you can begin to understand the community's skepticism when faced with non-Native academics standing at the front of the classroom for Indigenous studies courses or any program, workshop, or class with the word Indigenous in the title. In addition to Senator Sinclair's question above, outsiders can ask themselves several more questions when trying to determine whether the individual sitting across the table has the expertise that is claimed: "How were they trained – where, by whom, in what language? Are teachers Indigenous-minded or 'West-minded'?"[13]

Our Knowledge Keepers still actively contend that authentic *onkwehonwę'néha* is conveyed orally and enlivened through daily practice. In Haudenosaunee communities, acquiring expertise in *onkwehonwe'néha* requires a lifetime of mentoring, practice, and study. This practice occurs on the land in concert with the rest of our community members. Proficiency and mastery develop over decades. There is no acceptable self-definition; there is only community recognition and/or verification. For us, expertise is not only defined by intellectual pursuits but must also include action and performance. In contrast, colonial expertise accrues after a few short years of higher learning, heavily focussed on reading and regurgitating text. The ship expects you to "brand" yourself an expert after a few short years of study and to add letters of confirmation after your name the moment that you graduate. Therein lies the crux of the problem.

In our community, Haudenosaunee cultural and ceremonial expertise is completely transparent. The only people who can bestow and bequeath such designations are our fellow Haudenosaunee citizens. Although we appreciate the attempts to increase intercultural sharing and understanding, we draw distinct boundaries for those who would usurp our voice, space, practice, and knowledge for their own personal gain. As with our leadership protocols, the fastest way for people to discredit their claims to expertise is for them to stand up and self-proclaim themselves to be experts.

As a growing body of authentic Onkwehón:we scholars decolonize these colonial spaces, we force the institutions to grapple with the limits of their experience and knowledge of us. We point out the absurdity of their assumed institutional superiority in the face of local community members who habitually demonstrate their expertise and cultural eloquence (often without degrees but with the full recognition of the community). Conversely, there is prolific evidence of the academy's cultural illiteracy, as it has consistently demonstrated that it has zero understanding of how we internally define the cultural adept, let alone any capacity whatsoever to assess Onkwehón:we identities.

As the prevalence of the pretendian complex has risen to the surface in the academy, the question of how to authenticate Onkwehón:we identity has clearly led to a difficult discussion in colonial spaces and institutions. This bureaucratic unease has resulted in waves of opportunists taking advantage of the grey space in between the ship and the canoe. It is worth noting that their trepidation is to be expected, as institutional knowledge of Onkwehón:we and *onkwehonwe'néha* is practically nonexistent. Hands-off approaches like self-identification policies do not address the problem but instead exacerbate it. And finally, it has been almost three decades since Niles Bird Runningwater first articulated the following recommendations (using US terminology) for resolving this problem:

> Provide a space on the employment application for self-identifying individuals to list their tribal affiliation(s).
>
> Construct a heritage sheet that would accompany the employment applicant who is self-identified as "Native American," "American Indian," or "Alaska Native." This will allow the applicant an opportunity to provide verification of their tribal community involvement, tribal

> enrollment, social recognition, blood quantum, etc. This heritage sheet should also be accompanied with a statement by the institution regarding the ramifications of committing ethnic fraud.[14]

We can see these hires for the tricksters that they are – tricksters who dance the story of the fool for us. Through misdirection, they entertain settlers, performing just enough Indigenous vaguery – like waving eagle feathers about or performing non-nation-specific spirituality like smudging – to convince the outsider of their authenticity. It is nothing more than performative camouflage and charlatanry. Like any good con artist, these imposters have identified knowledge gaps and exploited them. Hiring committees, scholarship juries, granting agencies, and so many others lack the nuanced understanding and experience required to spot and flag even the most pronounced, inauthentic markers of Onkwehón:we identity.

This dance of distraction serves a societal function. Tricksterism is supposed to disturb our peace and to gnaw away at us until we face our shadows. Tricksters show us that something needs to change. The mirror that they hold up reflects back our collective folly, urging us to take action. If we examine their artifice closely enough, their dance reveals the gaping holes in institutional policies and invites us to close the gaps that pretendians have exploited for far too long.

The Haudenosaunee do not acknowledge or recognize any governmental influence or self-identification process for determining identity or expertise. We reject all colonial attempts by individuals, organizations, or governments to tell us who we are. We assert our sovereign discretion to determine membership in our nation and to confer Confederacy citizenship. We will let you know who is (or is not) a citizen of our nation and the Confederacy, and we will let you know who is (or is not) culturally fluent. This is a contentions issue, as membership and enrolment in band and tribal councils are determined by colonial governments, often in direct contradiction of ancestral processes. Although imposters might be emboldened to exploit the academy's folly and proclaim an Onkwehón:we identity, anyone who tries the same thing within our community is quickly corrected and often rejected.

To be clear, we are not discussing the dispossessed and the displaced. We need to recognize how myriad historical factors have deprived many of access to their birthright and created a tangled web of identity confusion. We seek to reconnect the lost generations to their Haudenosaunee cultural legacy. In 2019, in response to further proposed amendments to the Indian Act, the Haudenosaunee Confederacy issued another press release outlining our citizenship law and jurisdiction:

> There are two ways that one is recognized as a Haudenosaunee citizen:
>
> 1. Persons born of a Haudenosaunee mother. A person is considered a Haudenosaunee citizen at birth provided that he or she is born of a mother who is considered to be a Haudenosaunee citizen with a Haudenosaunee clan transferred at birth.
> 2. Persons adopted into a Haudenosaunee clan.
>
> … [Haudenosaunee sovereignty] includes the legal and moral authority to define Haudenosaunee citizenship regardless of where the Haudenosaunee citizen is domiciled. The Haudenosaunee, as a distinct and sovereign people, has the exclusive right to determine their own citizenship and nationality.
>
> Since time immemorial, Haudenosaunee identity and nationality has been transferred matrilineally through the mother's clan family.[15]

Fortunately, our community's genealogical experts have spent their lifetime untangling the knots in our clan lines that are the result of settler colonialist interference. We need to ensure that the dispossessed who are following the white roots of peace back to the sheltering branches of the Tree of Peace have a safe space and an opportunity to do so without being compromised by the discussions directed at exposing the antics of the con artists. We recognize the tension and emotional turmoil that these conversations create for the lost generations. For them, we must ensure that we do not create more suffering and that we help them to reconnect. We need to celebrate their return and to welcome them home.

Ka'satstenhsera (Empowerment) through Scarcity

Gae Ho Hwako's son was my first love. I spent more time with his family than my own. I more or less moved right in and made myself at home. We lived with his grandmother and grandfather, and the house was often a space of learning. People from across the Confederacy would stop in and talk about the Longhouse and ceremony. I learned a lot during this time. I developed a special relationship with Gae Ho Hwako's parents, Cassie-kenha and Oliver-kenha, and thought of them as my own grandparents, often referring to them as Grandma and Grandpa. When the partner relationship broke down, the most difficult part was leaving the rest of the family. I had come to think of them as my own. The loss was immense.

A few months later, I was working in the yard at my mother's house when a van pulled into the driveway. The side door rolled open, and I was happy to see Cassie-kenha's smiling face beckoning to me. When I walked over, I saw Oliver-kenha sitting on the other side of the van. He simply looked at me and said, "You're our friend, too!" And he smiled. The tears were immediate, and I choked up. She smiled, told me to come and visit, and closed the door. As they pulled away, I was left to think about their words and their actions. It did not take long for me to simply pick up where we had left off. My visits were practically daily.

I was welcomed into the fold of the Jacobs family – a traditional Haudenosaunee family who had maintained their connection to our languages and ancestral ceremonial practices. Gae Ho Hwako's entire family are some of the most influential people in my life. I feel privileged to call them mentors, teachers, family, and friends. Their willingness to share their time and teachings has grounded me and completely transformed my view of both the world and the meaning of life. I am forever grateful.

Because of his position as a chief in the Confederacy, Oliver-kenha was often required to travel to different communities for different meetings or ceremonies, and I was happy to drive for him. I was exposed to everything. I learned more driving them to do errands than most people learn in a classroom, and I would recommend that everyone become a helper. It is the time before events start that is the most precious – the time when people are just quietly musing and thinking about what needs to be done and talking about the hows and whys.

In particular, I remember one short conversation that we had. While I was calculating his age, I realized that he had been born during the Great Depression, and I asked him what it was like. He simply responded, "Meh, we didn't really notice it much." I was floored, mind-blown. I have thought about that simple statement and the power behind it a million times. What might have seemed like intense poverty to some was just a way of life for us. Such mild commentary underscores both the effectiveness of a communal distribution of wealth and the power of traditional teachings to provide for the needs of our people. I see incalculable strength in that simplicity.

My mom once told me that the construction of my uncle Donny's house was the last time that the community had held a community house-raising. And my sister told me about how the men and women did everything that it took to build a home, with the children playing and everyone eating together. There is an immense strength in simply doing what is needed to take care of each other. Everyone we knew had large gardens. We picked vegetables and fruits and gathered nuts every year. We knew where all the best spots were, and my mom always rushed us to get there before everyone else realized that it was harvest time. We canned everything and stored the harvest for winter. We had a large freezer and were locavores long before it was cool. Necessity bred power.

When I was older, my circle was filled with medicine people sharing natural plant medicine lore and home remedies for everything. I began to see the power of nations of people who could house themselves, feed themselves, and heal themselves. And as I entered the academy, I began to understand the challenge that we present to the colonial state. For a culture that controls people with fear, it makes perfect sense that our self-empowerment is viewed as a pre-eminent threat. Things began to make a lot more sense. What some might consider scarcity is viewed by others as abundance and strength. Because Indigenous communities had to maintain alternative subsistence economies in order to survive, we now find themselves in a powerful position as we watch the capitalist system decline.

I remember one South American healer who mentioned that it is the city people who will be most effected by the mass disruption and said that they will go crazy. We caught a glimpse of this at the start of the Covid-19 pandemic. The hoarding of toilet paper was an absurd yet powerful indication of how fragile the supply system really is. Surrounded by concrete, most are wholly disconnected from the land and are completely dependent on a fragile supply chain. The fear and greed that we witnessed are a warning sign for us all.

There are still small pockets of Onkwehón:we who outright reject all notions of capitalism or interference by mainstream society and who choose instead to subscribe to a subsistence-based economy. Although some may live poorly in financial terms, they embody an incredible wealth of traditional technological knowledge that speaks volumes to the current generation of Haudenosaunee youth. Many of these people tend to be our healers and medicine people, and most want to participate in settler society as little as possible. They are also the leaders of a growing worldwide decolonization movement.

A few years ago, I visited with another beloved mentor and friend who is now in her eighties. I was pleasantly surprised by her new home and remarked on it. She remained wistful and longed for her older and simpler home. I recalled a decades-old discussion with her about electricity and running water and how she had resisted technology into her seventies because she did not want to become used to the conveniences. She said that she did not want to get used to the ease and become dependent on them because it would be difficult to give them up when she got older. She said that this kind of life makes you weak. Again, I was astonished. The combination of internal fortitude, physical strength, and technical knowledge required to maintain such a lifestyle is inspirational. It is also not an uncommon story in our communities. These kinds of resistance become symbols of decolonial pride that drive an ever-growing population of Onkwehón:we who are seeking to live off-grid and outside the capitalist system.

An expanding number of Haudenosaunee are turning their backs on the modern conveniences of Western society and adhering to our revitalized ancestral practices. These members of our population are the most vocal and active in pushing back against the system. The decolonizing movement responds directly to the four main pillars of colonial oppression: religion, education, the legal system, and the market economy. We are actively extricating our lives from participation in settler society's tangled web. Workshops and teach-ins that expand on our ancestral knowledge of hunting, fishing, gathering, and growing continue to rise in popularity. Our reconnection to natural food cycles and to health and healing grounded in the natural world has become commonplace. Traditional plant knowledge empowers us to learn to heal ourselves naturally without Western medical intervention. Our land base is vital to the continuation of our species, as is the need to protect Mother Earth from the nearly constant attack of outside forces.

An Onkwehón:we epistemology is a resilient, anti-colonial, survival-based expertise that has been sharpened and refined by centuries of resistance.

There is an intense Haudenosaunee legacy of refusal to ask an outsider for permission or approval for anything. Instead, we will continue to listen to our cultural teachings and to fulfill our responsibilities as defined by our ancestors. We will survive and thrive "outside" of the colonial, patriarchal, capitalistic machine. As "outsiders" on the ship, we recognize that mainstream society is not environmentally, emotionally, or economically sustainable.

It is tiring to recognize that we are still performing Indigeneity for the state and writing massive arguments to assert our basic, fully agential human capacity for both knowledge and expertise. We are still viewed as a repository of resources that can be mined and exploited by the academy. It is still necessary for Onkwehón:we scholars to deconstruct state assumptions that we are less capable, less evolved, and unable to produce anything of value. Although the act of justifying our existence is still commonplace, we are poised to raise this incredibly low bar regarding our abilities a little higher.

There is also long-stated concern throughout the Haudenosaunee Confederacy that youth who leave the community – the canoe – in search of a higher education on the ship will lose their Onkwehón:we identity and be both indoctrinated and then consumed by colonial machinery. Although less common now, there is a local attitude that belittles Western education, and there is an oft-stated fear that our youth will no longer think like us. An infamous quote (at least in Haudenosaunee circles) from the writings of Benjamin Franklin captures the general sentiment that our community has long held about the merit of a Western education. It is also a beautiful example of the oratorical prowess and diplomacy of our Haudenosaunee statesmen. I have attended dozens of lectures by highly respected Haudenosaunee scholars who continue to share the following words with our communities, lest we forget:

> We are convinced, therefore, that you mean to do us good by your proposal, and we thank you heartily. But you who are wise must know that different nations have different conceptions of things; and you will therefore not take it amiss if our ideas of this kind of education happen not to be the same with yours. We have had some experience of it; several of our young people were formerly brought up at the colleges of the northern provinces; they were instructed in all your sciences; but when they came back to us, they were bad runners; ignorant of every

> means of living in the woods; unable to bear either cold or hunger; knew neither how to build a cabin, take a deer, or kill an enemy; spoke our language imperfectly; were therefore neither fit for hunters, warriors, nor counsellors; they were totally good for nothing. We are, however, not the less obliged by your kind offer, though we decline accepting it; and to show our grateful sense of it, if the gentlemen of Virginia will send us a dozen of their sons, we will take great care of their education, instruct them in all we know, and make *men* of them.[16]

Although there was an era when teachings were underground and heavily guarded by the few, there is now a burgeoning openness in our Haudenosaunee communities. Now, those who were historically dispossessed of their culture have a duty to return and learn about it, and the traditionalists who have safeguarded our knowledge must welcome us back with open arms.

Is it possible that the inverse is more true – that Onkwehón:we seekers and scholars who regularly engage in battle with the colonial machine will instead return with their tools of resistance now sharpened through constant confrontation that has deepened and strengthened our original, anti-colonial stance? As we turn our mind's eye toward the revitalization of *onkwehonwe'néha*, those same battle skills that we have learned while engaged in constant combat with institutionalized colonialism can be redirected to empower our communities.[17] Armed with an enhanced skill set, we aim to resurrect our ancient frameworks and to augment them in the contemporary context through modernized metaphorical longhouses replete with everything that we need for cultural survival. Additionally, as more members of our Haudenosaunee traditionalist community, like Gae Ho Hwako, enter the colonial domain and successfully maintain their Onkwehón:we identity while fulfilling their Onkwehón:we responsibilities, we prove not only that we are capable but also that we can adapt, thrive, and succeed in both locales. We become seasoned soldiers protecting Haudenosaunee jurisdiction and asserting Haudenosaunee sovereignty over our knowledge.

To expand this thinking into more contentious territory, we can ask whether it applies to the Canadian state's body politic. Is it possible to successfully fight and win this same battle within the electoral system? Seemingly, all who have tried have failed, seduced into service to the state through appeals to ego, money, and control. What other tactics do we not know about?

Why did they fail to remain in service to our people? What kind of mind does it take to remain authentically Onkwehón:we while working to subvert the political framework for our benefit and to commandeer the ship? What mechanisms would we need in order to safeguard those traditionalists who try? How do we make sure that our leaders remember, first and foremost, to honour our people? I have no answers.

In Haudenosaunee communities, the common political and governance discourse reconnects us to the teachings of the Kayanere'kowa (Great Law of Peace). Every day, our communities work to resurrect and enact the principles of the Kayanere'kowa and to proclaim it as the only truly democratic form of governance in the history of the world. Although settler society continuously attempts to destroy this knowledge, we continue to herald its legacy as the antidote to the perils of the modern world, and the fact that this knowledge still exists is a testament to its inherent power. It is arrogant of non-Indigenous society, through its socio-political theories, methodologies, institutions, and superstructures, to try to force its labels upon us, thus branding us as part of its social constructs or as residing within them. On each occasion, we must reiterate our separatist principles and reframe the politics of noninterference.

We have a human responsibility to maintain and protect the unique femininity of our Mother Earth, particularly her fertility and ability to carry and sustain life. Every land reclamation is in her defence. This stewardship responsibility is repeated in our histories, speeches, ceremonies, stories, songs, dances, iconography, wampum, treaties, and declarations. It is our duty to resist a dominant society that commodifies, commercializes, rapes, and consumes the landscape without regret. We stand on roads, and block trains, and yell it from the rooftops. We create spectacles to amplify our voice so that you might hear her voice and remember. As Vandana Shiva writes, we have "begun to recognize that this dominant system emerged as a liberating force not for humanity as a whole … but as a Western, male-oriented and patriarchal projection which necessarily entailed the subjugation of both nature and women."[18] Or in the words of Carolyn Merchant, "In investigating the roots of our current environmental dilemma and its connections to science, technology and the economy, we must re-examine the formation of a world-view and a science that, by reconceptualizing reality as a machine rather than a living organism, sanctioned the domination of both nature and women."[19]

In a few short centuries, we the Haudenosaunee find ourselves ushered toward total planetary collapse at the hands of the citizens of this ship and their cargo – their ontology, axiology, epistemology, and methodology. I have begun to wonder whether the mantra of the Tekeni Teyoha:te (Two Row Wampum) has reached its natural conclusion, as it appears that our ancestors severely underestimated the unsustainability of the ship and its inhabitants when we agreed to travel alongside them on the river of life. Did we not realize the extent to which the ship's unbridled capitalism, racism, colonial oppression, and patriarchy would jeopardize our first responsibility, the responsibility to practise gratitude to the Creator and humility before creation as stewards of the lands and waters? And finally, at what point does our primary human responsibility take precedence over the political premise of noninterference as prescribed to us by the Tekeni Teyoha:te?

Journeying as Ceremony

I believe that, as Haudenosaunee, we are not in danger of losing anything – not our culture, not our language, not our tradition, and not our "land." In the 1990s, when I began working with Gae Ho Hwako, this may have been considered an outrageous statement. But today, there is prolific evidence to support such a claim. There is a growing population of hardworking, tenacious Onkwehón:we who have dedicated their lives to the maintenance and transmission of onkwehonwe'néha. *An ever-growing community of people have empowered themselves and are empowering others to reclaim all those cultural elements that the state sought to erase. There are thousands of people who, together, have imagined and reimagined our ancestral legacy in modern contexts.*

Over the past few decades, I have surrounded myself and engaged with modern "traditionalists" from Indigenous nations around the world. I have met thousands of artists, educators, and professionals who are fully committed to the recovery and revitalization of ancestral knowledge and practice. I am proud of us. I am inspired to do more and be better. I extend my heartfelt gratitude to a sea of people from countless communities who have so freely shared so much. You have completely transformed me. And you continue to change me today. I am thankful that the Creator placed you in my path. I would not be who I am and where I am today without your love and trust. In respect of protocol, I seek to define my territorial and cultural boundaries. I want to be careful to remember where my voice belongs. I want to name those to whom I am accountable. I want to ensure that I do not unintentionally speak for others or usurp their voice. I do not want to reach into their basket and take what is not mine. I acknowledge where I belong: "Kawennakon ni: yonkya'ts, Ohswe:ken nitewake:non, Wakskare:wake tahnon Kanyen'kehaka niwakonhwentsyo:ten" *(My name is Kawennakon. I am from Six Nations. I am Bear Clan. I am Mohawk).*

In the early 1990s, I was introduced to the idea of journeying as ceremony during university. I had the great fortune to meet and befriend several medicine men and women from a variety of communities across Turtle Island. These men and women would have an indelible impact on the course of my life and on the woman I would become. The first Dakota man I heard speak in our community about the Unity Rides was Birgil Kills Straight. He travelled with a man name Arvol Looking Horse. I would later learn that Arvol was the nineteenth-generation Keeper of the White Buffalo Calf Pipe Bundle and chief of the Lakota, Dakota, and Nakota Sioux Nations.

As best as I can recall, Birgil said that through vision quests, he was told that the spirits of those massacred at Wounded Knee could not rest and needed a ceremony. He was told to create a ceremonial staff and to retrace the path of these ancestors on horseback over a four-year cycle. He was inviting us to join the ride. He told us that when the staffs returned to Devil's Tower, the people would awaken. I can remember wondering what the heck that meant. And it would be twenty years before I would get an answer.

Birgil said that riding along the route would gather the ancestral spirits and that the ancestors would follow us back to Devil's Tower, where they could be put to rest. The ride itself was a simple affair. You got up early, broke camp, and circled up. During circle, everyone offered their prayers for protection and a safe journey. As you rode, you prayed. When you held the staffs, you prayed. And when you stopped to make camp for the night, you circled up, set the staffs to rest, and prayed.

The first journey was called Mending the Sacred Hoop. It lasted for four years, and after that, the Wiping the Tears rides began in 1993. As the first four-year cycle came to a close, a Cree man asked to take the staffs north to travel through Cree territories for four years. As the Crees closed their four-year cycle, another gentleman from British Columbia asked to take the staffs out west. And in their fourth year, the BC delegation crossed the entire country, riding back to Six Nations and knocking on the door of the Confederacy in their final year.

In recognition of Haudenosaunee ancestral practices, which relied on runners not horses, the rides became runs, with the staffs travelling throughout our territories for two years and then down the coast to Virginia before eventually travelling back to their homelands. Although I did not attend any Unity Rides in Cree territory, I was lucky to participate in and to support almost every ride at different points over several years. The staffs travelled back and forth across Turtle Island for twenty years.

A few short months after their return to Devil's Tower and the closing ceremony, the world would watch and wonder at a unique uprising and display of Onkwehón:we pride as our people gathered for impromptu flash mobs everywhere. I was struck by the thought that this occurrence was no coincidence. This awakening was foretold and was a confirmation of Birgil's vision. A spontaneous and revolutionary movement captured the hearts of our people as we drummed and danced in the malls of cities large and small across North America. Outsiders were perplexed, but for us it was a triumph. It was an observance that we had survived centuries of violent colonial oppression and that we had found (and/or were finding) our joy, as foretold. This phenomenon would eventually be dubbed Idle No More. I see a direct correlation between the return home of those ceremonial staffs and the beginning of a new wave of revitalization.

By universal design, years later I was led to Gae Ho Hwako, her family, Winnie-kenha, and Awehaode Communication. It was there that my journeying would continue in Haudenosaunee form and that together we would organize several caravans throughout our traditional territories to reignite the Peacemaker's Journey and to retrace his path as he shared the message of the Kayanere'kowa (Great Law of Peace). There was no way that I could have predicted that I would still be organizing journeys thirty years later.

The Haudenosaunee Confederacy was formed when the Peacemaker, with the help of Hiawatha, journeyed to each of the Five Nations to promote the messages of peace, power, and the good mind. Jake Thomas-kenha – whose name as a condoled chief of the Cayuga Nation was Hadajigre:ta (Descending-Cloud) – was a teacher, an influential cultural interpreter, and a historian. He was famous in Haudenosaunee territories for recovering the practice of recounting the story of the Kayanere'kowa and the surrounding controversy that ensued when he agreed to document and video record the recitals. There is a long and well-documented history of dishonest practice between the academy and the Haudenosaunee. This historical relationship between the settler state and the Haudenosaunee has soured our taste for intercultural sharing. There is also well-chronicled Haudenosaunee resistance to documenting ceremonial practices and teachings at all. Jake-kenha challenged this community taboo.

When Jake-kenha passed away, the stories of journeyers and the recital videotapes provided the tools that others could pick up and dust off to continue some of his life's work and help us to recover recitals of the Kayanere'kowa. As founder of the Peacemaker's Journey, Jake-kenha created even more controversy when he agreed to take several caravans of Onkwehón:we and non-Onkwehón:we students across the original territories of the Haudenosaunee in Ontario, Quebec, New York State, and Pennsylvania while reciting the Kayanere'kowa. Journeyers retraced the path of the Peacemaker and visited historic, sacred sites throughout the original homelands. At each site, orators recited the history of each location and provided translations for speakers of English.

The Peacemaker's Journey is a formative experience for all who undertake the trip. Everyone who participates remarks about how it fundamentally changed and shaped their understanding of the Kayanere'kowa. Even decades later, we talk about how it changed the way that we talk about and view our histories and the confederation of our nations. When you place your feet upon the land while one of our speakers tells the story of what happened in that place, the Kayanere'kowa comes back to life and speaks to you. You can no longer dismiss it as a fanciful story or myth. The journey experience stands the story back up in its rightful place as part of historical events reaching back far beyond colonial contact to ancient times.

Every day is an epiphany on the journey, and each year something new reveals itself to us. It is a pilgrimage on par with any other ancient religion throughout the world. Indeed, it is absurd for foreigners to think that we would not have sacred sites all throughout North and South America and that we would still know where they are, be able to recite the oral histories for those sites, and continue to honour those spaces. There are several sites on the journey already designated as heritage sites and a few where further protections are needed. There are several Haudenosaunee who are working with the local populations to acquire heritage designations that prevent further encroachment and that provide protection from development.

In 2017, Hickory Edwards and I were invited to Kanatsiohareke, near Fonda in New York, to meet with Sakokwenionkwas (Tommy Porter) and hear about a dream of his. Sakokwenionkwas is the founder and spiritual leader of the community of Kanatsiohareke and is a member of the Great Law of Peace subcommittee. He told us that he had dreamed that our youth were walking and paddling the path of the Peacemaker, and he asked whether we would help to organize a journey by foot and canoe. He also asked us to present his dream to, and request support from, the Great Law of Peace subcommittee, whose members had been mandated by the Haudenosaunee Hereditary Council of Chiefs and Clan Mothers in 2010 to revitalize the recitals of the Kayanere'kowa.

The Great Law of Peace subcommittee agreed to support and work alongside the Peacemaker's Journey committee to organize the walk and paddle in the summer of 2020. Due to Covid-19, this undertaking has been postponed indefinitely. This journey will start with a gathering in Kenhte:ke (Tyendinaga) that will include previous journeyers and organizers who will be invited to share their pictures, videos, and remembrances. Our leadership has been invited to burn tobacco, offer words of encouragement, and listen to the people as they set the tone for the journey. They have also agreed to deliver recitals in the language of the land at each stop throughout our traditional homelands. This means that as we travel through the Kanyen'kehaka (Mohawk Nation), our leaders will recite in Kanyen'keha. As we travel through the Onenyo'te'aka (Oneida Nation), their leaders will recite in Onenyote'keha, and so on.

We will focus on collecting the minds and stories of many and bundling them together to achieve *ska'nikonhra* (one mind, body, and soul) in order to capture and revitalize the history of the Peacemaker's Journey. *Ska'nikonhra* is a Haudenosaunee cultural tenet that urges groups of people to seek the consensus of all. Negotiating total consensus is critical to maintaining peace, and peace is one of three core pillars that support the continuation of the Kayanere'kowa.

Over the past two decades, I have crossed paths with many past journeyers who have immediately stopped me to express how important the experience was and how it changed their lives forever. How? Why is that? What is so important about reciting ancient histories in ancient languages and in the original homelands? Why is the current discourse of complete transformation so pervasive? What was different about life before and after the journey? Which aspects had the most impact? What story, what lands, which sites, and which speakers influenced you the most and why? It would be interesting to write this story for an all-Haudenosaunee audience, with everyone else as a secondary reader. It would be even more interesting for us to begin capturing these modern histories in our own languages again, written in Kanyen'keha for the Kanyen'kehaka and translated into our other ancestral languages. This is the next logical step in my journeying ceremony.

If we expect to create legitimate and original Haudenosaunee works, we must start with a rejection of the colonial languages, templates, and terms that constrain our ways of thinking, and we must consider the associated cultural disruption provoked by ancestral language loss. Challenging Eurocentric assumptions means that we recognize that there are rarely direct translations of terms or concepts between colonial noun-based, monosynthetic languages and Onkwehón:we verb-based, polysynthetic languages. We remain anchored to contextualizing Haudenosaunee terms, and we argue against validating Haudenosaunee concepts via English-bound constructs and against reverting to a Euro-colonial base for understanding. It is a dangerous assumption that the demand for cultural translation is harmless.

As Onkwehón:we scholars, it is crucial that we protect our cultural legacy as often and as vigorously as we protect the land and waters. The colonial extractive industries operate the same whether operating in physical or metaphysical realms. They are as consumptive and destructive to our Mother Earth as they are to the human minds, bodies, and souls of those of us working in the academy.

As a young woman, I would often hear that the cultural teachings were in the language and that Kanyen'keha is the language of the land itself. This idea was intriguing, but I had difficulty understanding what that actually meant and why the idea was so pervasive until learning the root-word method and how the language itself "thinks."[20] *Kanyen:ke can be translated as "the land of the flint." Kanyen'keha is the language or animation of the land of the flint, and Kanyen'kehaka are the people who speak the language of the land of the flint.*

This account suggests that the language of Mother Earth was here first and that we are the human vehicles of her language. We can hear and understand what she is saying, and we can think and interact with her in a way that is foreign to our settler-colonial allies.

But what would it mean to teach them our language? What would it mean for the planet if we helped to decolonize their minds and helped them to understand the language of our Mother Earth? What would she tell them, and would they listen? How would it change the way that they mingled about on Turtle Island, and how would capitalism, patriarchy, and colonialism fare? What would it be like to completely flip the script and Indigenize their experience? How would it feel to create a completely new program wherein the settler-colonial "they" were expected to write a forty-page treatise in Kanyen'keha for presentation to a panel of Kanyen'kehaka experts in order to prove that their ship's cargo – their epistemology, ontology, axiology, and methodology – was valid and defensible within the framework of onkwehonwe'néha *and the worldview of the canoe? When we fully manifest that dream, we will have manifested authentic Indigenization.*

Decolonizing our minds and our writing requires a Haudenosaunee response to colonial ontology, epistemology, axiology, and methodology. As this chapter and book proceeds in English and according to the academy's protocols, we are mindful of the constant need to untangle and deconstruct colonial patterning. Until we resurrect our languages to a point where such papers are written first in our ancestral languages and then translated into a form of English that mimics our linguistic paradigms, our minds will remain colonized. While we recover from the unmitigated apocalypse enacted upon our bodies, lands, and minds through the centuries of colonialism, a rigorous decolonizing practice applied in all quarters is the balm that heals and sustains families, communities, and ourselves.

Creating intercultural understanding depends on the efficacy of the cultural translator to bridge two worlds and to facilitate understanding between the Haudenosaunee and colonial populations. With effort, Onkwehón:we scholars navigate between the canons of both philosophical traditions. We must acknowledge the unpalatable act that Onkwehón:we scholars undertake each time we are required to strip, dissect, and disconnect *onkwehonwe'néha* (the ways of being of the original people) from *onkwawenna* (our original languages) to serve up politely manageable colonial soundbites for institutional consumption. We undermine the beauty, richness, and power that comprise the wholistic Onkwehón:we conceptual frameworks in order to satiate endless colonial appetite for our knowledge. The academy must consider the distasteful nature of the constant expectation that the interpretation of this knowledge be locked "in a cognitive box delineated by the structure of a language that evolved to communicate the worldview of the colonizers."[21]

It is because of the work of people like Gae Ho Hwako, Winnie-kenha, and their families that our nations sit ready to begin a new age of Haudenosaunee intellectualism that is uniquely ours. Our cultural reclamation is complete.

Tsi nen:we enkwanoronhkwake tahnon wa'tkwanonhwera:tons.

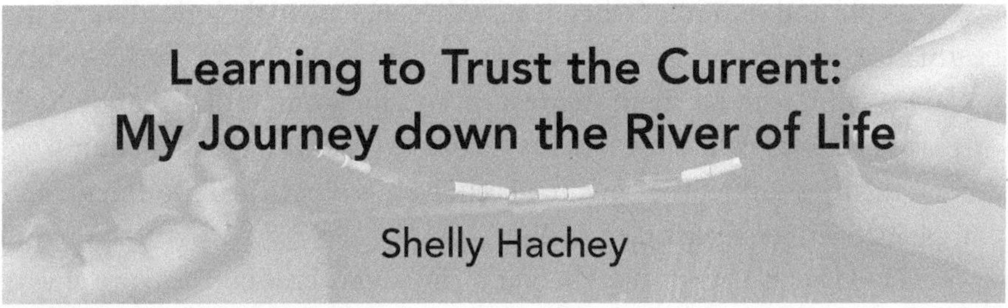

Learning to Trust the Current: My Journey down the River of Life

Shelly Hachey

My journey down the river of life has often forced me to question my identity. Born upon the rocky waters of colonialism, cultural genocide, and attempted forced assimilation by the dominant culture, I was drowning, without family or community to guide me toward safety. Just as Gae Ho Hwako teaches, I was "caught up in the confusion and hardship of straddling the space between the Indigenous canoe and the ship." I now stand with great humility at the edge of the river of life, looking into the waters that once seemed so rough and inescapable.

Through reflection and the guidance of Elders like Gae Ho Hwako (Norma Jacobs) and Awnjibenayseekwe (Banakonda Kennedy-Kish Bell), I was able to pull myself up out of the waters and take up my intended place within creation. Their teachings have helped me to understand that we come to this physical world for a purpose and set out on a path agreed upon by Shogwaeyadisho' (the Creator) toward connection and the experience of being alive. As Gae Ho Hwako says in the next circle of the book, "We are those sacred spiritual beings who descended from the Sky World to work on this spiritual journey." This belief gives me space to love myself unconditionally and without shame. Getting to this place, however, has not been easy, and I have a long way to go in my search for spiritual connection and healing.

My name is Shelly Hachey. I am an Indigenous woman from Six Nations of the Grand River Territory, a Haudenosaunee of the Oneida Nation, a member of the Turtle Clan, and a settler Canadian from Haldimand-Norfolk. I was told that my parents fell madly in love and that I was the product of that love. Unfortunately, I do not remember them, as my mother died when I was five years old and my father when I was thirteen. Due to their deaths and the traumatic breakdown of my family systems, I was absorbed into the child welfare system, where I spent the rest of my childhood, isolated and alone. The years between when my parents died and I became a young adult were among the most difficult of my life. Feelings of sadness, abandonment, and complete loneliness consumed me.

Gae Ho Hwako's words reverberate: "The waters around them are always dark and deep … because of the interference related to colonialism." Since I was brought up in a system designed from a colonial point of view, the only concern was for my physical safety, without a second thought given to my emotional, mental, and spiritual well-being. I was one of those many Indigenous children who were brought into a growing child welfare system that is connected to the Sixties Scoop and, before that, to the residential schools. As Cindy Blackstock states, the "systemic ignorance of the impacts of colonization often resulted in mass removals of Aboriginal children and their placement in non-Aboriginal homes – often permanently. This pattern of mass removals became known as the '60's scoop.'"[1] Transferred from foster home to foster home, I always had a place to lay my head and food to fill my belly, yet I was never given anything to fill my spirit; I was hollow. I aged out of the system an assimilated "Indian."

I know from personal experience in child welfare and from my education in Indigenous social work that the colonial ideology of permanency through placement in a foster home has negative long-term effects on Indigenous children. As Roger Paul, a cultural teacher, storyteller, and youth worker of the Penobscot Nation, says, "When a child is raised outside our community, that child knows there is a part of their life missing. That missing piece is their culture."[2] An attachment to culture and language is an attachment to your identity, and this is something that needs to be considered if we are to ensure the best interests of Indigenous children as well as tribal sovereignty. Permanency raises a lot of controversy. In the words of Sandrina de Finney and Lara di Tomasso, "As complex and multi-layered as the concept is in general child welfare terms, 'permanency' must be unpacked still further when it comes to the needs of Indigenous youth in government care."[3] Although permanency may be important in Western-Euro child welfare systems, it accounts only for the physical safety of the child, without any consideration for spiritual or cultural preservation.

Because I was brought up in a climate where Canadian national and provincial governments have been engaged in eradicating Indigenous cultures, it was nearly impossible for me to discover, let alone embrace, who I was as an Indigenous woman. The Government of Canada's intention was clearly stated in the policy of its first prime minister: "The great aim of our legislation has been to do away with the tribal system and assimilate the Indian people in all respects."[4] The active erosion of Indigenous cultural traditions accelerated with the assimilation tactics of the residential school system, which for many is ground zero for the violence of colonization. Their violent mission was epitomized in the early 1900s in a statement by the deputy minister of Indian Affairs, Duncan Campbell Scott: "Our objective is to continue until there is not a single Indian in Canada that has not been absorbed into the body politic."[5] When these schools began closing in the 1960s, child welfare took over for them, and to this day Indigenous children are overrepresented in the child welfare system.

As I travelled down my path, facing my own personal struggles under the omnipresent shadow of colonialism, I entertained the thought of being with my mother in spirit. I spent many nights alone, longing for the warm embrace that was waiting for me just on the other side of my suffering. I did not want to be in this physical place, this reality filled with so many violent divisions, where families were traumatized, the value placed on Elders had diminished, and we had been severed from the collective strength of our cultural traditions. I often felt that the only way out of these rocky waters would be to go home to the spirit world where I came from originally.

Gae Ho Hwako teaches that this is the place where we chose our earth walk. This teaching tells me that I came to this earth the way that I am for a purpose and that, as a result, I need to embrace all parts of myself, all that makes me who I am. I feel this teaching in the core of my being, yet it also raises for me difficult, perhaps unanswerable, questions. Why do I have to live on this turbulent river of life? Why are we mired in so much colonial violence?

We can tread water only so long; this is something that I learned first from experience, then through the Elder teachings of Gae Ho Hwako, and more recently from Awnjibenayseekwe. As she writes, "My grandmother shared a simple teaching with me that saved my life. She told me, when you are in a strong current it is folly to swim against it, swim with the current, at the same time, gradually move little by little out of it. I followed that teaching as a girl swimming alone in Lake Superior and I survived … It is easy to look at our contemporary situation as a strong current taking us down."[6]

Exhausted and without spiritual, mental, emotional, or physical wellness, I was drowning. I was at the point where I could no longer fight against the current. A choice was before me. I could either stop swimming and be consumed by the water or trust the water and let it take me where I was meant to be. Almost instinctively, as I was not connected with Elder teachings at this time, I began following the guidance of Awnjibenayseekwe's grandmother. I would "swim with the current [and], at the same time, gradually move little by little out of it."

I often describe the birth of my daughter as the day when my life began, although I now understand that this was the day when I began to live. This gift of life was everything that I needed to stop fighting the current and to begin trusting the water. I had travelled so far down the river alone that when my daughter was born into this world and was placed on my belly, the world seemed to hold its breath for a moment, and when it exhaled, everything was different. I looked at my daughter and watched her experience her first moments in this place, and I knew then that I would never be the same. This was the day when connection and the experience of being alive lifted my spirit. It was the connection of becoming a nurturing mother, of coming into relation with the being referred to by Gae Ho Hwako as E tinoha ongwesidage'dra gwe' (Mother Earth).

I understand now that I was never alone in my suffering but was closed off to accepting the warm embrace and unconditional love of E tinoha ongwesidage'dra gwe' and, as a result, also closed off to accepting my gifts and supportive relations. The years that followed my daughter's arrival were filled with new experiences of love, purpose, and a whole new level of fear. This unshakable bond of unconditional love that I have for my daughter is the same kind of love that I had been in denial of. Just as my child openly and unquestioningly accepts this love from me, I too needed to learn how to openly accept this love from E tinoha ongwesidage'dra gwe'. We have since been travelling the river together, both inching closer and closer to a shore where we trust ourselves and each other.

When my daughter was old enough to go to school, I found myself facing yet another choice: I had to decide what I was going to do with my life. Being a mother was the only thing that had ever brought me joy and happiness; however, I was ready to consider the possibility of something more. Guided by my experiences within the system, I decided that I wanted to be a social worker and to help children navigate the child welfare system. I enrolled in the Social Service Worker program at my local college, having no idea what lay ahead for me. I had no idea that I was signing up for something that would not only change my outlook on life but also define it.

I remember my first day; I was terrified and convinced that I would fail. My culture, history, and identity were far from my mind. During my practicum, the college brought in outside teachers to run seminar groups for the large number of students in my cohort. This was my first exposure to Indigenous culture, and it began with a smudge. I realized that I had been placed with the Indigenous students and seminar leader, and I was mad. I was ashamed of my Indigenous culture, ashamed to admit my place, and I went to great lengths to hide and avoid my truth. I was brought up to believe that I was lucky to have been raised in Canadian society and that I was not like my "savage" brothers and sisters. I could be saved. I believed this lie for a long time; most of my earth walk has been in this place of uncertainty, never knowing the history of my people. I did not know what a residential school was or about the Sixties Scoop, the Millennial Scoop, or treaties like the Two Row Wampum; none of my history was told to me. This guided my hatred, shame, and fear of my place and my culture. I had been easily assimilated.

The stereotype of Indigenous people being in need of assimilation for their own good had convinced me that I was not one of them; I was civilized. I watched as the smudge bowl came around the room and felt myself tense up. I did not want to participate. We were asked to identify ourselves, and I was filled with rage. I felt deep hatred toward Indigenous people, and I refused to accept that I was one of them. During the rest of my time in college, I was mildly exposed to Indigenous culture, still only holding onto the superficial connection as symbolized in the dreamcatcher above my bed. I graduated and applied to university to pursue a "higher education," and there began a journey that became so much more than what I was expecting.

When I began my studies for a bachelor's degree in social work, I was open-minded and only slightly annoyed that so many Indigenous courses were mandatory in the newly created program at the Brantford campus of Wilfrid Laurier University – just up the river from Six Nations. My spirit must have been opening up more at this time because I did not feel the rage as intensely as I once had. Also, I was being lifted up as an Indigenous woman in educational spaces. This was a new experience for me; what had once been a very clear negative attribute was here seen as a good thing. Liking the attention while also constantly fighting feelings of not being accepted, I slowly began to embrace my Indigenous culture. At the same time, I did not feel comfortable identifying as Indigenous, as I felt trapped between two worlds. As Gae Ho Hwako teaches in relation to the perils of "straddling the space between the Indigenous canoe and the ship" of the Two Row Wampum, the water was dark and confusing for me. As I fought the feelings of an internal conflict that was connected to colonial processes, I continued learning about the history of my people from the canoe, and with that learning, I could no longer remain angry.

I often say that once you know, you cannot unknow. In the required courses on Indigenous worldviews and Indigenous-settler relations, not only did I come to understand what colonialism had done to my people, but I also came to directly connect my child welfare experience and feelings of drowning to that history. I felt compelled to reach toward the canoe, desperately trying to grasp the wooden oars that guide that vessel. Convinced that this was the piece of me that had been missing all along, I decided to pursue a minor in Indigenous studies; I wanted to know everything.

As I look back now, it seems that every one of my experiences have been guiding me toward the purpose and path that my spirit laid before me in this life. It was through reflection and connecting to my spiritualty that I began to trust this new path. No longer fighting the current, it was here that I began to embrace my journey toward a shore where I could stand with my children.

The first person I ever heard speak from the space of being in between the vessels on the river of life was a professor I learned from while pursuing my bachelor's degree, someone for whom I have the utmost admiration and respect. I remember being brought to tears as he taught me about the Two Row Wampum. I felt as though I was not alone, like I had found someone who understood how difficult it could be in this space to situate myself and understand who I am. Since that time, the Two Row has taught me many things. It taught me the history of settlers coming to this land. It taught me humility in the face of the suffering and pain that have been endured due to broken promises and attempted peace treaties between nations. It taught me the values of peace, friendship, respect, honour, purpose, and love.

My child welfare experience and mixed ancestry place me on the Two Row Wampum in a unique way. The ship welcomed me with open arms, so long as I was assimilated and was willing to perpetuate the false history of peaceful relations on the river of life. Meanwhile, the canoe had boarded up its doors so tight as a means of protecting cultural practices and traditional teachings from being misappropriated that I felt that I could not take up a place on either vessel without giving up a piece of who I was.

Despite these life-giving teachings, I continued to fight feelings of inadequacy as I began to understand why I could never be fully in the canoe. And so I continued to search for my purpose. Not knowing my place in the world made me feel worthless. I had been discriminated against for being Indigenous, and I had been accused of being too white and whitewashed. I hated this feeling of disconnection, and up until my fateful meeting with that professor who talked about the space in between the vessels of the Two Row Wampum, I felt alone in those feelings. I had been resistant to sharing my story and using my voice because of my fear of being judged and not accepted, but I gradually came to understand that it was not my burden to carry. I could no longer allow the negativity of others to dictate who I was. I could no longer take on the burdens of others as I made my way toward the shore.

It was in the last couple years of my degree program that I also came to learn from Gae Ho Hwako and her teachings about the Thanksgiving Address, the healing process of reflection, the need to stay strong in our values, and the relation of all these things to *ǫ da gaho dę:s* (the sacred meeting space) between the ship and the canoe. As she says, "It is always about nurturing *ǫ da gaho dę:s* between us so that we can communicate with one another and be really clear about who we are in these relationships. We each need to discuss and understand what the other is saying by asking ourselves, 'Do I really understand what you mean and where you are coming from?' As our conversation evolves, we can come to a real understanding of what the other means. This is what we refer to as *ganigǫhi:yo* (a good mind), and it is needed to come to *ǫ da gaho dę:s*."

From the moment that I heard these words, I began a journey on which I would not be able to turn back. These teachings felt like they were talking to me, so I shared them. After completing my bachelor's degree, I was pulled toward furthering my Indigenous education for several reasons. First, I felt that the current of my life was leading me toward nurturing those sacred healing spaces not only within myself but also, by doing so, in the world. Second, I yearned to stay connected to Indigenous culture and ceremonial practice, and I knew that the only place that I had been able to foster these relations was in school. So I applied for admission to an indigenized master's program in social work at Wilfrid Laurier University and was accepted.

Unlike my undergraduate and college experiences, whereby I unexpectedly came to learn about my Indigenous relations, I now made a conscious choice to learn more. It all began with a culture camp on the land, and I was terrified. Although I was embracing the change, I was afraid. I knew that I would be affected in such a way that my life was never going to be the same.

Many people, like myself, have had no connection to ceremony or cultural practice, and I personally have had no means of connection to these experiences outside of an educational institution. That fact confuses and evokes emotions in me. Educational systems supported the eradication of who I am as an Indigenous person by colonizing knowledge, by teaching social workers to occupy space in the child welfare system, and by means of a host of other assimilative educational practices in the university that Kawennakon (Bonnie Whitlow), Timothy B. Leduc, and others in the circles of this book describe. More than that, I had been internalizing this forced identity confusion in ways that continued to create self-doubt and a lack of connection to Indigenous knowledge, culture, and land.[7] Yet here I was in a "higher education" institution experiencing land-based ceremony. This was mind-blowing and beautiful, and it has fostered hope in me for a different way forward on the river of life. If we can change systems by rewriting policy, practice, and procedure from an Indigenous way of knowing, then we can reclaim our knowledge and take up our rightful place in creation.

As I prepared for camp, I found myself lost in thought, overwhelmed with the possibilities of the discovery and growth that were to come. I felt happy and open to new ways of knowing and seeing the world around me. I arrived at camp and began to see so many beautiful people, many of whom welcomed me with smiles and excited faces. I was neither mistreated nor excluded by my peers, yet insecurity washed over me in waves of overwhelming fear. I had struggled with my identity for so long that I thought, "They are all going to hate me. They will all see that I am an imposter, not traditional, no status, no culture." I yearned for the comfort of home, the safety of my partner's arms, and the loving acceptance of my children. I almost convinced myself to pack up and leave. I was afraid to stand in my own shadow and be who I was; I will be forever grateful that I did not give into fear. I decided to continue trusting the current as I no longer had the strength or desire to fight against it. My path was leading me exactly where I needed to go.

The teachings that I received from the university's Elder-in-Residence, Awnjibenayseekwe, taught me how land-based ceremony is healing. At culture camp and during the ensuing program, I prayed by the water, attended ceremony, and spoke with Elders and Knowledge Keepers. These experiences helped me to see myself as a valued part of creation. Allowing myself to be vulnerable and open to these teachings, I came to understand where I was on the river of life and what I needed to be working on.

The guiding words of Awnjibenayseekwe helped me to come closer to the shore, which I could now clearly see: "Mutually working together can change outcomes, change narratives, change practices, and greatly increase room for inclusion. Indigenous perspectives believe there is an inherent desire for balance, harmony and well-being in all our relations. This requires a respect for life, valuing integrity and the autonomy of the individual, and of the collective as a whole, reaching and expanding to all our relations. This is a vision worth reaching and striving for."[8]

Having participated in land-based ceremony, it was time to open my spirit up to a new way of learning as I began the academic portion of my indigenized master's degree in social work. Gone was the need for definitive assertions and indisputable facts; I embraced a traditional, wholistic way of learning through my first steps of exploration into Indigenous ways of knowing and understanding who we are and how to stand in our cultural integrity against colonial forces. The great irony is that the same "higher education" institutions that supported the child welfare system that had severed my relations were now giving me a kind of *ǫ da gaho dę̱:s* for renewing in me an Indigenous sense of self and for helping me to see what my lifework would be moving forward.

The teaching that I learned from Awnjibenayseekwe and others in this indigenized social work program made it clear that spirit and heart come before knowledge and mind. We start with spirit, as our mind is not in one place but in the whole of our being. If you take the circle in each direction – spirit, heart, mind, and body – you will see how each part goes into one another; like with a clock, each is connected.[9] I am very grateful for the privilege of being a part of this unfolding process of coming to a new way of knowing that has so much more life than what I was taught on the ship. Dawn Martin Hill says that "restoring traditional healing practices and knowledge is a pathway to both empowerment and health for communities."[10] That is exactly what this program did for me. The sweat and fasting ceremonies taught me to take up my space not only in the circles of our class or this book but, more broadly, also in the circle of life.

The teachings of Awnjibenayseekwe that I reflected on challenged my beliefs about my mixed heritage. They made it clear to me that neither mixing the two nor adapting one to the other is healthy, as doing so undermines diversity. We are on the journey together with people in relationship, and mixing cultures can undermine their integrity; it can undermine my spirit, who I am. Mixing is what colonial systems often did to get the land and wealth that the settlers desired. The exchange is constantly happening, and we are responsible for honouring this exchange by respecting the integrity of our cultures and all life. This respect is central to the relational accountability that underlies the Two Row Wampum.

We each have a responsibility to do our own work, and in order for relationships on the river of life to be maintained in a good way, both vessels need to be engaged and respectful. This place of exchange has to be mutual, and Gae Ho Hwako would say that when this condition is met, we come to *ǫ da gaho dę̱:s*. Awnjibenayseekwe has a similar understanding but says that we ignite the Third Fire:

> The image of the Third Fire expresses the concepts of interconnection, interdependence, mutuality, and co-operation. It is the third place that belongs to both, not one or the other. It is within this conception of interdependence, mutuality, and co-operation that we can explore the possibilities of kindness, kind honesty, and of kind, honest sharing. Kind, honest sharing is a strength and is the cause of good relations. Enacting these principles, placing ourselves in that place that recognizes our interdependence and our mutuality, can open each of us up to changing the narrative between Indigenous and Western social constructs, that would allow diversity and new pathways to co-exist alongside each other.[11]

I am not in the canoe, not fully, and I can never be because that is another's place. Nor will I ever belong on the ship. I refuse that path because my spirit is not open to the possibility of that life. But as I struggle with all this through the support of Elder teachings given by Gae Ho Hwako and Awnjibenay-seekwe, I have begun to get a different sense of where I belong. My work on self, on identity, and on my vision has me wanting to change systems, role model thoughtfulness, and live and work wholistically because my spirit has been awakened to its true purpose and intended path. Everything that I have been through has led me to this purpose; every experience, good and bad, has taught my spirit something that it needed to know in order to swim to this shore and take up my place.

The gift of my experiences of living in and working in the child welfare system has lit a fire in me. I have a purpose and a way of knowing that have grown from these experiences. The deconstruction of current ways of knowing and teaching upholds Indigenous knowledge as credible and worthy of respect.[12] Estelle Simard writes about culturally restorative child welfare and how this practice is fundamental in rebuilding Indigenous communities.[13] She talks about the term "split feathers," which refers to the loss of culture, community, family, and connection to spirituality that is experienced by the children and families affected by the child welfare system.[14] As one of these "split feathers," my place lies in gathering and finding lost children and their families and then reconnecting them to the Elders, the Knowledge Keepers, and the communities that can reclaim the culturally "displaced" and "uprooted."[15]

The privilege of my educational journey has guided me back to my identity and created a space where I can begin to advocate for our people and bring them home. Many others are out in the rocky waters, like I was, lost, drowning, and afraid. I want to set my moccasins firmly in place and do the work that needs to be done. That is my responsibility as one of the "split feathers."

I have come to understand and accept my place as a person who walks between worlds. I know that I have a purpose, and I honour that. I honour the people who have come before me and have helped to hold me up. I am telling my story as someone who once was assimilated by the Canadian government through the child welfare system. My culture and my history were not just denied to me but were also portrayed in a way intended to make me truly believe that they were inferior and of no value.

I was born through no fault of my own as someone seen as a burden and problem to society. I suffered unspeakable losses, and instead of being provided with support and guidance toward a fruitful future, I was forced to fight against my identity, against myself, and against colonialism. As I began to understand these issues, I stopped fighting the current and let go. As I stopped fighting, I was able to gain the strength and perspective to slowly move out of the current. I am sharing my story in this circle of *ǫ da gaho dę:s* as somebody who is finding her way back to her culture and her place. I did not allow the assimilation tactics that I was born into to win or defeat me. My very existence represents a failed attempt to bring about the cultural genocide of an entire people at the hands of the Canadian government – to end what Duncan Campbell Scott famously referred to as "the Indian problem." I have a long way to go in my search for spiritual connection and healing; however, I trust that the path that I am taking is the one that will lead me exactly where I need to be.

I once believed that I was nothing, but with family, guidance, culture, and traditional teachings, I am discovering that I am everything. I embrace and honour who I am, my place in creation, and my connection with spirit. I trust the current to take me exactly where I need to be. As I take up my place on the shore, no longer in the rocky waters between the ship and the canoe, I am filled with gratitude. This is the path that I agreed upon with Shogwaeyadisho' (the Creator) when I set out, and there is much work to be done here.

Unravelling Our Roots: Wholistic Paths in Two Row Education

Timothy B. Leduc

I feel a deep resonance when I hear Gae Ho Hwako (Norma Jacobs) speak of how the umbilical "cord of males is buried out in the woods" and how traditionally the strength of men arises from their responsibilities to "work hard in the woods." Although these cultural teachings were not part of my upbringing, it did seem that my father's greatest joy came from spending as much time as possible walking in the woods. I get this habit from him, and so does my son, Etienne. I see his joy in the fun and peace that he expresses while climbing the trunk of a fallen white pine, tracking creeks to break ice in winter, or using sticks to pool the water as it melts. I feel it as I witness a friendship grow between him and these woods, a way of relating that has a deep ancestry in our family, in the Indigenous cultures of these lands, and in the human species around the world.

Each time that we visit and climb upon the fallen white pine that I talked of in the book's introduction and offer tobacco in a spirit of thanksgiving for all that it gives even now in its death, a deep peace settles in. That is one good reason that I come to this fallen tree regularly, although perhaps now with more intention after Gae Ho Hwako's guidance to spend time here. Walking the length of the tree's horizontal trunk, which is about ten feet above the mucky creek, we come to a closer view of its crown, which snapped off upon its violent crash. The needles that remain attached to the trunk have now turned brown, although they remained green and yellow for a few seasons longer than those beyond us on the branches that broke off from the pine. The decomposition of those branches nurtures the emergence of a sapling in their midst, and Gae Ho Hwako's teachings ask me to support this renewal by reflecting on the peace and friendship that are needed to replant our roots in E tinoha ongwesidage'dra gwe' (Mother Earth) – in her *river of life.*

The cool air of fall is like an old friend who visits each year, drawing us into the smells of cold mud, decomposing leaves, and fallen trees. From my earliest childhood, autumn was a time of cutting and piling wood. For weeks, there would be chainsawing, splitting, wheelbarrowing, and piling. Once the snow and cold air of winter arrived, my responsibility as the oldest son was to bring the wood into the house and, in time, to tend the fire. I can still smell the smoke that was ever present during the winters of my youth and can still recall the feel of intense heat in the rooms close to the fire and the shift to coolness in the more distant rooms. Although these remembrances arise in relation to Gae Ho Hwako's teaching, I need to be clear that I grew up with no cultural instructions associated with wood, fire, or tobacco. There was nothing beyond the discipline of working hard in the cold and tending the fire.

Something about the expanding circle of *ǫ da gaho dę:s* (the sacred meeting space) stirs a desire in me to offer what I have learned from this white pine to my son, Etienne, and by doing that, to offer him stories for coming into relation with this sacred space. In the process, I am reminded of the care and love that I need to hold when sharing with anyone who wants to approach this circle. I do not mean care and love in the paternalistic, colonial sense of a father watching over and controlling others but simply in the sense of someone who wants to support others in the kind of spirit that I feel with those I care for, like my children, or that I feel from Gae Ho Hwako in relation to all of us gathered in this circle. That is the quality of spirit that I feel when I come with Etienne to this bush and fallen pine, and it is what I am hoping to lift up as I reflect on the importance of connecting with our ancestral roots in these times of climate changes.

Sitting among a few white pine saplings that are near the shattered crown, I cannot help but recall the concern of Gae Ho Hwako about "straddling the space between the Indigenous canoe and the ship" of the Two Row Wampum: "If you have one foot in the canoe and one on the ship, when the waters roughen, you will have to decide where you stand." There is a spirit to this teaching that I feel drawn to honour. If you are not grounded in a culture that can help to root your ways of living and relating, then even in the best of times, life can be a struggle. But it also tells us that the difficulties of being without cultural roots can intensify when you have to withstand storms, whether they be the centuries-long impacts of colonial violence or the more recent emergence of extreme climate changes and the Covid-19 global pandemic. Going one step further, this teaching also suggests that all this turbulence is arising in response to the ways of the ship's uprooted culture.

As I honour this teaching on straddling the space of the Two Row Wampum, I also struggle with what it means for those with mixed and adopted ancestries who emerged amidst so many colonial violations. I think about this question in relation to residential schools and the continuing violent legacy of child welfare that Shelly Hachey talks about in the previous chapter and that I teach in my classes. I hear Gae Ho Hwako again: "Many of our people … have been influenced by their education and do not know much about their own Indigenous cultures … Many on the ship have the same concern, and I have heard some talk about all the institutions and historic politics that are impacting their ways of living. How long is it going to take for them to unravel where they have come from and why their family is here now?" There is so much value in struggling with these Two Row teachings in relation to the core of who we are and what our spirit is trying to lift up in this life.

In a way, I have come to see clusters of my family roots caught in this fallen pine, and those are the stories that I want to tell Etienne. On the one hand, our "whiteness" gives us the privilege of cover amidst the colonial storm, except when we raise our voice in solidarity, such as when I teach in the university, support the writing of a book like this one, or confront the ship's racism, patriarchy, and species chauvinism. On the other hand, it was a desire to understand the Indigenous relations in my paternal ancestry that eventually brought me toward the canoe and eventually to Gae Ho Hwako. In the mid-1990s, as I prepared for my employment as a social worker in northern Indigenous communities of Labrador, my father questioned me in a frustrated tone about why I wanted to do this work, and in that exchange, he brought up the French-Indigenous relations of his parents. His words stirred me, for as a social worker in Labrador, I came to live in a Roman Catholic mission house, a dwelling that also raised my mother's French Canadien connections to Catholic nuns and missionaries. The life path that I had chosen seemed to be dredging up ancestral conflicts at my core.

The steps that I have taken toward *ǫ da gaho dę:s* would have been futile if some from the canoe had not initiated the possibility of such a relationship. Before I met Gae Ho Hwako, it was the lifework of the late Cayuga chief Jacob Thomas that was significant for me. It was in university that I first became aware of Thomas's teachings through his students William Woodworth and Dan Longboat, and later I learned of his influence on Gae Ho Hwako. He became a professor and an Elder in 1976 at Trent University in Peterborough, Ontario, just as Gae Ho Hwako has for periods of time taught in the university. Teaching Haudenosaunee culture and language, Thomas "attracted both Native and non-Native students." Starting in 1986, he also fostered initiatives along the Grand River with the Iroquois Institute and then with the Jake Thomas Learning Centre. It was in these centres that he more fully grounded his teachings "in Iroquoian philosophy, values and traditional teaching," as the organizational structure was "modeled on the Kaianerenko:wa [Great Law]."[1]

From within the shade of these initiatives, Thomas offered cultural workshops and ceremonial teachings on the Great Law, eventually organizing a Peacemaker's Journey, which Gae Ho Hwako and others, like Kawennakon (Bonnie Whitlow) (see her earlier chapter in this circle of the book), supported after his death. There is in these teachings a deep sense of the importance of connecting with difficult truths as part of the process of coming into good relations. Although Thomas critically pointed out the ways that "white people ... keep historic truths hidden from their people" and thus foster the repetition of colonial violence, he also said, "The Creator has given each of us gifts to help one another. There is a bridge for all people to cross, a common belief to bring us together."[2] I hear echoes of Thomas's teaching when Gae Ho Hwako talks about how a bridge to *ǫ da gaho dę:s* can be fostered by reflecting on our ancestral roots to discover the difficult truths that they hold and the gifts that they offer.

By reflecting on our mysterious journey into relation with this white pine, we can replant within us a sense of responsibility to give our gift back – to give something that may support a good response to the storms that blew this tree over. As Gae Ho Hwako explains, her Ongwehowe name means "ancestral females holding the canoe before me." Gae Ho Hwako is a name that guides her lifework by positioning her "in an ancestral line of great women of the Wolf Clan in the Cayuga Nation," thus giving her the responsibilities "of empowering myself, my family, my community, the nation, and the Confederacy." This is what it means to nurture and maintain "the sacredness of life by honouring our culture." Her words bring to mind Thomas again: "No one arrives in this world without a purpose. That is why the Creator gave us a culture. He meant that we should keep that culture going … The Creator has given each of us gifts to help one another."[3]

Each exposed root carries for us teachings and stories about that which severs us from good relations, as well as about what is needed to sustainably replant our lives. Such a wholistic approach to Two Row learning has long been denied, suppressed, and virtually forgotten in the educational systems of the ship. From Etienne's elementary education to the university where I teach, we tend to be schooled in information transmission rather than in the kind of reflection that can contextualize and wholistically ground our knowledge. With this recognition, a question arises: how do I foster a more conscious relation with nature through an education grounded in the trees, fire, and creeks – a wholistic education rooted in E tinoha ongwesidage'dra gwe'? I hold this question in my heart as I bring Etienne to this fallen white pine and listen to the questions that he in turn asks while playing here. It is his curiosity that helps me to uncover the ways of a wholistic Two Row education, and so in what follows, I begin with Etienne's questions before opening to a few children's stories that we often read together. All of us in the circles of this book have unique stories about roots and renewal in our modern world, and I hope that Etienne's questions and stories will offer one more model for approaching *ǫ da gaho dę̱:s*.

"Dad, what are those roots, and why do you come to visit them so often?"

> Wood wide web. Trees like to keep in touch with each other. It's not just roots that link the trees in a forest. They are also connected through fungi – the living things we know as mushrooms. Fungi are sort of like plants, but they cannot make their own food. Instead, they make a network of threads called hyphae (pronounced hi-fee), which break down food. The hyphae can swap food, water and even messages with tree roots. In return for the fungi network, trees give water and food to the fungi.[4]

As I sit with these roots, it is clear that there is so much mystery here to learn from. When the white pine was planted in the ground, they brought the tree sustenance while also stabilizing its tall straight trunk through the seasons as the winds blew through the forest canopy. The roots interconnected with fungi to make what some call a "wood wide web," as the "fungi operate like fiber-optic Internet cables" and in mature forests "can cover many square miles and … transmit signals from one tree to the next, helping exchange news about insects, drought, and other dangers."[5] So in an ecological sense, these roots once provided the white pine with sustenance, grounding, connection to other trees, and through fungi relations, ways of communicating with the broader forest community. But when I spend a little more time with Etienne's question, it seems that the uprooted tangle also teaches us about our ancestral roots and ways to connect with stories, a kind of cultural hyphae for learning who we are on this river of life.

Being born on the lands of the Passage de Taronto near the mouth of the Humber River, not far from where Étienne Brûlé portaged with the Wendat, my partner and I gave our son his name in remembrance of the first French Canadien who came to these lands and the complex stories that he carried. His journey began in the year 1610 at the age of eighteen when Samuel de Champlain sent him to live with the Wendat as part of a cultural exchange that saw Sauvignon, the son of a Wendat chief, visit France. After one year, the young Wendat had seen enough of the inequities in French society and returned to his people. As for Brûlé, he preferred the egalitarian ways of his Indigenous hosts and spent the rest of his life in Wendake, the lands nestled between Lakes Huron, Erie, and Ontario.[6] His life became entangled with these white pine roots, both with the teachings of their peaceful potential and with the reality of their colonial violations.

When we bend down within the uprooted pine mound to place tobacco, we are following a relational teaching that connects us to the time of Brûlé. It was from the Wendat that he learned the language of these lands and the ways of being that they fostered, such as offering "tobacco, which they throw into the water against the rock itself, they say to it: 'Here, take courage, and let us have a good journey.'"[7] Offering tobacco to water, a tree's roots, or fire is a way of prayer that can guide us through our lives. As Thomas writes, "When we burn the sacred native tobacco, the smoke rises to the sky world and to the Creator. This is a sacred connection. Other cultures shared this same connection."[8] It is through doing this that a sacred space is opened for learning from E tinoha ongwesidage'dra gwe', the beings of creation, and our ancestors. It is one way that we can approach the peace of what Gae Ho Hwako and Thomas call *ganigǫhi:yo* (a good mind) and thus approach *ǫ da gaho dę̱:s.*

When we stop amidst a grove of white pines and take time to notice how we feel different in their presence, we are just beginning a relation that, if nurtured, can open in profound ways. This is what Gae Ho Hwako is pointing to when she writes, "If this energy [of peace and friendship] can pass between two people, it certainly can also pass between those trees and the people. The trees begin to shape how we behave – how we respect and honour one another." I have felt this effect in my life, and that is partly why I feel responsible for bringing my children into this urban ravine forest. I want to nurture relations with these beings and to experience the diverse ways of knowing that they make possible. I want to foster a living relation with this tree of knowledge.

Teachings of this kind are carried in the textures of the land under our feet and in the root mound before our eyes, and this is the kind of living language that Brûlé was learning in Wendake. Although he became an important cultural interpreter through his education in the Wendat's language and traditions, he also became someone often suspected by French officials of having ill intentions because of his shifting alignment. When describing his participation in the rock-water tobacco offering, the missionary Gabriel Sagard wrote that "we rebuked him sharply."[9] Subsequent *coureur de bois* (forest runners) who followed his path were likewise looked down upon by French governors and Jesuits. As one stated, "I could not express sufficiently to you … the attraction that this savage life of doing nothing, of being constrained by nothing, of following every whim, and being beyond correction has for the young men."[10] For missionaries, there was nothing more dangerous than engaging in land practices like a tobacco offering, such as occurred when *coureur de bois* maintained a canoeing rhythm through song and pipe smoking, which were considered to be acts "of prayer, mimicking the common Aboriginal custom of offering tobacco to spirits."[11]

It was not only Brûlé's openness to the Indigenous sense of land relations that led him to be seen as a threat to French interests. During his first decade in Wendake, after traversing the Passage de Taronto, "Brûlé got so separated from the others that he could no longer retrace his steps nor find the trail, and thus he continued to wander through the woods and forests for some days … almost despairing of his life."[12] This experience of being lost led to his capture by the Seneca and an extended stay that almost ended in his death. Before being released to his Wendat hosts, he agreed to facilitate a process by which the Haudenosaunee could become "friends with the French and their enemies."[13] In the midst of ongoing conflicts with the Haudenosaunee and their colonial allies the Dutch and then British, this alignment of Brûlé left him suspect.

To come to an agreement to extend peace, Brûlé would have heard the Seneca talk about the Wendat Peacemaker who had brought a vision of peace to the Five Nations at a time when they were killing each other and about the Great Law carried in a white pine whose roots reached in the four directions. Although well versed in a Wendat language that is connected to the Haudenosaunee, he would have been lost again amidst these white pine teachings, which were new to him.

Thinking about his challenge, I turn to my learning with Gae Ho Hwako and the insights of Thomas on the inseparability of culture, land, and language. For Thomas, a true translation needed to come "out from your heart" in ways that went beyond "a simple search for word equivalents." To maintain the spirit of "thinking in Indian," he took "time to explain more obscure concepts as he went along, all the while trying to keep his place in the narrative sequence." The translation needed to evoke a heartfelt relation with the land from which the language and teaching had arisen. As Thomas explains, "Using your culture is showing your feelings … You can't divide culture and language; they work together. The old people used to say a long time ago: 'Language opens the door to your culture.'"[14] Speaking the Ganǫhǫnyǫhk (Thanksgiving Address) and offering tobacco are ways to foster a relation with the spirit of the "wood wide web" – a spirit that we can just barely still sense in these upended roots.

A similar careful attentiveness to the spirit that we experience with this fallen pine is what was meant to underlie the earliest international treaties like the Two Row Wampum, and this attentiveness is what Brûlé would have had to reach for while listening to stories of a Great Peace. Coming to deliver a translation with "heart" would have had its difficulties, as would have attending to the meanings of an Indigenous language for those steeped or re-educated in objectifying colonial languages like English and the French that Brûlé grew up with. The process that Thomas described is meant to sink us into our roots so that to go back on our word is to go back on ourselves, our ancestors, and creation. In a historic context where the residential schools had uprooted so many, he was convinced, despite the pitfalls, that traditional teachings – like those about the Tree of Peace – needed to be spoken "in English in order to reach the largest number of younger Iroquois and interested non-Natives."[15] A relational connection to these stories is what brings heart into them, and something similar would have been occurring as the Seneca shared with Brûlé and as he in return committed himself to extending the roots of peace.

Unfortunately, what Étienne Brûlé brought back led not only to the failed efforts of the 1620 peace embassy but also to his death in 1633 at the hands of Wendat allied to the French, who were opposed to a peace due to the potential implications of shifting trade routes. Such stories are for me the cultural hyphae that, through reflection, bring us into participation with these teachings. Brûlé's characterization by French officials as a scoundrel and traitor is related to the way that he confronted colonial assumptions by learning an Indigenous language and challenging French political interests. But he is more than an individual ancestor, as his story is tangled with those roots that brought me to live in Toronto not far from Étienne Brûlé Park on the Passage de Taronto.

Although French is the first tongue of my mother, whose family name is Valade, and although my father's surname is Leduc, French was not spoken in our house. Nevertheless, at age four, I was sent to a French Catholic school. After a few weeks, my parents were told that I was not interacting with anyone and that it would be better to send me to an English school. The latter experience was better, but I was still often seen as backwards, shy, and in need of years of speech therapy to get rid of a phantom French lisp. This experience set me up for a life-long struggle with French culture and the French language, such that I continually attempted to pick it up, but my mouth and heart simply would not embrace it. And although I use words of Gae Ho Hwako's Cayuga language here and have used words of other Indigenous languages in previous work,[16] I carry a linguistic uncertainty when I try tentatively to speak Indigenous languages or French. This familial disconnect from French culture and the French language brought me to Toronto, and I have come to learn something about the ancestral depth of this struggle from Brûlé.

Over the last decade of my father's and his parent's lives, they talked of their connection to Catholic mission communities along the Kaniatarowanenneh, the great Saint Lawrence River. Intertwined with genealogy, my grandfather's stories indicated that the village of Saint Regis was the birthplace of his mother, Lucie Florence Plamondon, in 1895, his grandmother Adeline Desrochers in 1861, his great-grandfather Antoine Durocher in 1824, and other family relations before that. These relationships partake of a pattern wherein about 40 per cent of French Canadiens have "at least one Amerindian in their family trees."[17] Whereas my grandfather's Saint Regis relations connect back to Ignace Plamondon, who was born upriver in the Wendat community of Lorette in the mid-1700s, my grandmother also shared stories that stayed with me. She told us that her grandmother Emelia Delorme was a mix of Mohawk and Wendat, and although the genealogy information is sparse (no dates or place), it is a surname that seems to have connections to communities across the river. What also makes her ancestral lines difficult to follow is that her paternal grandparents changed their surname to Watters in the late 1800s to better blend in with the British of Upper Canada, thus hiding their French ancestry in an English context.

Beyond their words and this family genealogy, so much remains unclear to me about the nature of those relations and what they mean for Etienne. Despite this uncertainty, I hold onto two things that seem clear. First, prior to the twentieth century, these branches of our family had much closer Two Row relations. Second, we are a people uprooted from our culture in many ways. As a result, I turn to the Indigenous and colonial stories of these lands during the time of my forebears to help place them in the changing relations of the nineteenth and twentieth centuries.

Long known to the Mohawk as Akwesasne (lit. "place of partridges"),[18] my grandparents' use of the name Saint Regis for the community across the river reflected their connection to the Roman Catholic mission that came into being at Tsi Sniahne (Snye or Chenail), "where the Racquette and St. Regis Rivers joined the St. Lawrence River" and where thirty people from Kahnawake arrived in the fall of 1754.[19] Although I have no experiential connection to Tsi Sniahne beyond a name that I heard my father and grandparents talk of, something about these rough waters speaks to the uncertain ancestral positioning of my paternal family, the teachings on the perils of straddling the space of the Two Row Wampum, and the disconnect of my son, Etienne, from his French Canadien ancestry. I envision the people arriving at this confluence of rivers with an offering of tobacco to its natural power in the spirit of gratitude that has been taught by Gae Ho Hwako and Thomas and that was learned by Étienne Brûlé with his Wendat guides.

My paternal relations connect us to the waters and missions of the wampum alliance known as the Tsiata Nihononwentsiake, or "the Seven Nations of Canada, the Seven Fires, and the Seven Villages."[20] Inspired by the great white pine that came to hold together the Six Nations, this belt represents a peace between seven Jesuit mission villages of Abenaki, Algonquin, Wendat, and Mohawk origins that include Saint Regis and Lorette. But there were a couple of significant alterations to the Tsiata Nihononwentsiake, as Darren Bonaparte clarifies: "Instead of being united by a pine tree or heart at the centre … the icons on this belt were united by the cross of Jesus Christ." Perhaps of greater significance, there "was no path of peace directly linking the fires to the cross that stood alone."[21] A sense of what was missing can be seen in the words of the Jesuit priest Father Pierre François Xavier de Charlevoix as he described the 1701 Tree of Peace negotiations held in Montreal: "This ceremony, as serious as it was for the Savages, was for the French a kind of comedy, which they enjoyed very much."[22]

Disrespect is woven into this history of a missing "path of peace," to which I connect the story of Étienne Brûlé's failed peace. It was in 1625 that the imperialists in the French court shifted New France toward their vision of a Roman Catholic agricultural colony, and Brûlé was given the choice of "returning to France or settling on farms on the lower St. Lawrence." He decided to live in "the only home he knew, Huronia," and that was the last time that Brûlé was heard of until 1633 when news arrived in Quebec City that he had been killed by Wendat aligned with the French Crown.[23] Something that I was barely conscious of compelled me to follow an ancestral pattern that moved me away from the province of Quebec and my beloved home next to the waters of the Kaniatarowanenneh. That is how I came to call the Passage de Taronto home in a spirit similar to Brûlé's embrace of Huronia, and it is from here that I edged into relation with the white pine roots and hyphae of Thomas, Gae Ho Hwako, and this fallen tree that my son and I regularly offer tobacco to.

"Dad, why do you like this white pine so much?"

One great longhouse, one family
All Nations came … they came to see.
They say Peacemaker bid them come
This family torn apart
To meet beneath a Tree of Peace
"Come hear me – heart to heart."[24]

For two decades, I have been coming into this forest, and for much of that time, I have regularly come to commune with this once standing tree. It all began unconsciously years before I appreciated stories like those that Gae Ho Hwako tells of the white pine's central role in Haudenosaunee culture and those that we read in David Bouchard's illustrated book *The Great Law: Kayaneren'kó:wa* (2014) as Etienne drifts into sleep. Although my experiential connection to Gae Ho Hwako's culture is tenuous in relation to direct community, cultural, and ancestral connections, a long relation with trees, bush walking, and fire gave me a way to listen to and appreciate her teaching. I slowly learned that we need to bring our stories into these relations, as reflection on our truths and sharing is what allows us to lift up the peace of the Two Row Wampum and then to approach *ǫ da gaho dę:s*.

Picking up a white pine's five needle cluster from the ground, I am given an opportunity to recall the story told of the Gayensra'go:wa (Great Law), as briefly shared by Gae Ho Hwako, about how the Five Nations came to carry a stronger power through the peace of confederacy than they had possessed while divided. In the words of Thomas, "Five bound arrows symbolized the complete union … [T]hey had bound themselves together in one mind, one body, one head, and one heart to settle all matters."[25] It was under the pine's white roots that the Peacemaker instructed the people to gather the weapons of violence, which had divided the Five Nations, and to bring themselves under the branches of this tall evergreen as a reminder of their responsibilities to nurture peace. Thomas's name as a condoled chief was Hadajigre:ta (Descending-Cloud), a name that connected his responsibilities to the Peacemaker and to the first chief of this name – just as Gae Ho Hwako's name places her in a line of ancestral women holding the canoe. This story and related ceremonies are meant to bring one into personal, cultural, and national relation with a line of peace.

Driving west from Toronto toward Gae Ho Hwako's community of Six Nations takes us along a highway that hugs the shores of Lake Ontario until we eventually come to the lake's western reach and, beyond Hamilton, to a busy turnoff whose sign opens me to another vital French Canadien story. On the exit sign for the Lincoln Alexander Parkway, there are directions for connecting with Rousseau Street. This is a reference to Jean Baptiste Rousseau, one of the last French Canadien *coureur de bois*, who had followed his father in trading along the Passage de Taronto with the Mississauga over the latter half of the 1700s before relations with Chief Joseph Brant and the Six Nations brought him to the Ancaster area. It was from these life-long relations that Rousseau learned the Indigenous languages of these forests and came to embody a similar tension to that experienced by Brûlé, and therefore Rousseau's story offers some valuable insights for navigating the missing "path of peace."

Whereas Brûlé's life was marked by his difficult positioning between the French and the Wendat, Rousseau lived in a different time, one that led him to navigate relations between the British Empire Loyalists and the Haudenosaunee of the Six Nations. Mediating his relationship was a friendship with Joseph Brant (1743–1807), who was both a Pine Tree Chief representing the Haudenosaunee Council and a captain in the British Army during the American Revolution of 1765–91. Following the British losses and surrender of the war, Rousseau helped Brant to survey lands for those allied Haudenosaunee who decided to relocate from their homelands. Recognizing their support, British general Frederick Haldimand signed a land grant on 25 October 1784 known as the Haldimand Tract. It stated, "I have at the desire of many of these His Majesty's faithful Allies purchased a Tract of Land … upon the Banks of the River commonly called, Ouse, or Grand River, running into Lake Erie; Allotting to them for that purpose six miles deep from each side of the River beginning at Lake Erie, and Extending in that proportion to the Head of the said River, which them and their posterity are to enjoy for ever."[26] This closing reference to "for ever" echoes the same words often spoken in regard to the Two Row Wampum.

Because of Rousseau's life-long relation with the Indigenous languages of these forests, he was seen by the arriving British as valuable to their interests.

In a 1793 letter, Lieutenant Governor John Graves Simcoe wrote that Rousseau has "all the necessary requisites for that office, and is equally agreeable to … [Brant] and the Mohawks as to the Missassagas … the only person who possesses any great degree of influence with either of those Nations."[27] As a colonial official, Simcoe was accustomed to looking for "influence" that would support his military mission, and he therefore appointed Rousseau as his personal interpreter for surveying the forests. That said, Rousseau's close relations with Brant and others also led him to be seen by Simcoe and subsequent governors as unreliable. He was sometimes suspected of leaking information and was accused in 1799 of blocking British plans to interfere with the Council of Chiefs in the governance of the Haldimand lands.

When the Six Nations arrived on the Ouse, the lands were rich with animal and plant life, "the climate not harsh, and water and wood were plentiful."[28] For all these reasons, it attracted "white settlers," some of whom had fought under Captain Brant during the American Revolution and others of whom "were white captives who refused to go home."[29] In fact, Rousseau eventually married Brant's adopted daughter, Margaret Cline, and they would name their son Joseph Brant. The Rousseau-Brant family was initially given a lease along the Ouse, although that was given up when they moved to land near the present-day highway sign indicating the turnoff for Rousseau Street. Many who came to the Ouse were squatters looking for good agricultural land, which they were able to occupy with the support of colonial officials who actively undermined the Haldimand Grant. By the time of Canada's 1876 Indian Act, the Grand River lands of the Six Nations had been reduced through appropriations and other pressures to the current 46,000 acres of the original 950,000.

Similar dynamics played out where I was born along the Kaniatarowanenneh. In the 1780s, Brant helped to negotiate five kilometres of land along the river's north shore for use by the Mohawk of Akwesasne to continue trade with their Anishnaabe allies of La Petite Nation. The Nuttfield Tract negotiation was under duress, as the Akwesasne chiefs had objected to the white Empire Loyalists who had settled in what became the city of Cornwall,[30] but they "were told that since the French government had never actually 'granted' us the land or given us a written title, the British government wasn't obligated to recognize our claim."[31] Across the river, a related dynamic unfolded toward the end of the 1800s on Tsikaristisere (Dundee Lands). As with the Haldimand lands, 20,000 acres were leased to non-Mohawk, who refused to return the lands when the lease ended. An 1888 "surrender" of Tsikaristisere for $50,000 was negotiated after the fact, but it has recently been found that the sale was invalid and that a new land claim is needed.[32] These lands are associated with my grandfather's family in Tsi Sniahne, and it was in the time of this surrender and the Indian Act that they moved across the Kaniatarowanenneh to lands between Cornwall and Montreal.

As with Jean Baptiste Rousseau and Étienne Brûlé, the ancestors of my paternal grandparents are quite likely mixed into this history of white squatters, adoptions like those that Gae Ho Hwako teaches of, and marriage. Such people were also often used to extend Canada's colonial appropriation of land, and over time they accepted the privileges that came with hiding these relations. There are good reasons that Indigenous communities are suspicious of people with such ancestral roots, not to mention the uncertainty surrounding Joseph Brant, whose vision of a different relationship was continually violated by the colonial ship. These dynamics are one reason that, in Rick Monture's words, "there remains today considerable debate among the Grand River [Haudenosaunee] community itself as to how Brant's legacy should be assessed."[33] Toward the end of his life, Brant would lament, "We wanted nothing more than what we enjoyed before the American War, the land we then lived on was our own and we could do what we pleased with it … I am totally dispirited."[34]

If we walk along the Ouse in Brantford, not far from where I teach social work, we come to the Mohawk Institute, a place where Canada's destabilizing and genocidal residential school system began in the 1830s. The school was originally envisioned by Brant as a place for bringing Haudenosaunee culture into relation with British knowledge of "husbandry and the mechanic arts."[35] This intention was connected to his early life in eastern New York State and to his English education at the Moor's Indian Charity School in Connecticut, which later became Dartmouth College. Although the school's mission "was to Christianize and 'civilize' the Indians" with the intent of "sending them back to their own country as missionaries and teachers," the Mohawk leaders who sent Brant there had a different intention.[36] He was to learn the English language and to learn about English culture so that he could be a cultural mediator, with his Mohawk name, Thayendanegea (lit. "two sticks bound together"), signifying the mediating role of his life. In contrast to a sovereign approach to education that could weave together the best of both cultures, a project for which his son John Brant secured funding,[37] the Mohawk Institute inaugurated a different quality of education.

A century after Joseph Brant's death, these schools came to their full coercive expression in the early 1900s under the guidance of the deputy minister of Indian Affairs, Duncan Campbell Scott: "Our object is to continue until there is not a single Indian in Canada that has not been absorbed into the body politic."[38] Beyond the intention being problematic, the follow-through was neglectful. In 1907, an official inspection of the Mohawk Institute led to this report: "I cannot say that I was favourably impressed with the sight of two prison cells in the boys [*sic*] play house. I was informed, however, that these were for pupils who ran away from the institution, confinement being for a week at a time when pupils returned."[39] Over the first three decades of the twentieth century, Canada's own records "estimated that up to 50% of Indian children died in the schools from disease or maltreatment," yet "there is no record of children's aid ever intervening."[40] Their true intention is described by Canada's Truth and Reconciliation Commission (TRC) in these words: "The Canadian government pursued this policy of cultural genocide because it wished to divest itself of its legal and financial obligations to Aboriginal people and gain control over their land and resources."[41]

Although there was a Christian zeal to the residential schools, they were also steeped in the industrializing spirit of their time. As the TRC explains, "The model came from the reformatories and industrial schools that were being constructed in Europe and North America for the children of the urban poor."[42] It is in this context that my dad's father spent some of his childhood in the Nazareth Orphanage in Cornwall. The local Children's Aid Society was instituted in 1897, and the orphanage was opened a decade later by the Sisters of St Joseph to house the rising numbers of, in the society's words, "destitute children." My grandfather would occasionally recount how hard the orphanage could be on children, recalling that the nuns at times locked him in a small enclosure for a day when he was "bad." But that is just one side of my familial connection to this history, for I also have immediate ancestral lineages associated with the Sisters of St Joseph, the Grey Nuns, and other missionaries – an intimate connection to the Tsiata Nihononwentsiake alliance's missing "path of peace."

Isolating punishments were common across these reforming institutions, whose outward mission was to re-educate children on the margins of a so-called "progressive" society for integration into the emerging industrialism. I am reminded of Ursula Franklin describing the emergence of industrial education in the nineteenth century.[43] The assembly line called for a repositioning of people toward a capitalist production model, and this shift required an education that could supplant the preceding longstanding wholistic approach to work as crafts. Whereas an immersive education in particular crafts situated the individual in a creative process from inception to final product, the industrial system required people to become specialized, automatized parts of a production process that could be numerically measured. In residential schools, this legacy is evident in the numbers and "+" signs found etched into the underside of wooden tables and chairs at the Mohawk Institute, for rather than reflecting an interest in math, they indicate one Indigenous youth liking another, with their government-issued identification numbers replacing names.

"Let us continue free as the air." These words were written by Brant as his life approached its end in 1807. Each passing year increased his suspicions about the true intention of British officials whom he once thought were allies. His letter concludes, "It seems natural to Whites, to look on lands in the possession of Indians with an aching heart, and never to rest 'till they have planned them out of them."[44] In a sense, Brant straddled the space of the Two Row Wampum in the midst of an intensifying colonial turbulence, and his mixed-up legacy is related to these violations. The ship's approach on the river of life has from the beginning been fundamentally different from the kind of "sacred obligation that commits both parties to maintain respectful relationships and share lands."[45]

The friendly quality of the relations between Brant and Rousseau follows a pattern that stretches back to Étienne Brûlé and is connected to Gae Ho Hwako's adoption teaching and those of other Indigenous nations. As described in Anishinaabe stories, "the French traders seemed to come wearing the face of brotherhood. They seemed genuinely friendly and respectful. Perhaps this was because of their closeness to the Earth and her waterways. The Ojibway were so sincere in their acceptance that they adopted some of these French people into … the wa-bi-zha-shi'-do-i-daym' (Marten Clan), the clan of the warriors … [T]he responsibilities of this clan would be a worthy test of the sincerity of the newcomers."[46] These factors are connected to the difficult relations that both Brûlé and Rousseau had with colonial officials, and thus they model for us a potentially different path toward renewing a "path of peace" on this river of life. In following their cultural hyphae, we may find ways for replanting our sacred responsibilities as set out in the Two Row Wampum.

"Dad, why did this tree fall? Is it still possible to replant like the seeds we plant each spring?"

> Trees living in a forest grow best if all the trees are healthy. If one tree is in trouble, the others help it … If a tree is damaged and starts to die, its neighbors will pass it food to keep it alive. Trees grow wider until they reach the next tree. This creates a roof of branches and leaves that protects the forest from storms. If too many trees die and leave gaps, strong winds can enter and wreck the forest.[47]

There is so much to Etienne's question, so I begin my response to him with another: "Do you remember that big windstorm that blew down signs and created all kinds of damage in Toronto?" He was four years old when my relationship with this white pine was changed by a windstorm that brought it down on an early May day. The wind gusts of a hundred kilometres per hour toppled many trees and caused about $400 million in damages to the city. Such extreme storms have long been part of life here, but with each passing year, their intensity and frequency are escalating. It was because of our human role in these climate changes that we walked as a family in the 2019 Climate March, with Etienne and his sister, Iona, joining other children as they carried signs asking adults and leaders to change paths. This is how I want to start reflecting on Etienne's question.

Looking around at all the fallen white pines and oaks that crisscross these ravines, it is clear that with each passing year, the canopy of this urban forest is becoming more open to the intensifying global storms and local impacts of modern ways. We live in a time of more extreme weather events, of expanding losses in biological life that some characterize as the planet's sixth mass extinction event, of quickening uncertainty for Indigenous peoples in a melting North and in flooding island nations, and of conflicts over energy extraction and consumption, as highlighted by pipeline protests. For Gae Ho Hwako, this growing storm that swirls around us is connected to a kind of forgetting not only about the colonizing forces that continue to open up this forest but also about our human responsibility to lift up the Ganǫhǫnyǫhk. As a result, in her words, "uncertainty and confusion grow."

Gratitude is the ground of the Two Row Wampum's sacred contract, and this foundation gives us a different sense of what is being violated and what needs wholistic renewal in our ways of learning. Neither of my "higher education" experiences in social work or environmental studies came close to the reflective spirit that Gae Ho Hwako teaches. In my social work education of the mid-1990s, the ship's human-centric focus resulted in excluding from our sense of the "social" all that is of the land and waters. My chosen profession had also taken over for the residential schools with what is known as the Sixties Scoop, which placed Indigenous children in the child welfare system. As highlighted by Shelly Hachey in the previous chapter, that these inequities continue is reflected in the overrepresentation of Indigenous children in child welfare, in the disproportionate funding of Indigenous children, and in an overreliance on Western conceptions of social work policy and practice.[48] Even if I had been taught to reflect on social work's role in colonialism, the idea that child welfare was connected to land would not have been in the picture because land was not part of social work education – neither land's role in violent social policy nor the more recent awareness of land's healing potential.[49]

It was these gaps that guided me away from social work and toward a doctorate in environmental studies. Although the grounding of environmental-based learning and the interdisciplinary breadth were freeing, my learning with Indigenous teachers still highlighted for me the lack of a wholistic tradition in the university. I found myself writing and teaching about how environmental studies is often constricted by powerful disciplines like geography, national predilections like resource economics, a technological pragmatism that supports unending economic growth, and fragmentary colonial worldviews that tend toward appropriating Indigenous traditional ecological knowledge outside of cultural teachings like those shared by Gae Ho Hwako.[50] These conflicts are today epitomized in the way that Canada's government under Prime Minister Justin Trudeau has tried to initiate a pragmatic approach to pipeline development that repeats colonial dynamics with

Indigenous communities, all while trying to project an image of global leadership around the Paris Climate Accords of 2016.

There is a pattern here that connects the tendencies of my "higher education" experiences to the starker and violent education of the residential schools. Compliance and isolation were dominant features of the prescriptive education in these schools filled with children whose names were replaced with numbers. Although Ursula Franklin concedes that industrialization gave the modern world "a wealth of important products that have raised living standards and increased well-being," it simultaneously laid the groundwork for "a culture of compliance" that continues to specialize and isolate our knowledge, education, and lifeways[51] – not to mention how it supports the accruing of wealth in ever fewer hands. In other words, the unique disciplinary divisions and isolated pragmatism of my environmental and social work education partake of these colonial dynamics that are the fabric of the ship-based university system.

Offering a stronger Haudenosaunee view on the prescriptive education described by Franklin, John Mohawk writes that the ship's belief in "an unbroken story of cumulative improvements" that have brought us to the present is "an exercise in creative history," one that denies the continued low-intensity war against regional economies, cultures, and lands.[52] The goal of residential schools was to melt away Indigenous culture, stories, and ceremony without regard for impacts on individual lives, families, communities, or nations, even though some of them were once allies and supposedly even friends on this river of life. In the words of the Truth and Reconciliation Commission, Canada "pursued this policy of cultural genocide because it wished to divest itself of its legal and financial obligations to Aboriginal people and gain control over their land and resources."[53] There is a deep contrast between, on the one hand, the violent education that isolated and killed so many children for the wealth of land and, on the other hand, the wholistic, land-based education that Thomas, like Gae Ho Hwako, wanted to lift up. As Thomas wrote, "This melting pot that people speak of will create a loss of our identity and our connection to the Creator."[54]

Just like an old tree, an Indigenous Elder's roots are planted deep in the life of his or her cultural ancestries and in the relational knowledge that they make possible. The Two Row Wampum's river of life is so much more than "resources," for these waters are the lifeblood of E tinoha ongwesidage'dra gwe' and thus nourish all our roots through the Two Row's wholistic teaching. Although the economic appropriation of land and resources has been central to the Canadian nation and underlay the policy of the residential school system, the truth work of the TRC opens us to a different view on the ground of our lives. In its words, "Other dimensions of human experience – our relationships with the earth and all living beings – are also relevant in working towards reconciliation."[55] This is an understanding that flows like a current throughout the teachings offered by Gae Ho Hwako and Thomas. In fact, the source of Thomas's "bold steps" in education was the "wellsprings of energy and imagination" that came from his cultural roots in the great white pine.[56] This is the spirit that Brûlé and Rousseau also came to learn about from the languages of the waters as they offered tobacco. Such an education in the Elder hyphae of the land will inevitably bring us into conflict with the centre of power on the ship.

Informing Thomas's educational work were these simple words: "Wisdom is meant to be shared, and society is in great need. Now is the time to listen to our elders."[57] In 1992, he "took the unprecedented step of reciting the Great Law on the Six Nations reserve in English" to about 2,000 people, "a large number of them non-Iroquois."[58] Such an approach in the context of colonial violations made him controversial "in Iroquoian communities, a person at once respected for the extraordinary breadth of his knowledge and much in demand as a speaker at traditional events, but also criticized for 'popularizing'" Indigenous ways.[59] His response: "If they [whites] want to learn it, they have a right to. That should have been done 500 years ago, to study and respect the Confederacy. Maybe we wouldn't have the problems we have today." A "moment of decision … was at hand," and Thomas "believed there was no choice but to take bold steps."[60]

So is it possible to replant this tree and to nurture its growth in the wake of these storms? Answering this second part of Etienne's question requires a particular kind of reflective education that is intimately related to the teachings of this white pine. As Thomas related, "When we talk of our traditions, we never hide the truth of our history from our children. We are honest about our faults and share this with our people. But do white people do that? We speak the truth to help our people become better human beings. Whites keep real history away from their people. They hide poverty, theft, and murder from others. Instead of learning from the past and changing it, they create repetition by denying historical truths."[61]

In fact, it is the ship's inability to speak "truth" about broken promises and about the succeeding waves of uprooting violence that fuels the concern about Thomas's "bold" educational steps. I have come to see Thomas as an important teacher because, like Gae Ho Hwako, he held this tension and thus offered guidance toward a wholistic Two Row education. Reflecting on their teachings in relation to my family, to Rousseau, and to Brûlé, Etienne's namesake, I see a living ancestral pattern of people trying to reach beyond the margins of a ship that is always finding ways to convert more of us to its religious, economic, and political missions.

The 1895 birth of my great-grandmother in Tsi Sniahne was the end of my family's direct connection to an Indigenous community, for she was born in a period that coincided with the worst abuses of Canada's 1876 Indian Act, land appropriation, the residential school system, and unending waves of social violence and land theft. These violent forces, which deepened the gulf between Indigenous and non-Indigenous communities and increased uncertainties for those who navigated between those worlds, were surely related to the general move of our paternal family toward communities of the ship. Although on my dad's side we have close family from the community named after Brant's Indigenous name, Thayandenegea, who were born Mohawk, the reality is that these relations lived for years just west of those Mohawk lands. From my position, this is one more reminder of paternal ancestral patterns that are continually positioned on the ship side of the Two Row Wampum, although the reality is that we have always been on Indigenous land – on Turtle Island.

We should feel proud to honour, rather than hide from, this reality, and we should do our work from there. Our roots and hyphae have been planted on the colonial edge of French-Indigenous relations for centuries, and that is what has brought me to the circles of this book in a unique way – one that over time I have come to see as offering a way to re-envision truth and reconciliation here in Canada on Turtle Island. With every step that I take on this path to replanting our roots, I feel called to stand with Gae Ho Hwako and Thomas as teachers because of how they embody the white pine in ways that I can learn based on who I am. Given my respect for their teachings, I also need to reflect deeply on their concerns about straddling the space of the Two Row Wampum when offering these teachings in colonial languages that are connected to the "melting pot." It was due to similar concerns that Thomas was criticized for going too close to the ship and for offering too much – a concern that I also hear in the clear words of Kawennakon (Bonnie Whitlow) on "pretendians" offered earlier in this circle of the book.

Etienne, we must listen closely. We have not grown up in Indigenous communities, directly experienced colonial racism and violence, or lived the cultural ways that make one like Gae Ho Hwako a person of the Longhouse, a Haudenosaunee. We are also not of those Métis nations around the Red River who had time and space to realize themselves as a unique culture, before suffering their own abuse at the hands of Canadian policy. Rather, like Brûlé and Rousseau, our *coureur de bois* French Canadien ancestors always returned to the Great Lakes and Saint Lawrence River waters that they called home, lived in relation with the communities of the Tsiata Nihononwentsiake, and then, lacking a sense of community or culture, hid in isolation as fear of the Indian Act, Métis suppression, and other colonial changes gripped people. In fact, it would seem that this system of fear had as one of its intentions expansion of the gulf between the vessels of the Two Row Wampum in order to inhibit the relational learning and transformation that are central to *ǫ da gaho dę:s*.

For all these reasons, we must remember the stories of relations between French Canadiens and Indigenous peoples that your name carries, but we do so in a context where we are also severed from the French language and culture. Without the fear and hiding described in our ancestral stories, we would have a very different sense of who we are as Canadiens and perhaps be further along the path of enacting relational accountability to the land and our Indigenous Elders. We need to continue searching for that balance. This is why I only go so far when approaching the canoe that Gae Ho Hwako holds, despite the beauty of her Longhouse culture and river of life teachings. Meeting in *ǫ da gaho dę:s*, I have come to appreciate that the restraint of relational noninterference is fundamentally about a passion to foster the diverse gifts of life here so that we can replant our sacred responsibilities in the spirit of the Two Row Wampum's original intention.

"Dad, can you be quiet? I've heard enough!"

> Peacemaker's final words were clear …
> *"Now go and bury your 'weapons of war'*
> *Beneath the White Pine of Peace*
> *And welcome all who will live by 'the law'*
> *The one law … the Great Law of Peace"*[62]

These uprooted tendrils offer many stories and teachings, but I have to better understand when Etienne has heard enough. My academic tendency toward lecturing rather than storytelling often gets in the way of enjoying the relations of this forest. In the words of Gae Ho Hwako, "We used to climb trees; they want us to climb them, clutch onto them, and swing from them." Without that playful joy, the spirit of thanksgiving cannot arise in our hearts, and a wholistic Two Row education is probably impossible. So I tell him to go back to his tree climbing, and I promise that another day I will tell him more stories about his roots.

A spirit of gratitude is the mother root that can help us begin to internalize the values necessary for clarifying our responsibilities to *ge' gyo kwa* (the people), to the Great Tree of Peace, to the river of life that is the blood of E tinoha ongwesidage'dra gwe', and to the mystery of Shogwaeyadisho' (the Creator). Without a rooted sense of gratitude for all the beings that make our life possible, our forest canopy will become more and more open to storms as we stop learning what our heart is saying. Although there is much that can be learned by feeling our way semi-consciously into relations with a white pine or a local river of life and its trails, like the Passage de Taronto, my learning with these beings deepened as I came into a living reflective relation with Elder cultural teachings like those of the Thanksgiving Address and the Two Row Wampum.

It is exactly because urban living makes gratitude for our place in creation seem so distant from our thoughts that I try to find ways of offering my son, Etienne, something to make these teachings less tenuous. Although I am forever thankful for the generosity of Gae Ho Hwako and for the wisdom shared by Thomas, I am also aware of the colonial violence that spreads so much confusion. I have felt those dark stormy waters that Gae Ho Hwako refers to deep within my being. For a time, I tried moving closer to the canoe as my grounding, but the imbalance of that action felt less right than the aridity that I feel on the ship. It became clearer that I cannot pick up a Haudenosaunee teaching like the Great Law as an object to be possessed and appropriated, but I will follow Gae Ho Hwako's guidance to our own roots so as to come to the learning of *ǫ da gaho dę:s*.

Peace, friendship, respect, sharing, and other life-affirming values are the roots that need tending, and this task should be approached through bringing our unique ancestral stories and ways into these transformative relations. I cannot let myself or family be constrained by the ways of the ship that go against good ways of relating on this river of life. "There is no fear with a good mind," Thomas said, adding that when in "a bad mind, fear is always following you."[63] It is in those moments that the privilege of our white skin can prompt a desire to hide or isolate oneself, as some of our ancestors (and many others like them) surely did in the face of being called, like Brûlé and Rousseau, traitors and scoundrels. We need to go beyond this privilege and keep standing with those friends and family for whom hiding is not only not an option but also known to be a violation of the spirit that we choose to culturally embody in this life amidst all the beings of the Thanksgiving Address.

Thomas and Gae Ho Hwako are right: wholistic work, education, and living cannot be accomplished out of fear. It is the generosity of the Thanksgiving Address, not fear, that brings about the unity of a good mind; fear brings only more violence, confusion, and division. As one of my favourite quotes states, "Peace is unity in diversity. There is no peace where there is no diversity, and there is no peace when there is only diversity."[64] This is the intention that we lift up when we offer tobacco to these roots.

I give these stories to Etienne as reminders that this land we live with is, as was the case for his namesake, "the only home" we know. The way of cultural ancestors like Brûlé and Rousseau courses through his veins. Their stories tell us about the difficulties and wonders that they experienced, about the mystery of this world and our place in it, about conflict, confusion, and hiding, and about the responsibility of being who we are while affirming the diverse relations that we find ourselves in relation with as we traverse the river of life. The words of Thomas echo: "It does not matter what colour we are, we need to come together. Mother Earth has suffered so much abuse."[65]

All of these stories and teachings are in the name Etienne! By reflecting on our ancestral roots and hyphae, we can approach a wholistic Two Row education in *ǫ da gaho dę:s*. But as I close this reflection, I need to recognize a vital limitation to everything that I have learned so far from these paternal roots: if I am to honour the matrilineal source of Gae Ho Hwako's teachings and confront the patriarchal source of colonial violence, I need to recognize that the mother roots of my family arise from a woman of the Canadien ship. For now, I am done, but I will unravel these maternal roots for Etienne's sister, Iona, in the final circle of this book after Gae Ho Hwako's teachings on "E tinoha ongwesidage'dra gwe' (Mother Earth)" and "Geihnyenoh de yo ki ye'nya dohn (Spiritual Helpers) and Shogwaeyadisho' (the Creator)."

A Prayer: Two Road

Awnjibenayseekwe (Banakonda Kennedy-Kish Bell)

I have been wondering about our youth and about youth as a whole. Through my children and my work, I have encountered and heard from many young people who are discouraged. Some are even angry, yet they are dreaming. Almost in the same breath, they are reaching, longing for a future without the deprivation and destruction of life all around them. These young people quest right in the middle of their confusion and despair. They do so with imagination, thoughtful hope, and straightforwardness.

Indigenous youth are dreaming of a covenant of friendship and peace called the Two Row Wampum – seeing, experiencing, and exploring this long-ago agreement as a relationship with settlers across Turtle Island. They believe the covenant was and remains a sealed, sacred, stated promise: "For as long as the grass is green, as long as the rivers flow, as long as the sun rises in the east and sets in the west, we will travel two paths."[1] Belief and trust in the Two Row Wampum still holds fast.

The Anishinaube have a prophecy we refer to as the "Two Road." In this prophecy, the people were told of the coming of the light-skinned people. They would wear the face of friendship, or they would wear the face of death and greed. If they came with the book and the sword, there would be great struggles, loss, and destruction.

If they came in the spirit of friendship, a great new nation would be born. This new nation would not result in the undoing of one or the other but in a rising up of the great diversity that is within all of creation, within all the cultures of humanity. It is a vision that recalls for me the words of the Oglala Sioux Black Elk: "The first peace, which is the most important, is that which comes within the souls of people when they realize their relationship, their oneness with the universe and all its powers, and when they realize at the center of the universe dwells the Great Spirit, and that its center is really everywhere, it is within each of us."[121]

In this telling, there are many circles of dreamers young and old reaching for the canoe in the water ways of our ancestors, not for the ship. There is an awareness, born out of a longing, that is reimagining, re-engaging their future to revitalize culture and ceremonies – to sound the drum, the songs, the dances of our ancestors, to call in the healing of our First Mother, of ourselves with all our relations, to take up our place with respect and reciprocity once again in creation. Here, in the Two Road, is the principle of the Third Fire, what Gae Ho Hwako describes in her Two Row teachings as *ǫ da gaho dę:s* (the sacred meeting space).

I dream of coming together at the Third Fire, where we stand in who we are, celebrating our diversity by kindling our own fire with the Strength of Kind Honest Sharing. I know from my own experience of our ceremonies that our drum, our prayers, our songs, and our dances reverberate in the living of my life – in the way I love, share, and do my work.

My love for the beauty and simple grace of my canoe and the abiding relationship that I am brought to with water and sky in the arms of our First Mother restore me, filling me with gratitude again and again. This relationship with the canoe helps me navigate the grief and loss I have experienced due to the legacy of our ongoing one-sided Two Road relationship.

I am Canoe
Laughing waters embrace
Caress me

You
Move the paddle
To move me

Ahead

Under blue skies
In the green
Of pines, spruce, cedar, and balsam

I remember
The hands that shaped me
Feel the difference
In the hands that direct me
They move me away

Toward
A place called forward

Away

From being touched
Worked with
To being used
To being useful

No experience
Of me

Alive

No encouragement
Or acknowledging words

No call
For the good medicine
Of the earth
Air, water
And spirit
To lead us

Just the quickening press
To move forward
To claim
To conquer
To get
Pelts, hides, gold
And silver
Timber
Land
And labour

Resources
Lifeless

Great-grandfather trees
Great buffalo
Lakes
And rivers
So many veins across this land
No longer

Dams redirect
Dry up rivers and lakes
Clear-cut
Leaves parched land
And erosion

And memories
Of grandeur and majesty

I am left
To grieve
The beauty, lost
For the songs
Of my paddle

Of my people
Of the land

Spirits now
Not flesh and blood
Or pumping rhythm
I grieve
That I carried the voices
Who stole
Earth songs
Water songs
Bird songs
And wind songs
Of all directions

Confused the seasons
Stopped the dialogue

With our mother
Our relatives
Our ancestors
I grieve

Yet
Remember
With gratitude
Experiences
Before
The endless degradation
The endless rape
And the take, take, take

I lie on my side, now
My beauty fading
Ribs exposed

I bare witness
To the destruction
To what is lost

I carry the history
And I remember
The hands that made me
Long in the earth now
I too
Am returning
To my mother
To spirit
To her songs

Still abiding
Deep in the earth of her

Still pulsing
At the centre
Spirit
Her past, present, future
In spite of all
Whole

Still alive
Still rising
In the breath
Of you and I

And I hope

Once I dialogued
With the water
The winds and seasons
With the hands that formed me

Struggled and bent
To the men
Who drove me
Stole me

Felt the voices
Silenced
Witnessed
The mass burials

Yet
The spirit
Of creation
Of all my relations
Still engages
Still responds
Still emerges

I am still
I am silent

At my centre
Still longing
For the touch of the rivers
Of lakes
Longing
For the push and pull
Of the wind
Of the paddle stirring me

And now
As sun warms me
New hands
Touch me
A voice

Admires me
Gently, caringly
Moves me
Washes
Scent of pine gum
Glue spreading over me
Gathering me
Together

I am waking
Trembling
In the cool light
Of spring
To the sound
Of water
Moving like thunder
Anticipating

Could it be
A new beginning
You and I
Rising up together
Cleansing, healing
Singing renewal
With our mother

Megwetch Gitchi Manidoo (thank you Creator) and all my relations.

Ḛsḛhsgwaowhaneh: An Invitation to Expand the Teaching

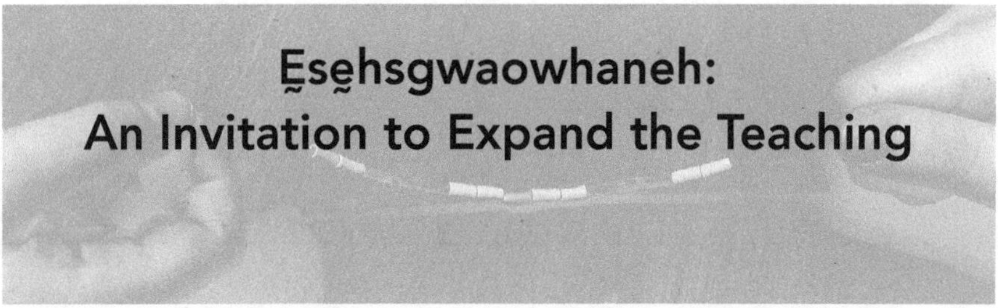

> You need to expand the teaching or story beyond what you hear and see; it is about clarity, questioning, and seeking answers.

The string is now passed to you, the reader, to "expand the teaching" in relation to your own experiences, stories, and knowledge. Is there a part of Gae Ho Hwako's teaching that really resonates with you or perhaps something from one of the responses? Begin by reflecting on that in relation to your story. In this way, you can help us to expand the circle of truth, sharing, and healing.

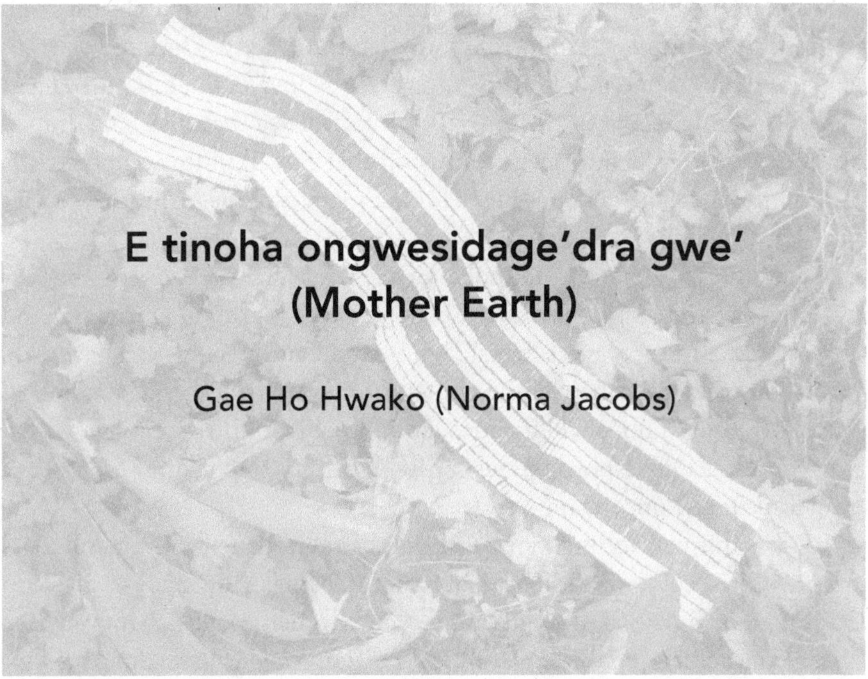

E tinoha ongwesidage'dra gwe' (Mother Earth)

Gae Ho Hwako (Norma Jacobs)

> She is a life giver, as all life begins with her! She teaches us about values, boundaries, forgiveness, encouragement, patience, love, laughter, strength, and *awehaode'* (soft, kind, embracing words). Her *awehaode'* embrace us with those winds that keep us strong in ourselves, ever supporting us with provisions of comfort. She is our foundation; we walk upon her body every day, ever so gently massaging her so that she can provide us with the luxuries of life. E tinoha ongwesidage'dra gwe' connects all the roots of the plants, trees, flowers, and medicines. All the roots are interwoven so that they can supply their energy to everything. We never go without the nurturance of her love, which is our very existence. We say *nya weh* (thank you) to our Mother Earth for all that she provides. Let it be that way in our minds!

Today, I looked outside to see the love that is given and nurtured by E tinoha ongwesidage'dra gwe' (Mother Earth). It is late fall, and the trees, shrubs, grasses, rocks, medicines, fences, and buildings are all covered with frost. As E'dehka gakwa se dwa ja (Our Eldest Brother the Sun) shines light on these frosted beings, they begin to sparkle with a new energy. A ceremony of love is being extended to those elements through this energy that cleanses and reminds them of their responsibility to give and receive. The sun's warmth enlivens them to open their arms to receive the love emitted in this sacred dance of intimacy, and in that moment, it feels like a shawl is being draped around the shoulders of our precious Mother Earth. In this embrace, she feels appreciated and acknowledged for her many ways of gifting and receiving – reciprocity!

Relieved of all her stress, E tinoha ongwesidage'dra gwe' exercises her extremities by stretching, massaging, playing, laughing, smiling, rolling, and moving side to side. She is exhausted but happy, and now she can have a replenishing sleep over the coming winter, from which another generation of trust, love, and honour will be born. Soon it will be time to awaken with a new energy as our responsibilities for living with E tinoha ongwesidage'dra gwe' come to life once again!

What is this new feeling? Something is changing. A new movement arises from within – cold, warmth, heat, queasiness, beings growing. The air is refreshing; her breath is strengthening. Our Mother Earth is happy, as the changes mean new life – a new energy and vision – and with it comes responsibilities and preparation. She draws strength and refreshment from the rain as the changing winds bring a sprinkling mist that blows ever so gently on her skin. This falling water sings a lullaby and cradles her gently, for her body is in a sensitive state that needs caressing and tender encouragement. Each day, she awakens with the excitement of a new movement, and through it all, she is supported by extended family: her Grandmother Moon, her Aunties and Ancestors the Stars, her Grandfathers the Thunder Storms, and the ever-changing winds that embrace her with their soothing messages.

I was always told that women have two roles. The first is to give life, and when we think about life as a woman, we know that much energy and wealth of knowledge exude from this foundation. As women, we give life, and we receive from this act our second role as nurturers of life. All we need to do is look out the window or open the door to see all the nurturance and health of creation that E tinoha ongwesidage'dra gwe', our Mother Earth, generates with her love.

Take care of your gifts, for you are so precious. This was my first awareness in seeking out my identity and gifts as a female. Then I moved to my clan, my nation, and my Ongwehowe name, Gae Ho Hwako, which means "ancestral females holding the canoe before me." It is a name that positions me in an ancestral line of great women of the Wolf Clan in the Cayuga Nation of the Haudenosaunee Confederacy. I have been given the responsibilities of empowering myself, my family, my community, the nation, and the Confederacy. I have been affected by the onset of colonialism and by all that it did to our culture, but I have held strong to our culture, language, values, and beliefs. I was told by my mother that it was important to know my cultural ways so that I would be able to help explain them to people, and it is these experiences and responsibilities that I hold as a mother, grandmother, Haudenosaunee community member, Longhouse Faith Keeper, and Indigenous woman.

The times are changing, and we are all changing. It is so beautiful to be part of these changes – these healing processes that we often do not think about in terms of ourselves. We always look outside of our stories and experiences to see these things rather than looking within and appreciating who we are as people in all this change. Where do our beginnings come from? How did we get here? What are we doing here? It is such an honour to be able to reflect back and say, "This is who I am, and this is my journey." We should be appreciative of being on this journey. There are lots of people of our age and younger who no longer have this great opportunity because they have been called home.

Everything is just so beautiful. This is a great day, as life is happening; births are happening. The moon is in a place where it is continually filling up and emptying itself, just like a pregnant woman. It is so beautiful to see how new life is always on the verge of happening. We should be able to celebrate these days of new beginnings and to take joy in the babies who come to bring us – to remind us of – pure laughter and joy. We should be able to look with our eyes at the future that they bring and to remember how we missed out on things and how we want to make it better for these coming faces and for those still unborn.

There is such wonderment in how a baby comes to be through its birth in the waters of women – not just of its mother but of all those who have birthed human life. We were all birthed on those same waters because we are each connected to our mother. That is why Haudenosaunee culture is matrilineal. Life begins with women, and so we honour them because of their capacity to bring life into this world. We celebrate women so as to remember that we are part of something greater than ourselves. Conception is a great and mysterious time when two drops of fluid come together. There are billions of drops of fluid, but these two drops are attracted to one another and join, egg fertilized by sperm. Looking at it closely, we can see that it is an amazing experience.

Sadly, I did not grow up with these teachings to celebrate and look forward to giving life. Colonialism took us away from those teachings that would have allowed us to enjoy the experience of becoming a mother. Without our teachings, having a baby was about being ashamed. Missing out on the beautiful teachings carried by our ancestors, we became overloaded with the negativity of being pregnant and able to carry life within ourselves. So for me, it was not until I gave birth to my last baby of six children that I began to learn our teachings and could celebrate what a great thing it was to be pregnant and give life. But to celebrate, I also had to grieve for those times when I did not know the preciousness of pregnancy and how my attitude and behaviour could impact my babies – my children. Through this grief, I learned to celebrate how great life is.

Sometimes, the baby cannot move through its mother, as it is sideways or upside down. Our women have traditional teachings for home birthing; they know about natural birth and how to move the baby so that it can be born in a natural way. We are able to do that by gently touching and moving the baby in the direction that we want it to go with our hands. During pregnancy, we also have lots of medicines that we can take for cleaning out our system and making our organs, bones, and muscles more flexible so that we will have an easier time giving birth.

Everything is supposed to be in honour of the baby that is growing inside the womb; that place inside is as sacred as the outside. Mother and baby are there to nurture one another, and so they need their proper foods. There are certain foods that we should not take into our bodies when pregnant because they cause congestion or do not agree with the baby. Such foods are not the natural foods that we have long eaten, like corn, beans, and squash, which our people should enjoy because they are part of that beginning support for us.

Everything that creation offers to that new life is sacred and pure. Our babies are held in a sacred space for nine months so that they can develop. So much has changed today. Now, you can know the identity of your baby before it is born, but in our traditions, that is a sacred time for us to be thinking about whether it is going to be a girl or a boy. It is special to have that experience of being overwhelmed when the baby is born and saying, "It's a girl" or "It's a boy." We often miss out on that now because we have already been informed. The experience is not as sacred anymore.

My second daughter was born with a caul, a clear membrane that can cover a baby's face and sometimes its whole body. It is like a transparent casing or blanket. When she was born with it covering her face, the doctor asked, "What do you want me to do with it?" I said that I did not know anything about cauls, so he should just get rid of it. But afterward, when I got home and told my mother that my daughter had been born with a caul, she said that it was a special gift that would allow her to read people's lives. The caul is great medicine, a gift that a person is given to help people and the community. I felt so bad that I had not known this teaching and that I had let the caul be incinerated. Because I had missed out on that, my daughter also missed out. It reminds me that when my babies were born, I was so afraid and not in a good place because I did not know my culture.

With my last baby, it was the first time I realized that there is a tree of life on the sack of water that holds the baby so gently during pregnancy. When my daughter was born, they held that sack up for me to look at. I was just so amazed because it was such a pure white, and I could see the tree of life. I did not know what to think, and I was just so overwhelmed. I was also angry at myself that I had not seen it before, but I guess that it was just time for me to see it now and really understand the greatness of our journey. When my baby was starting to travel down the birthing canal to be born, I came to learn that she was covered with the medicine of being in my body, of being born the natural way through the vagina. This was another thing that I had not known before, but when the baby is coming, you can smell the medicine. A baby's birthing is tremendous; it is like a flower opening up. When the birthing space opens, the baby's head looks like the centre of the flower with its fuzzy hair. It is so amazing to see life beginning on this human journey.

When you hear the baby take its first breath and yell out, it is announcing its arrival here to all of creation, which is already inside the room. All of creation comes to see what journey this baby has participated in. The water is there again to wash the baby off and to begin the baby's introduction to all the elements. We introduce them one by one and give thanks for the gift that each brings to this earth walk, which the baby now joins. We celebrate the support, guidance, and direction that each offers this child in its journey through this life. That moment of delivery is a precious time when we are able to receive babies in a good way by introducing them to all the elements and by acquainting the elements with the new babies.

When our babies are born, we put a bonnet on them to keep the sacred space of the soft spot on top of the head open for all of the good energy that is coming to this earth walk from the Sky World. It also keeps the negative energy away from the baby because the soft spot is where the spirit is still moving back and forth between the spirit world and the earth. We want to protect that sacred soft spot on the head in order to keep the baby strong as it comes into this life. During the first eight weeks, the baby gets to recognize and know the voice of its mother, and so mothers traditionally did not go anywhere. Today, when our babies are born and we come out of the hospital, where do we go? We go to the mall, and they are already out in the community. But in our teachings, the mother should be at home during this time, learning about the baby and the gift that it brings forward.

If we hear the baby crying, we can hold its little finger, and it will calm down in seconds. It can become stressed, as it is not used to this new life after being safe in the womb, so grasping onto that little finger calms it down. When our babies come here, it is said they already know their journey and that it is shown on their hands. Everything that they are going to learn on this journey into the Longhouse is held in their hands. They are curious right away, and they start asking questions as they cry, gurgle, or murmur. If you listen to them closely, you will hear the question and will try to respond. So they are already trying to communicate to you, to the parents, or to whoever is in their surroundings. They are asking who they are, or what the day is like, or who knows what other kind of question. But they are already asking questions; they want to build that relationship.

Because we are responsible for giving life, we cannot separate birthing from being a leader. This act connects us to the social, environmental, and political systems. It connects us to the abundance of harvest. I cannot just talk about birthing. There are so many other things that I need to include, for when we give life to our children, we are also preparing them for a place in leadership – whether it be in politics, economics, culture, or whatever. We are giving them all these tools, a great bundle to carry. We say, "I'm putting these teachings here; you select which ones you want to focus on." We do that in our lodge during the first eight weeks of life so as to build this relationship with the baby because we are trying to identify its skills. How do I know you?

New babies also wear a buckskin bracelet because they are now on their earth walk, and we have to ground them in that way. They need to be connected to the earth as the source of life. We are also supposed to wrap them in a blanket or cradle board, what is called a *tikkanaagan* by the Anishinaabe north of us. They are wrapped tight in these casings because their muscles are developing. And when they get to the point of movement, they break out of the cradle board and are able to unwrap themselves. They are working at their body's development, and they need time to adjust to this life. If you leave babies unwrapped, every sound or movement can make them jump because they are not used to the human energy. As babies grow, we can continue to wrap them, and they will continue to unwrap themselves. This is more natural than having your baby in a bed or a buggy or dressing it like a little doll. We let it be a baby, and we enjoy the pure energy that it brings to us, the happiness, smiles, and joy of seeing you, of recognizing your voice and knowing that you are Mom, that it can trust this earth walk because it knows who that is.

Women are always trying to care for everybody, sharing what they can. Women are multi-taskers, and this is a responsibility that we see in E tinoha ongwesidage'dra gwe'. She connects all the roots from the plants, trees, flowers, and medicines. All the roots are interwoven so that they can supply their energy to everything. When I look at all this, it makes sense to me why we women are multi-taskers and how our energy and work are different from that of men. We are always thinking about our future and what will nurture life. How do we make changes for the better?

❈ ❈

> It is great that we look forward to celebrating the annual return of the hanging fruits, first greeting their leader, known as the *jihso'dak*, wild strawberry! We layer our soft words to her so that she will again bring into our presence her medicine and sustenance. She reminds us of where we come from and our responsibilities, not only to ourselves but also to all involved with the continuance of life. She brings her families to build relationships with everyone, and it is our responsibility to go and meet her in that sacred space so as to honour one another. It is fun searching for the ripe berries and seeing all the humps in the field as the people bend over or squat to pick the berries. The *jihso'dak*

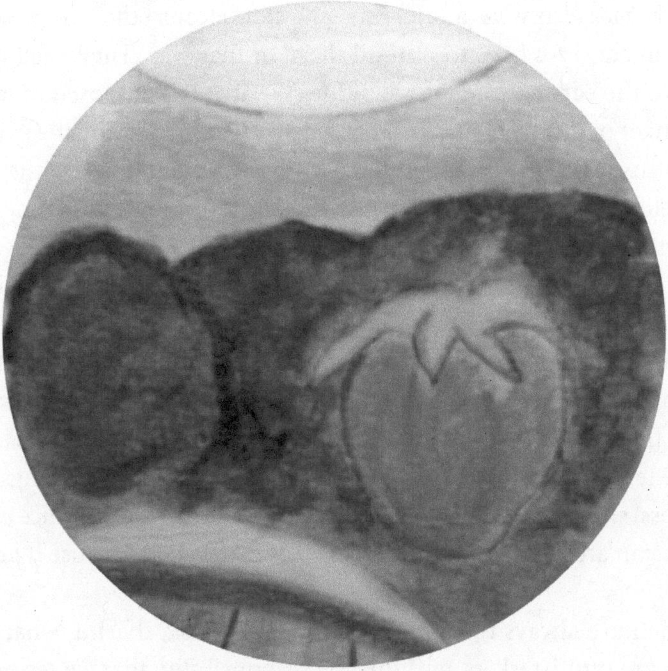

The *Jihso'dak* (Wild Strawberry) in the Ganǫhǫnyǫhk (Thanksgiving Address). Drawing by Gae Ho Hwako (Norma Jacobs).

> begins a cycle of growth, as she provides a pathway for the other hanging fruits to journey this way and to receive the benefits of meeting us pitiful humans. We say *nya weh* (thank you). Let it be that way in our minds!

The Two Row Wampum is not just about the past but also carries instructions for how we should try to live every day – how to discipline our ways of living rather than always trying to develop further and to consume more, in the process spreading confusion in the world. We are to remain true to those values, stories, teachings, and protocols that we had when we came to meet the ship. The Gayensra'go:wa (Great Law) is one of the philosophies that has kept our culture and traditions strong and intact throughout the centuries of colonial conflict. We honour its teachings by working with the land, gathering the berries, and offering the first words of the Ganǫhǫnyǫhk (Thanksgiving Address) to all the beings we depend upon. With all this sustenance and with the ceremonies to remind us of our responsibility to give thanks, we were a healthy people who had a way of life that was complete for us in all our relations, whether they be with the *jihso'dak* (wild strawberry), the waters, other nations, or E tinoha ongwesidage'dra gwe'.

The *jihso'dak* is the first gift of life, the first gift of food each spring that we celebrate as our closest connection to this earth walk. My body is spiritually aware of the seasons and what they bring in regard to health and wellness for all aspects of self – mentally, emotionally, spiritually, and physically. I pay close attention to the changes of the environment because the environment gives to our well-being. The strawberries come to see how you greet their return as visitors coming back to our lands, and through this return, they remind us of our families, of our great-great-grandmothers who have long shared stories of all the relationships that we celebrate.

I remember as a child going out to look for the *jihso'dak* and giving that first gathering to my grandmother. It was fun searching for the ripe berries and seeing all the humps in the field as the people bent down or squatted over to pick the berries. I see those humps today on the modern berry farms, and as I look around, my memories bring back stories and teachings! The return of the *jihso'dak* brings forth thoughts that have been shared with me, and I use my mind in a good way to relate with the berries as human beings because they carry an *ancestral* line that is their life energy.

I always have a feeling of messages approaching. Maybe it comes on the wind as I feel an energy that causes me to go to the fields and check for berries. Before doing that, I will have been watching the earth come alive after the long winter and seeing the green foliage from plants and trees like the willow and the maple approach in response to the spiritual calling of their sacred responsibility to all our relations. In past years, I have seen the strawberries blossom, so I know where to look for them. I prepare myself by giving thanks and greetings for this second gift of healing remedies from creation – the first gift being the maple sap that cleanses, rebuilds, and replenishes our bodies and minds. It is the maple that prepares us for the arrival of the *jihso'dak* at this time.

I walk to the field in a good mind because I am going to see where my relatives and families are. I get to the edge of the field, and I give thanks, as I have a sacred responsibility to ask whether I can approach this field to search for the berries. Walking in, I see the many plants, but there are no berries in sight. I walk in farther and bend down, and then I see something red hiding behind a leaf. I am overjoyed! I grasp the tiny fruit, and I feel honoured that today is the day when we are to greet each other. It feels like a great love, so fulfilling, and I experience the joy of seeing a great spiritual friend.

We look at each other and smile. "It has been a long time," I say, "and I was not sure if you were coming back for a visit or if I would be here to greet you." I hold her close to me. "Where is your family?" I ask. I move more leaves and see more strawberries, and they dance with happiness. I pick them and bring them home so that they can meet my family. I will have lunch with my family, and we sing songs as the meal is prepared. We sit and share our journeys, talking about where we have travelled and about how the *jihso'dak* has brought good medicine for us to share.

I have learned so many stories that I can apply to gathering the *jihso'dak* and its flowers, to gardening, to tapping trees, and to birth. Because every element in creation gives sustenance to babies' lives so that they can be born and be healthy, all of creation is involved in their birth. All of creation gathers around to see the results of all of this work that the elements have participated in by nurturing, feeding, and cleansing the new being. It is important to make these connections for babies and to celebrate their health; that is how it should be. We must enjoy the medicines, the tapping of the trees, the power of water, and the return of the *jihso'dak*.

I think to myself that these stories and our visitors, the *jihso'dak*, are too precious to keep to myself and my family; they should be shared. The community is informed that our precious relations have returned and that their presence needs acknowledgment. The community gathers, and our relations join us. We greet each other and celebrate that we still have life and that we are medicine for each other. The prayers that we share are for our health and well-being. The songs that we sing express our gratitude for this day. Happiness and reflection exude from our "being." We remember our journeys, stories, and songs, and we recognize that we are those sacred spiritual beings who descended from the Sky World to work on this spiritual journey with E tinoha ongwesidage'dra gwe'.

We are honoured to share our medicine as we unwrap our bundles of instruction from our councils and the Creator that prepare us for this journey of life. We have been told of the hardships of humans, disease, conflict, and the struggles of the ego. Our stories remind us that we live with two energies and that we need to choose which one will enhance our lives. Across all our Indigenous territories, we tell stories about our journey into this world. They teach us about the importance of being conscious of how we live with each other. Is what we are bringing into our relationships beneficial for others or not? How we approach these stories and this question is always a choice that we are asked to make.

All these teachings ask us to learn about ourselves and the preciousness of our bodies. They tell us that our bodies have been created in such a way that all the organs enhance each other and the body through their responsibilities – just like we, the people, enhance each other. The heart does not take on the role of the kidneys or the liver; it has a certain responsibility in connection to all of our other organs. When one thing goes wrong, all the organs are affected. Our bodies are sacred in their own right, for they allow us to walk, see, hear, care, and give life. They know how to do all of these things naturally every moment, and so they support our journeys on this earth walk. Nothing in this world stands alone.

Inside our bundles, we find love, encouragement, compassion, and a good mind, all of which give us spiritual strength and hope for our walk through this life. We sit across from the fires of our ancestors, sharing truth. We smile and embrace as our time together comes to a close. This is not goodbye but rather an offering of layers and layers of prayers until the next time our paths cross – perhaps next spring when the red *jihso'dak* is again seen hiding under green leaves.

❁ ❁

> We are so fortunate for the changing winds that warm and cool the earth and work to accommodate the changing seasons. They come and wrap around us like a blanket, holding us strong and giving us comfort. We are fortunate that we have not experienced the horrendous destructions of tornados or other strong forces of wind in our lands, although we have been forewarned that these things will happen when we fail to ensure our responsibilities of thankfulness, respect, and humble recognition of the limits assigned to us by the Creator. We say *nya weh* to the winds for being with us through our journey of life. Let it be that way in our minds!

Beware the storm! This thought comes to mind over and over again. Our mother's skirt of beautiful colours has been torn and dirtied by the violations of her sacred space. Her dark, long, flowing, and shiny hair is where the eagles and many varieties of winged ones nest and give birth to their young. The shrubs protect her like the lace on her skirt from the sweat and dust as she plants, nurtures, and brings to harvest the gifts for the people. Her bosom nurtures all life – plants, animals, and humans – with the food and medicine that give us health. Her beaded moccasins are adorned with many flowers, butterflies, humming birds, blue jays, and other varieties of birds that live among the plants. Our relations no longer have a nurturing and fulfilling habitat where they can raise their offspring because of the corruption, violence, abuse, and rape of the land, the very being of our Mother Earth.

There are always consequences for violating good boundaries, and that is true for how we relate to E tinoha ongwesidage'dra gwe'. Once a prestigious female, a bounty of love and magnificence, a woman in all her seasons, a beauty never to be replicated, she has now been rendered helpless in the wake of destruction. We will feel the discipline and pain of her red willow whip against our legs, our foundation. When that happens, there will be no mercy, no support or guidance, no encouragement or loving kindness, no strength. In their place will come uncontrollable winds, darkness, water imbalances, and silence. All of these things will happen because we have not respected the gifts that she shared with her family, with us.

There is not a woman who would surrender her life for that of her children without a fight. I remember carrying so many burdens – the mental anguish, anger, fear, frustration, manipulation, and untruths. I remember running away as I tried to protect myself but coming back because my children were there. I remember reaching out and grasping at anything available to strike back. Every woman who has lost her life has put forth a battle to protect herself and her children. She never gives up; she goes down fighting with every ounce of strength.

The ship thought that our land was rich, and with its industrializing ways, it moved as quickly as it could to take the nutrients from our Mother Earth by doing things like mining, oil drilling, and fracking. Our kids were sent to residential schools or adopted into non-Native families, and these occurrences deteriorated our connection to the ways of life provided for us. The ship's ways have become a detriment both to our people and to all the people of the world, who are now suffering directly or indirectly from the cultural and environmental impacts of ways that have not held our relations sacred. It is always possible to take in unhealthy food, to drink water that is polluted, or to trust people who have not come into our lives in a good way, so healing ceremonies are applicable in many ways.

When I was attending ceremony, I always wondered why our people looked so unhappy, sad, or withdrawn. I thought that our ceremonies were so precious, as they told us about who we are. I thought that we should be ecstatic, and this question stayed with me until I heard stories about their experiences in the residential schools. My grandmother was a key person in my life; she told me stories and taught me about listening, watching, and being me. She was concerned for my safety, so she made sure that I could learn to assess for myself whether I was safe. She was afraid of what would happen to me because of what people in the community had experienced in residential schools and other colonial institutions. I always thought that this concern with safety was a puberty rite of our culture – that we were not allowed to go anywhere until we were mature.

All of these things make me angry that the ship thinks that its ways are superior to those of the canoe – that it can objectify us in a system of greed that lacks the values of the canoe. I felt this anger as I gathered with other families at the National Inquiry into Missing and Murdered Indigenous Women and Girls (MMIWG), where we shared stories of agonizing pain experienced through the loss of loved ones. Some had been found, but others were still missing. I too had an expectant granddaughter who went missing and was found murdered after being strangled by her unborn son's father. He was later released after several appeals related to failings in the judge's court directions. I know the frustration and anger caused by disillusionment with a system of law that supposedly "protects" the innocent victims of crime. It is a joke! That was what I felt as I heard the excruciating pain of hundreds of families who shared their experience. It was overwhelming.

We grieved together at the National Inquiry, and we learned from one another about our strengths and dreams. We remembered our ceremonies and sang songs. We held onto one another and shared our caring with the families. We listened with our hearts and began to build a trust as we recognized our common pain and grief. We remembered our ancestors, those who came before us and taught about the importance of boundaries, values, discipline, and honouring oneself so that honour can be shown toward others.

Because the Two Row Wampum instructs us to travel down the river of life together without interfering in the ways of the other, we were also taught that if we choose to straddle the space between the ship and canoe, we can nurture a friendship and travel on these waters together; however, we should stay in on our own vessel by affirming its concepts and philosophy of life. I think about this teaching in terms of the diverse human relationships between male and female, female and female, male and male, and parents and children. It is a teaching that provides a process for understanding our relationships, which begin with a man and a woman, who should understand their values and then be disciplined in their minds and bodies before they come together to create another life. Those shared values that direct our relationships are important, and that is what the Two Row is about. We need to value what other people have without interfering, although we can always learn from each other through conversation.

How did I get here? From the onset of conception, I was birthed through sacred ceremony and the good thoughts and energy that come from within and in relation to our Mother Earth. As expectant mothers, we are always in a place of transformation, being cleansed so as to honour ourselves and the new baby's life! Because the expectant body is experiencing hormonal changes, increased appetites, and new cravings, as well as feeling nauseous, annoyed, and tired, Indigenous women share stories about these experiences between mother and daughter, and we listen to our Elders, aunties, and grandmas. These stories and teachings come from their connections to the older ones in the community. It is like *ǫ da gaho dę:s* (the sacred meeting space), where much is shared, this time between the new mother and her baby. We become like a potter spinning the potter's wheel and using water to mould the new creation with our values, stories, songs, laughter, and love!

Our minds reconnect the spiritual world to this human life as we enhance our relationships, opening ourselves to receiving and giving. What is good about the truth and reconciliation process is that it asks all of us to look at ourselves and examine thoroughly our minds and hearts. What needs to be cleared up within ourselves and our relations? It asks each of us to reflect back so as to clear up those things by regurgitating them and asking, "Was this real?" Reconciling with ourselves is an original law of the Haudenosaunee, and it was not something that we made up. The Peacemaker reminded us of the kind of life that we were intended to live, and he demonstrated how people of healthy mind, body, and spirit naturally seek harmony, balance, and peace. It is a spiritual law that has been instilled in our nations and their people, and it is this law that we brought into our relations with the ship.

We always seek clarity as we explain the teachings to our family, children, and community. This is what we refer to as *ganigǫhi:yo* (a good mind), which is needed to come to *ǫ da gaho dę:s*. We have long forgotten about this sacred space between the canoe and the ship of the Two Row Wampum – the space where we get information, communicate, acknowledge, and validate what we bring into relationship across our sacred fires. We have lost a sense of what is sacred in our everyday lives, as we have forgotten the importance of the Ganǫhǫnyǫhk (Thanksgiving Address), and thus there is growing uncertainty and confusion about the fate of future generations as we face the storm that is raging on E tinoha ongwesidage'dra gwe'.

I feel this storm also building up inside my being. I could have lashed out at those who disrespected my granddaughter's life and my unborn grandson in utero. They were my future, and they were destroyed by selfishness and lack of conscience. I had to grieve and cleanse myself with the medicines given to me by our Mother Earth. Walking in the mountains, I could feel the shrubs brushing away the surface pain. They let me know their love by offering themselves to me. Drinking the herbal teas, I began cleansing and healing my insides. I prayed to the water and asked for help in reminding our women to honour and respect themselves, to know their gifts and teachings, and to raise awareness about the violence against our women!

With all that was in me, I could have created a storm of lasting grief, always carrying the hatred of those who crossed the sacred boundaries of my family and caused them pain. That was not the journey intended for me. A Haudenosaunee woman, a matriarch, is the voice of all that she understands and experiences: the pain, grief, life, and ceremony. But she is also someone who does not understand violence, for she knows the power of compassion, forgiveness, and love. I still miss my granddaughter, and I will never see my grandson as a human being. But I also know that they walk with me every day in my travels. They appear sometimes to me as dragonflies or butterflies, and we have a conversation.

Through these relations and experiences, I can feel a tiny bit of what E tinoha ongwesidage'dra gwe' is experiencing right now with all the disturbances. I have no idea what she is feeling or thinking, but I do know that she is unhappy. I too have had to make choices about how to respond to these violations. Would I follow the good mind or take myself to a dark place by being destructive to others and causing suffering? I chose to follow the teachings of the Haudenosaunee people and move forward by working at positive things that would be beneficial for me, my family, my clan, and my nation. By doing so, I can be the storm that reclaims my rightful boundaries by living the good life!

In our cells, the original people carry a blood memory of the past, present, and future. I have been given many gifts that help me to exercise and establish my boundaries, my sacred space that was violated. I am woman; I am the storm that comes to cleanse our understanding of who we are. We will forever be here with E tinoha ongwesidage'dra gwe'. We wrap our bundles and gather our medicines, like the *jihso'dak*, that we have shared with each other, and then we begin to depart from one another with encouragement, hope, and most of all, hearts filled with renewal.

Although E tinoha ongwesidage'dra gwe' is compassionate and healing, our mother has limits, and she will defend herself in ways that society has not and will not be able to comprehend. She has lost her patience with the people who have not changed their attitudes and behaviours. We as women are the storm!

Woman

Identity confusion
Who am I? I am searching
For I have disappeared
Beneath the surface
Of destruction
No longer an organizer
No longer respected

I cleanse myself of
Humiliation, degradation, nothingness
Through tears, pain, laughter, and love
I reclaim my responsibilities
I gather my strengths
Genuineness, uniqueness
For I am
Woman

A woman of many responsibilities
Bestowed upon me by the Creator
To provide life, knowledge, nurturing
Sharing and respect
With the outcome
A whole person
Of self, family, community

So it was destined
Woman!

Daneto! / That is all!
Encouragement
Compassion
Love
Strength
Awehaode' / Soft, kind, embracing words

Teaching Them to Dance: Reclaiming Indigenous Parenting

Lianne C. Leddy

A little girl and her mother, in the midst of a pandemic, take a stroll through the woods. We are not in our homeland and, indeed, cannot visit our community or her grandparents. During these days, I worry incessantly about my daughter's increased screen time as, like many families, we struggle to balance work and family life while at home during the Covid-19 pandemic. On days when the worry gets to be too much, we do what we can to find refuge in a local nature park in order to get out of the house. This activity also continues work that my partner and I have done to ensure that our daughter knows what to do and how to conduct herself outdoors, just as Timothy B. Leduc talks about in relation to his son in the previous circle of this book. On our walk, we cross a bridge and stop to take a look. There is a lot of stopping with a three year old, and she is a constant, joyous reminder to take things more slowly, something that I have forgotten on my own life journey. In the bright morning sunshine, we take turns pointing out sunfish, algae, and cattails. "We can eat the roots of those, right, Mama?" she asks, already knowing the answer. And then we see a turtle swimming swiftly on a mission that we cannot guess. I stop for a moment, my face feeling the late-spring sunshine and holding this perfect moment. My daughter does not yet know the story of how, after a great flood, the world was re-created on the back of a turtle and how a muskrat risked everything to bring a pawful of dirt from beneath the vast waters to form the land that sustains us.[1] An eager student, she is learning how, as descendants of the original inhabitants of Turtle Island, we have responsibilities to the land and each other. Yet, despite the fact that she is still at the early stage of her learning journey, she sees wonder in this small, determined, swiftly moving turtle. For several minutes, we stand there watching it intently, talking about it, saying hello, and wondering where it is going.

The teachings of Gae Ho Hwako (Norma Jacobs) about E tinoha ongwesidage'dra gwe' (Mother Earth), or Shkaakamigokwe in Anishinaabemowin, remind us of the sacredness of giving life. Although I am an Anishinaabekwe, Gae Ho Hwako and I share the view that our connections to land and water are tied to our responsibilities to future generations. In keeping with Indigenous methodologies, I want to take a moment to position myself in this story.[2] I am a member of Serpent River First Nation and grew up in Elliot Lake, a uranium-mining town and now retirement community in northern Ontario. I am the daughter of an Irish Canadian man and an Anishinaabekwe. I currently live in southern Ontario on the Haldimand Tract with my daughter and partner, where I teach Indigenous studies at the Waterloo and Brantford campuses of Wilfrid Laurier University. Although my research has always had a focus on land and increasingly on gender, I have been working to reclaim Indigenous parenting practices since starting my family. As part of this ongoing work, I had in the past brought Gae Ho Hwako into my classes to talk about Haudenosaunee birth and parenting teachings, and I now reflect further on them in this book.

Before I begin, I want to be mindful of the fact that some Indigenous women find motherhood to be a reductive and confining role, and it is important to understand that nurturing others and community building need not be understood in strictly biological or mothering terms. Kim Anderson writes about the importance of recognizing and honouring Indigenous motherhood, arguing that "women can be mothers in different ways" as she documents the importance of aunties and role models and recounts other ways that women lead in community building and activism.[3] Nevertheless, a growing number of Indigenous scholars are attentive to how equating Indigenous motherhood with Indigenous womanhood can be essentializing and problematic. Métis scholar Emma LaRocque, for example, writing in response to Kim Anderson, argues that "such maternalization is totalizing and exclusionary."[4] In her chapter in the final circle of this book, Giselle Dias beautifully describes how her relationship with a spruce helps her to challenge heteropatriarchy as a queer Indigenous woman and how she is eager to "lean on and lift up two-spirit and queer Indigenous writers who give voice to identities and sexualities that exist outside binaries." Indeed, I acknowledge the problematic ways that colonial policies have imposed binaries on our communities. Furthermore, when "womanhood" is relegated to the role of "motherhood," such thinking can reduce choices and possibilities for women. More broadly, it is distressing how this connection is used to reproduce heteropatriarchy and abuse.

At the same time, raising my daughter has been the most empowering and transformative experience of my life, and I have taken to heart the works of Indigenous women scholars who see the possibility of resurgence through our teachings for the next generation and the necessity of reclaiming our own traditions to do so.[5] For me, motherhood has enhanced my own connection with creation, and most importantly, it has focused, with razor-sharp precision, my prioritization of decolonizing work, as it connects me (and my actions) to a future beyond my physical lifespan. Gae Ho Hwako's words on E tinoha ongwesidage'dra gwe' and motherhood remind me of Leanne Simpson's call for the resurgence of Anishinaabe thinking and being. She reminds us that "reclaiming Indigenous traditions of pregnancy, birth, and mothering will enable our children to lead our resurgence as Indigenous Peoples, to rise up and rebel against colonialism in all its forms, to dream independence, to dance to nationhood."[6] If, as Simpson tells us, resurgence is our first instruction and involves "dancing on our turtle's back," how can motherhood and respect for Shkaakamigokwe be our music?[7] Indeed, our children are gifts, and they have much to teach us. But how do we reclaim our ways of bringing them into the world and raising them to dance, especially when many of us are still working through decolonizing ourselves as individuals? In this chapter, I reflect on Gae Ho Hwako's teachings about women, pregnancy, and birth in connection to my own mothering experiences and decolonizing journey.

Journey to Birth

Gae Ho Hwako's account of the transformations that E tinoha ongwesidage'dra gwe' goes through – her constant changes to give and then support life – provides us with a beautiful understanding of how we undergo our own transformations as mothers. Just as we have our own seasons, we are also supported by our families and communities. Gae Ho Hwako's moving account of understanding that sacred journey only with the birth of her sixth child is as impactful as it is devastating. During my own pregnancy, I happily grew rounder and delighted at the transformation that I was undergoing. Gae Ho Hwako teaches us about the foods that expectant mothers should eat, and I was reminded of the care that I enjoyed from my family. My husband happily complied when I demanded meals made of fish and berries, like countless generations of grannies would have had at home. He generously acquiesced when I outlawed the hot sauce that he so loved because I could smell it from the upstairs of our house. When I visited my home territory and my daughter rebelled inside of me, unhappy with the bumpy road on Highway 17 near Sudbury, she was soon soothed by my aunties rubbing my belly, happy that I was able to experience this transformation. I found pregnancy to be a joyful time, despite the nausea, the fatigue, and my connections to emotions that I would normally have pushed through.

All of that soon changed. My own birth experience was terrifying – a colonized experience made all the more difficult to process because I also knew that it was necessary. My daughter, although almost full term, weighed only three pounds and thirteen ounces. After my C-section, I could not nurse her, and instead, she ate though a nasal-gastro feeding tube and was hydrated intravenously. I had to go to my room to mechanically pump my breasts first to encourage my milk to come in and again to obtain the milk that she needed to eat through her nose and then from a bottle once she was strong enough. I could not keep her in my room, close to me, but instead had to visit her in a corner of the Neonatal Intensive Care Unit, where I also had to contend with different nursing strategies, personalities, and expectations. Do not get me wrong; my daughter received truly excellent physical care, but I was constantly reminded of her condition and deeply felt my own body's responsibility for it.[8]

My daughter's roars at birth had in fact been reassuring. As Gae Ho Hwako teaches us, "When you hear the baby take its first breath and yell out, it is announcing its arrival here to all of creation, which is already inside the room. All of creation comes to see what journey this baby has participated in." The ultrasound that I had undergone a few days before her birth had already told me that she was small for her gestational age, and we had not known what to expect. These cries, then, brought immense relief as I watched one of the nurses carry her across the operating room. In fact, when she was weighed and turned out to be even smaller than the ultrasound technician had estimated, the incongruity of her loud, fierce screaming and her tiny size was made all the more apparent. Although it was a stressful time, her ferocity and engagement in the world were wonderful to behold. She pulled out her own feeding tube when she had had enough. She responded to particular noises in the hospital and immediately started to chatter. Paige stayed in the hospital for more than two weeks, as she had to reach feeding and weight milestones before being released.

I think a lot about what her condition at birth was meant to teach me, especially since Western science did not give me an answer as to its origins. First of all, it made me grateful for those first cries in the delivery room. At the same time, as I have written elsewhere, I could not welcome her to the world in the way that I had planned or nourish her in ways that I had expected. I felt a tremendous amount of guilt about what I perceived to be my own body's betrayal.[9] In our last writing circle for this book, I read an early draft of this chapter and broke down in tears. In our conversation, Gae Ho Hwako and Awnjibenayseekwe (Banakonda Kennedy-Kish Bell) helped me to realize that this outpouring was part of a grieving process that I was still working through. They helped me through what I thought of as a difficult moment, which I now see instead as part of a journey that was tied to writing and healing.

Perhaps, instead of treating my daughter's difficult birth as an experience to simply "get over" and work through, as I had done with other difficult experiences in the past, I needed to see it as more of a process. I had written a column and a previous chapter in an edited collection in order to work through the experience, as I had been self-reflexive enough to know that writing would help. However, what I had not fully considered, much less understood, was that this was not one isolated event that I could work through and forget; grief does not simply disappear. I credit the writing process of that collection for this knowledge and for the seed from which I was able to reevaluate my daughter's birth story and, most importantly, to see it as a way forward as I tried to decolonize my parenting journey.

As I thought about what was (to me at least) a revelation, I read Gae Ho Hwako's words about needing to bury the baby's umbilical cord. As I have written elsewhere, my daughter's cord and placenta were sent to pathology because of the cord's twisted nature.[10] This tie to her home territory was dissected and incinerated in an effort to answer why she was born the way that she was. Most frustratingly, this loss yielded no answers, as her pediatrician told me that the results showed that it was "an unremarkable three-vessel cord." These are words I will never forget because I had hoped that the dissection would give me guidance about what had happened during this pregnancy and what it could mean for any future baby. Instead, it meant that I went through what Gae Ho Hwako had experienced when she allowed her daughter's caul to be incinerated: a loss of something so sacred that it could never be recovered. Indeed, it also meant that, as Gae Ho Hwako says in the final circle of this book, "the ceremony of [her] birth was not closed." Perhaps this experience of loss was also the seed of what I needed to move forward. I would not recover the cord, just as I would never have the birth and infancy experience that I had envisioned for myself and my daughter. That was a reality that would never change, and instead, like dealing with all forms of grief, I needed to find a way forward rather than simply looking to the past for answers.

Reading Gae Ho Hwako's words led me to bury the belly button end of the cord at home, the nub that had stayed on my daughter's body until it dried out and fell off. I had kept it because I did not quite know what to do with it until Gae Ho Hwako came to my Indigenous gender class at Wilfrid Laurier University and shared the words written in the previous teachings. I hoped that this burial to close the ceremony and move forward might be a way to acknowledge the birth and also to give thanks to Shkaakamigokwe for my daughter's bright, shining existence in creation. It also brought to bear something that I had already been reflecting on: the importance of homeland.

The need to connect her to where we are from is deep and unrelenting. Therefore, I also hoped that this closing of the ceremony would help to bridge her southern Ontario suburban life on the Haldimand Tract with the fact that her homeland is on the north shore of Naadowewe-gichigami (Lake Huron).[11] Of course, this geographical displacement as a result of first my schooling and then my career is one of the many reasons why reclaiming Anishinaabe motherhood traditions is so important to me. I am far away from my own mother, aunties, and territory, and our quarterly visits home will not be enough to raise my daughter in the same way as I was raised. These generational differences, therefore, are not only shaped by technology and changing social expectations but are also deeply framed by our distance from our homeland. This distance has imparted another layer of complexity to my parenting journey, affecting what came after my daughter was brought home following her birth.

Home and Infancy

When we brought Paige home from the hospital, I was ecstatic. After she had spent more than two weeks in the Neonatal Intensive Care Unit, I could not wait to get her outside. I took her out for a walk and dressed her in so many layers that she developed a heat rash, one of the many lessons that the next year – and beyond – would teach me. I spent the rest of the day staring at her and, indeed, the next four months keeping her at home, as I tried to leave the house only for medical appointments or to walk outside. I was afraid of her getting sick and having to be hospitalized again. With the exception of visits from a strong and generous group of family and close friends – the extended kinship circle that supported me with care and gifts – we were alone at home most of the time. In fact, I delighted in keeping her to myself and did not pressure myself to do other kinds of activities until she was six months old. It was only then that she saw the inside of a mall, and I tried to keep the flap of her car seat cover closed on the occasions when we did have to go to the family doctor, the pediatrician, the development specialist, or even the grocery store. Even at six months, she still weighed less than twelve pounds.

Instead of running errands and participating in playgroups, she and I got to know each other. My initial impression of her strength at her birth was further reinforced despite her tiny size, as it was clear that she had an enormous personality. When we got home, she developed an interest in our cats. She made it her life's mission to extricate herself from my haphazard swaddling and always succeeded or made her displeasure known. She hated her bassinet and would have a deep sleep only on top of the bed or in her Moses basket. We soon called it "the wake-up bassinet," which was sometimes useful to get to a doctor's appointment on time but not as useful for sleeping. I knew that she was powerful, even as a fetus, but those first few weeks reassured me that she was going to be just fine, and I did not rush our time together.

Perhaps paradoxically, I worried constantly. It was stressful to try to manage pumping, bottle-feeding, and trying unsuccessfully to breastfeed, and we worried constantly about her weight. I have come to recognize that this worry, which was so pervasive throughout the first year, was also grief caused by the experiences that I did not get to have and by how totally confusing it all was. To add complexity to all of these emotions, at the same time, I felt tremendous joy, and I am still trying to make sense of this duality – how to hold the memory of such divergent feelings together at once. Fortunately, I had a supportive circle. I am reminded of Gae Ho Hwako sharing that she came into relation with Haudenosaunee teachings upon the birth of her last child and the subsequent births of her grandchildren. She reclaimed her teachings through these experiences and felt a similar sense of both loss and joy, which highlights another way that I have come into relationship with Gae Ho Hwako through her work.

My family was very supportive, and my parents doted on Paige after having made the trip to see us on several occasions. I soon took her to visit my colleagues at Laurier, where she was held with such love and watched so carefully that I was deeply moved. My first trip home with her was so that she could meet my grandfather, who had suffered a heart attack in January. Although I was nervous about driving seven hours with an infant by myself, I knew that it was important for her to meet him and her other relatives. I had responsibilities to her and to them, as it was time for me to introduce her to her homeland, and I am so grateful that I did. She got to meet her great-grandfather only that one time before he died a few months later. As he had been my last living grandparent, I made the transition from granddaughter to mother in the same year, a shift that rendered my roles, which Gae Ho Hwako has defined as both life giver and life supporter, much more prominent.

Raising a Daughter

In Anishinaabe thought, our children choose us from the spirit world. I think a lot about how my daughter must have chosen us to be her parents and why. I am neither patient nor indulgent as a person, much less a parent. As she is at an age when she not only takes her time on her journey but also does so at a runner's pace, I do my best to follow her lead. In addition to her strength, her other gifts include storytelling. Her chattering as a newborn soon gave way to an infant's babbles, and at seven months of age, she called me Mama. She had been making the sound for a few weeks, but it took her looking me straight in the eye for me to finally make the connection that she had clearly said Mama. She has been teaching me daily lessons through her words, her stories, and her simultaneous ability to take her time learning while moving quickly. She is also aware of her own power as she learns her place in the world, and I marvel at the big kid she has become. Her growth also brings an awareness of my specific responsibilities in raising a daughter, and I rely on the lessons taught to me by my mother, grandmother, and aunties. Parenting also takes decolonizing work that has required deep thinking and a reconsideration of what I had angrily thought of in my early adulthood as lost Anishinaabe traditions.

My Anishinaabe and Irish families are both Catholic, and although I was not raised with traditional Anishinaabe ceremonies, there were clear consistencies in the principles that I grew up with – something that we look for as we rebuild our communities in the wake of the trauma that Christianity and other forms of colonialism brought to nations across Turtle Island. As we move through our learning journeys to decolonize ourselves for and with our children, especially in urban contexts, I have grieved the colonial interruptions of our knowledge, ceremonies, and ways of being. But at the same time, as I look back at some of the important milestones that I have gone through on my life journey, I can see the seeds of core Anishinaabekwewag values. Although I lived in a nearby settler town, I was lucky enough to be raised close to my community and surrounded by the love and knowledge of my mother, grandmother, and aunties – an experience that I share with Kawennakon (Bonnie Whitlow), as indicated by her reflections in the previous circle of this book, and with many other Indigenous people who grew up outside their communities. Indeed, my aunties of Irish descent on my father's side are also strong, community-minded women who were important role models in my life. I was fortunate to be able to watch and learn from the women around me, and although I tend to focus as a historian on the negative and far-reaching impacts of colonialism on Indigenous gender relations, I also need to focus as an Anishinaabekwe on our survival in order to look forward.

One of the ways that I have been able to rethink this position is to see the seeds of our Indigeneity in the ways that we interact with each other and, in particular, in the ways that I was taught about my role and how to conduct myself in the world. I have a vivid memory of my first moon time, which I had not been looking forward to because I knew that it would mean the end of my childhood. My mother, however, understanding that it was going to be soon, had prepared me for this important time. When I told my mother that it had happened, she said, "This means you can be a mother now and you have responsibilities to yourself." I remember her words, more than twenty-five years later, because she made me feel empowered and safe. My aunties were excited for me. Although we did not follow the tradition of the berry fast because of colonial and Christian legacies, the women in my family taught me that this time marked a beautiful milestone. Words like "the curse" or "dirty" were never uttered. Instead, it was the beginning of a new stage of life in which I would have new responsibilities for my own well-being and also for that of my future children. My body was mine.

I work hard, like other Indigenous women I know, to reclaim Indigenous parenting practices, and I worry that I do not have enough knowledge to carry us on our journey together as a family. When that worry becomes too much, I remember my mother's words to me when I was twelve years old. They are a reminder, certainly, of Gae Ho Hwako's teaching about our roles. However, keeping in mind that not all Indigenous women have children, my mother's words also provide an important example of how we still have the seeds of knowledge and tradition, as Simpson writes, that our ancestors gave us. It is up to us to nurture them.

Conclusion

In this chapter, I have reflected on Gae Ho Hwako's teachings as they have resonated with my own life experiences of pregnancy, childbirth, and raising strong Indigenous children. As Simpson writes, "Our Mothers have always known that our rebirth, like any birth, is a powerful but painful process – a pain that fades into the background as the birthing ceremony comes to an end. Bringing the old into the new is our way forward. This becomes clear when, like Zhaashkoonh [Muskrat], we place our piece on the back of our turtle and dance a new world into existence."[12] Now, let us return to our turtle sighting. My fierce little Nish girl, no longer a baby and far from her homeland and her family, does not yet know the whole story of how the world was re-made on the back of a turtle. But it is a reminder to her mother to teach her.

Haudenosaunee Women in between the Generations

Kitty Lynn Lickers

It is through story that we learn the most about someone or something. Our minds demand stories. Often, we fight this need, trying without true success to learn by memorization or rote. It is the deep connection that I have to who I am and what I do that makes it imperative for me to tell this story. It is a connection that I have to my ancestors and to all my relations that demands I tell this story. As Gae Ho Hwako (Norma Jacobs) teaches through her stories, I feel that my spirit has come on this earth walk to tell this story. In her words, "We remember our journeys, stories, and songs, and we recognize that we are those sacred spiritual beings who descended from the Sky World to work on this spiritual journey with E tinoha ongwesidage'dra gwe' [Mother Earth]."

I am an Indigenous woman. Although I cannot state my clan, my father was a Bearfoot Onondaga man from Six Nations of the Grand River Territory. My mother was a first-generation Swedish Canadian of the Sami (Indigenous peoples of Sweden), although that has not been confirmed in a governmental way. I am clanless at this point in my life, yet that does not change my connections to family, community, other Indigenous women, and these lands. It is from this position that I hear Gae Ho Hwako, as with other Elders, teach of the Two Row Wampum and how "if we choose to straddle the space between the ship and the canoe, it will bring difficulties" and confusion. I have always found it difficult to hear this teaching that one can be only in the canoe or on the ship. I am led to wonder about its connection to my own struggles with being in between worlds and not being enough. I share this experience and struggle with many other Indigenous women who, like me, are forty to sixty years old, as well as with many involved in the sharing circles of *ǫ da gaho dę:s* (the sacred meeting space).

There are predominantly two versions of the story of women around my age. Early research on Indigenous peoples creates a historical picture of a strong, stoic, vocal, knowledgeable woman who holds her family and the community together.[1] This woman is most often pictured in photos taken in profile, head held high, as she haughtily shows the world her strength. Today, this strong Indigenous woman is displayed in the media as standing against the colonial powers of our time, often militantly leading her community to fight battles for water, land, respect, acknowledgment, and equality. The second more common image today is of a fragmented, broken Indigenous woman who is abused and lacking in every way.[2] There is no in-between. There is no space for us to be the whole and complex beings that we are.

The constant focus on colonialism does not allow for the study of Indigenous peoples or Indigeneity but rather constrains us within the violent historic and ongoing implementation of the Canadian state and its institutions. Lee Maracle writes about the "appropriation of Indigenous stories rather than the appropriation of voice."[3] I have pondered this "appropriation of stories" at great length. It is what I see, hear, and believe has happened to the stories of the women of my group. The voice that they have is about their everyday life and living, but the stories that they should know or do know of their place in the life stages are missing or have been appropriated or altered to the point that they no longer connect to us.

It is imperative that all women come to realize how we have been influenced by the colonial ship and its way of life. This is not a judgment but a truth about the world that we live in. I know women who are in between the two vessels but are nonetheless defined by their knowledge and connection to family, community, the land, and water. Their stories tell us that they are women who care to make E tinoha ongwesidage'dra gwe' the best that she can be. So the deeper meaning of our place on the Two Row Wampum is about being rooted in community and about sharing our knowledge and connection. It is not about how the women of the ship are troubled and confused, for the women of the canoe can also experience this confusion. The hope is that one day the dark in-between waters will hold a stillness and peace as all arms clasp, embracing our Mother Earth.

The stories that I tell here are about women and about me as a woman. They are about the intersectionality of colonialism, racism, feminism, patriarchy, gender roles, and sexism. They are about a search that I have undertaken for the understanding of an in-between space that I caught out of the corner of my eye. I did not seek out this story or this in-between space, but it was shown to me nonetheless just by living my life in community. I want to tell you about the awakening of self to this position with other women and about the impact of this awareness on my sense of who I am in community and in the social justice actions of my life. Hope inspires me to battle against a space that has altered not just myself and other women but also our families and communities over many generations. And so I try to tell a different story of who we are on the Two Row Wampum – on the body of E tinoha ongwesidage'dra gwe'.

Storytelling is a ceremony of love; I feel this love in my heart, in Gae Ho Hwako's teachings, and in the words shared by others in this book. The authors emphasize that no matter where people are, they are able to connect to the ancestors and coming generations because the stories will be carried on. Stories transform us in a way that is consistent with Shawn Wilson's understanding of Indigenous research as a ceremony that must be respected as a sacred act: "A ceremony is not just the period at the end of the sentence. It is the required process and the preparation that happens long before the event … It is the voice from our ancestors that tells us when it is right and when it is not. Indigenous research is a life-changing ceremony."[4] Such a ceremony calls me to reflect on an intersectional understanding of myself as someone who engages Indigenous ways of knowing while challenging the power differential with Western ways of knowing. It also asks me to share the wisdom of our stories, for they connect us to all that the world holds – the earth, animals, sun, and sky.

We carry our stories forward from our ancestors so as to give them to the future generations. Within my Indigenous culture, it is said that people must keep in mind the seven generations before and after us. The stories that I tell are not merely my own but also those of two other distinct generations of grandmothers approaching my age group. They include my story as well as my account of the stories of my seven-generation ancestral grandmother and my seven-generation granddaughter to come. So I am going to tell the story of my great-great-great ... seven-generation grandmother of the eighteenth century when she was in the same time of life as myself. It is a story that I have created by drawing on relevant research, on Haudenosaunee oral storytelling like that of Gae Ho Hwako, and on living reflections in my journaling about what the story means for me.

The hope is to offer a better story for my great-great-great ... seven-generation granddaughter, and so the future story that I tell is of my vision of what could be. With this story, I want to shine some light on what the shift to a world where everyone works together may look like, one where the notion of being on the ship or in the canoe takes on a deeper meaning. By telling these stories and reflecting on them in relation to my experiences, I can learn about who we are as in-between women, about where we have come from, and about our responsibilities moving forward. And so the story that I share in this chapter is a story about stories that position me in relation to my ancestors and descendants.

I usually love to write in my journal, but the get-together today has brought me to a very strange place in my head. The very people I had thought would offer me the most offered almost nothing. Maybe I was asking the wrong questions or asking in the wrong way. I did enjoy the activity of moving the herbs to big pots as we talked. Maybe I shouldn't have an activity. Maybe just snacks and stories ... I am tired, so maybe that's why I feel weepy about the few answers that I got. (Personal journal)

The walk into my present story begins by reflecting on when I was thirty and recognizing that it has been a long journey, one that I was initially unaware that I was even on. I came to realize that I was missing a part of me that made my inclusion in my own family and community tenuous. I had been away from both my family and my community for more than seventeen years. Although this absence alone had an impact, it was only a small part of what I originally perceived as my problem. I had difficulty making connections with other women. I was told many times that I needed to stop trying to change the world. I heard over and over again in action and words that I needed to understand that the ways of life on the reserve had a rhythm that was implacable, especially for women of my age. So for years, into that rhythm I fell.

It was at fifty-five that I felt I should take a stronger leadership role in my community. Both my parents were gone, and I was now the matriarch of our family. I did not have much to do in this role, as my brothers had families of their own and my children were grown, but I did have my precious grandchildren to learn from and teach. At the time, I was a supervisor of a community food-access program and taught self-sustainability classes for growing and preserving food based on Indigenous ways of knowing. Having nurtured a strong and capable team in this program, I decided to enrol in the Indigenous Women in Community Leadership program at St Francis Xavier University in Nova Scotia. It was here that I met a small group of middle-aged Indigenous women who were part of a panel speaking about violence and the roles that they embody in their separate communities across Turtle Island.

The women were articulate and intelligent, and they had a strong sense of who they were and what their place was in their individual communities. They shared a great deal about their important roles in assisting communities to understand their connection to land. Stories were told of reclaiming culture, making connections, sharing knowledge, and encouraging health through a return to cultural ways. What was shared makes me think of Gae Ho Hwako's words: "Women are always trying to care for everybody, sharing what they can. Women are multi-taskers, and this is a responsibility that we see in E tinoha ongwesidage'dra gwe'. She connects all the roots from the plants, trees, flowers, and medicines."

Despite the inspiring stories and strength of these Indigenous women, I heard them voice again and again an absence, a seemingly learned response of not knowing anything of merit. It was during this time at the university that my questions about being in between really began to arise as I observed the conversations of these and other women while assembling a simple children's book about a child interacting with a grandmother figure while planting a garden. As I gathered information for the book, I also wrote in my journal. At the time, I did not notice that most of what I wrote was on how I was feeling about these conversations. That is where my story of seeing the in-between space in the life cycle of middle-aged Indigenous women began in its fullness.

The women grow up and have children, their kids have children, and then the women are directed to that space or gap of not being connected to an absolute spot in the life stages. The primary problem that these women in the leadership program identified – despite being chronologically on their way to becoming Elders – was that they were not yet acknowledged Elders and, therefore, were unable to answer questions about connection to the land and unable to express knowledge about food sustainability and sovereignty or even about family matters despite having grown children. As I was of this age group and had a similar sense of things, our relations and discussion raised questions for me. Why do these women feel such uncertainty about their knowledge? What had occurred other than the obvious influences to get them to this place? What is the impact of colonial violence and community changes on our sense of self?

Over time, I came to realize that our minds and bodies had seemingly turned away from who we are. This awareness drew me back to my reading of the late Betty Friedan, who asked, "Is this all?"[5] In her book *The Feminine Mystique* (1963), she opened the conversation about women and their place in the world by seeking to understand whether childrearing and staying home were all that women wanted. Even though she was not discussing Indigenous women, her concern with what she called "the problem that has no name," the title of her book's first chapter, reflects a search for something more that is connected to what I was feeling within myself and also hearing from other Indigenous women my age. It is a search beyond how others – particularly men (especially white men) and academics – come to define us and how we internalize these constricting definitions.

The literature about this age group of Indigenous women reiterates what these women are, what they say, and what they do. Kim Anderson tells of Indigenous women of this age bringing sustenance to their community.[6] She talks of the life stages of women and the concepts around community and roles within both gender and social duties. Specific examples and stories are shared to describe the life stages as they have been known – from childhood through to adulthood and ending with Elders and grandmothers. As much as Anderson's book answered some questions for me about the specific roles of women in their lives, it also supported and reaffirmed my questions. Were the roles of women at my age the same in the past as they are in the present? In the modern age, becoming a grandmother can happen at the age of forty.

Does this event mean that we now move into the category of Elder and grandmother? What are we offering our community at this age today if our life stages are different from the past?

Sustenance in all areas of life is central to Indigenous women of my age, by which I mean sustenance not just as feeding and providing people with food but also as knowledge, culture, and connection. That is what I read in Anderson and what I heard again and again from the women in the program, who came from a diversity of Indigenous nations. Women of the in-between seem to struggle with being bringers of sustenance to their community in all areas of life, a struggle that seems connected to a breakdown in their matrilineal lines. They have been told that they perhaps are less than what they should be, not always directly but through actions from both sides of the Two Row Wampum. What they have internalized causes them to think that they are unable to fulfill the position that they are entitled to fulfill as women, mothers, aunties, and grandmothers.

The truth that those who are in between need to hear is that we all hold a role – that we are all capable of being the bringers of sustenance. Other questions arise for me. How will the women who do not speak up affect the future generations of Indigenous women? Why do these women feel that they are not "qualified" to share and teach? Why do they believe it to be an Elder's place to do so and not theirs? Times change, and the responsibilities within community change, especially in a place like Six Nations, where the population is large and where the impacts of colonial, Western living are very evident.

Indigenous ways of knowing and being include everyone having a space to be acknowledged, which allows for a wholeness that keeps everything in balance. When things are out of balance, they invariably crumble apart. What seems to be missing for these Indigenous women is something that is inherently part of who they are. What I am trying to recognize, understand, and convey through the story of these women is an in-between space that is filled with knowledge, laughter, connection, grief, resilience, disappointment, and life. I am talking about a wholeness that cannot fit into flat definitions of colonialism and intersectional violence. In the past, the connection to self, family, community, and all beings would have been intact because women would still have still been raising children. They would still have held a place in the life stages.

In telling my in-between story, I will give you a window into the stories of other Indigenous women who are, in essence, missing from the mainstream view. I am compelled as a woman, a mother, an auntie, a grandmother, and a strong Indigenous person to see if I can teach with these stories in between the seven generations so that I can do what Shogwaeyadisho' (the Creator) prompts my heart to do. I offer this knowledge to your heart so that you might understand what, as an Indigenous woman, I regard as teaching, learning, and sharing. The way of my people is a different path from what the university may teach. As Wilson writes, "We have tried to adapt dominant system research tools by including our perspectives into their views. We have tried to include our cultures, traditional protocols and practices into the research … The problem with that is that we can never really remove the tools from their underlying beliefs."[7]

Recognizing these constraints – which I also hear Kawennakon (Bonnie Whitlow), Shelly Hachey, Timothy B. Leduc, and Lianne C. Leddy struggle with in the chapters of this book – I am engaging Indigenous storytelling here as a ceremony that is my way of doing research and coming to knowledge that is useful to my community and the seven generations. The stories that I am about to tell of my seven-generation grandmother and granddaughter are not a "real" examination of any individual life, but by telling you "what could have been" and what "could be," I want to understand my in-between space and its vast impact on our sense of Indigenous women's roles in the life stages. Storytelling can give us a new and transformed sense of this space – one that no longer ties women to the prevailing definitions of how they are seen by themselves and the world. What I have learned from my ancestors and descendants is shared with the aim of impacting future generations through my experience of growing into the roles of this in-between space.

My Seven-Generation Grandmother

When I imagine my ancestral grandmother at my age, she is a Faith Keeper from the Longhouse like Gae Ho Hwako, but she is from the area east of us in the Saint Lawrence River basin that is the home of the Onondonga people. She speaks about an Indigenous way of life in an almost wistful manner because she has the wisdom to know that great changes are occurring. An equal number of both men and women are appointed as Faith Keepers, and they have a responsibility toward their clan, nation, and entire community.[8] They take care of the needs of the people by doing the ceremonies and feasts that remind us all to express gratitude for everything in our lives with the Ganǫhǫnyǫhk (Thanksgiving Address). Learning our stories and ceremonies helps us to care for each other and to remember the abundance that E tinoha ongwesidage'dra gwe' and Shogwaeyadisho' give to us.

In fulfilling their responsibilities, Faith Keepers provide a link across the seven generations. My ancestral grandmother would have had a strong voice, but her story would have been written down by the priests and not shared. The French missionaries were learning our languages and collecting stories in order to save the "savage Indians." This collecting was often done by missionaries who reported their work in colonial sources like *The Jesuit Relations*, published annually from 1632 to 1673, just as later academics like anthropologists would do in their journals. This practice was, as Lee Maracle says, appropriation of Indigenous stories, which was achieved in this case by keeping them hidden instead of proclaiming their ownership by others. In a sense, the way that this book lifts up Gae Ho Hwako's teachings and our stories reflects the proper protocol that should have been followed from the beginning of our Two Row relations.

An air of despondency hangs over the village of my ancestral grandmother as the tendrils of colonialism take away the life once known. Because of the impacts of the missionaries, her village is no longer based in a Longhouse, as was the custom, and instead they now live in small rough cabins that the missionaries built for the converts. Here is my imagined account of her words to a missionary when she was not yet an Elder but in her fifties:

> My life and way of being are no longer at the heart of my family. My relations have been removed, and what I think of as my home is no longer the entire land, as it had always been. You ask if my life remains the same, but it cannot. The strangers from the ship who claim that we are allies do not see what is happening to us, despite what they believe to be peaceful relations on the river of life. Changes are being brought about in everything that we do and understand.

We are being made to claim that we own the land, even while we know that the land cannot be owned by anyone. This act cannot bring about peaceful relations. The strangers say that we are free to live as we always have, but they have displaced the foods that we hunt, gather, and grow by taking possession of the lands. The way that they live without consensus and their desire to possess what is held in common have encouraged our young to change.

Many of our ceremonies are now being shielded from the eyes of those who should be our guests but who often show disapproval of our ways. Because of this interfence, the ceremonies are not being performed as they should be. We understand what each person offers to the nation, community, and self. We teach so that each person can understand his or her strengths, wisdom, and sense of belonging. But this understanding is changed by the strangers who come to trade, to tell of their God, and to impose a way of life that is not ours.

I know my place as a woman and a nurturer who provides sustenance to my family and nation. I teach the children and young men and women about the important role that they have in our way of life. I tell them how the teachings of the aunties, grandmothers, grandfathers, and Elders are most important and must therefore be listened to for our way of being to continue. The strangers say that we can govern ourselves, that we are able to live as we always have, but we cannot do so with all the influences that they have brought and imposed. They treat us like we treat our youngest and smallest, as if we must be humoured and taught the right way to live. But this is not the way of our culture.

My children have all grown, and soon I will be of the age to become an Elder. If I do not take up my responsibility to the culture, who in the future will know what knowledge is to be shared? How will I know what will still be there for my daughters and the generations to come? We cannot own the land; all we do is borrow it from the seven generations to come, who will then borrow it from the next generations. We have been taught to know the importance of acknowledging the seven generations before and after ourselves.

To be recognized as Elders, we must garner our knowledge and truth about who we are in relation to what the generations before have passed along to us. Their knowledge and teachings guide us to live in harmony with our E tinoha ongwesidage'dra gwe' by being our best selves, caring for each other, and providing sustenance to our community. Only when we know our place as nurturers who care for our families can we know where we come from and our responsibilities.

The *jihso'dak* (wild strawberry) knows its job. The heart berry of our people brings sustenance each spring, and with it comes hope for the future. We give thanks for its return with these words: "The *jihso'dak* begins a cycle of growth, as she provides a pathway for the other hanging fruits to journey this way and to receive the benefits of meeting us pitiful humans. We say *nya weh*, thank you, and let it be that way in your minds!" In saying the whole Ganǫhǫnyǫhk, we remember the importance of being connected, grateful for the world, and mindful of our roles. Like the *jihso'dak*, we are all here to carry on our place in the world, as those before us have done throughout the ages and as those still to come will do. We will share the berries with joy and gratitude.

We are taught the responsibility that we have to continue sharing our knowledge, teachings, and stories so that they are there for future generations of our people. This responsibility means that we must teach and tell the stories that will someday remind us of the most important pieces of who we are. With all our strength, we need to hold onto the knowledge that we are part of all our relations, all that makes up this life on Mother Earth. We need to respect and hold the land in the highest esteem and to remember that we must together take care of the land, for without it, we will no longer be a people.

I see not only the diseases and sicknesses that are taking our people but also the changes that the stranger's ways have caused for our people. We are being disconnected from what was given by the seven generations before us, and so our life is lacking in teachings about how to be a strong, sustainable person. I see how the diminishment of these teachings has caused our youth to lose sight of who they are and what they must do if we are to maintain our strength as part of Mother Earth.

"Live as you have always done." That is what the missionaries say to us. But then they also say that we must pray in their building, and they denigrate our culture of the Longhouse. We are told that giving thanks and sending our prayers on tobacco smoke are not enough or proper in the eyes of Shogwaeyadisho', whom they say we must now call God.

Approaching the responsibilities of an Elder, I know that I must tell the children about the Creator, our Mother Earth, and our way of being. We must continue to give thanks, but now we must do so while keeping the ceremonies hidden from those who do not understand what they are and what they mean to our people. The gratitude that we offer is more than prayer and more than recognition of the parts of our world that we live in. The Ganǫhǫnyǫhk is about caring for the future by living now as people who are responsible for sustaining the ways of this world so that they will continue when we are not here.

Our Haudenosaunee culture teaches and reminds us that we must always be respectful by expressing gratitude for the time that we and all our relations have here. We practise gratitude so that others will also have sustenance in their time. It is important that the stories and, in particular, the Ganǫhǫnyǫhk be recited again and again so that we are reminded of who we truly are, especially in difficult times when they are needed. They guide us to do what we must do as we take up our position in the generations. Mother Earth suffers, as do we, when we do not take part in her relations through the Ganǫhǫnyǫhk. She sustains us with all that the Creator has given.

I see the way that the strangers take all they want and try to own the land, even though we know that they should leave some for the Creator and Mother Earth. I see how the bountiful foods, animals, plant medicines, fish, and fowl dwindle with alarming speed to fulfill the desires of these strangers. I see too how some of our people support and accept this way, which is not of our Longhouse culture, because it brings their own increase. Through this acceptance, they are losing their ways of connecting to Mother Earth as they source food and clothing from buildings, while also forgetting the skills of the hunt and planting. No thanksgiving is being practised, as the goods and money of the strangers have quickly replaced the disappearing sacred hides of animals.

Why do I tell you, a missionary from the ship, of these things? My heart knows that it will change nothing. Nothing will change until we all have to face a Mother Earth who is so injured that we will have to fight together to save her and us. Prophecy says that we will sleep and then awaken after many years with only the barest of time to do what we must by garnering the help of many. Will my Elder's words help when that time comes? It will possibly be too late, and only the Creator will be left to take care of us from the Sky World but not here on our Mother Earth.

How will I say to my daughters and their daughters, "Please understand the place that you have on the earth and take what the earth offers but with thankfulness. Take only what you need, and always leave enough for the Creator, all the relations of Mother Earth, and the generations to come. There may be a time when there is not enough for you, but you should still leave what must be left"? How do I tell them to do these things when all around us are strangers with the idea that we need to have, to take more, and to leave nothing behind? How can I make them understand the importance of working with the seasons that bring the *jihso'dak* and with the other patterns that Mother Earth has sustained for eternity?

I have no more to say. I just have a weight in my body telling me that all is not as it should be. What is this weight? Is it the heaviness of responsibility and duty or the somber weight of knowledge? I am not sure, but it is there.

Who will you tell my words to? Why do you depict them as things on that thin hide with that stick that makes marks to look at, not listen to? I may never see my daughter's daughters, but I hope that they can live the best life provided for them by the Creator and that they will continue to offer the Thanksgiving Address.

This is all that I want to say to you for now.

In Between the Generations

The fairy party was a fabulous success, and my information gathering went well. The storytelling with the kids was part of it. It filled my heart so much to watch them leaning closer to hear my stories. I was thrilled when I was talking about my children's book project and one of the older kids sitting with a parent said that it was about time someone asked kids what they thought. I have to admit that I still didn't get responses from those women I thought would have lots to share. A couple of them actually said that it wasn't their place to share knowledge because they weren't Elders. Their words felt like a punch in the stomach. Was I also doing something I shouldn't? How can I possibly be the right person to share the knowledge that I believe I have to share when I am just an old half-breed – that is, unless we can figure out Ma's family heritage as Sami? Then I'm what, a fabulous designer Indigenous baby? This idea occurs to me often enough that I am starting to worry about myself. Hopefully, my next gathering will be different. Everyone seems thrilled about the book idea. (Personal journal)

Telling the story of my seven-generation grandmother gives me a way to understand the living history of my challenges as an in-between woman – the challenges that I recount in my journal entries and in my reflections here. Her grounding in the seven generations and the thanksgiving teachings is something that the Haudenosaunee and many other Indigenous communities are now known to live by. When she shares the teaching that the *jihso'dak* is "the first gift of life," I imagine that her teachings as a Faith Keeper are connected across the generations to the words of Gae Ho Hwako, who says that the *jihso'dak* is "the first gift of food each spring that we celebrate as our closest connection to this earth walk. My body is spiritually aware of the seasons and what they bring in regard to health and wellness for all aspects of self – mentally, emotionally, spiritually, and physically."

In our Haudenosaunee culture, such teachings are connected to the Great Law of Peace, which teaches us to think and act with the best interests of the seven generations at heart. It asks us to have a good will and good mind and to be patient and understanding with others. This teaching is central to the challenges that I kept hearing from in-between women who did not know whether they could share cultural knowledge because of their separation from the seven generations and their culture. Indigenous ways of knowing and being would have given my ancestral grandmother the wisdom to see the effects of colonization and the coming difficulties for Mother Earth and her people. Indigenous ways are about being connected to all our relations and, through that, understanding who we are.

When I began noting the concerns carried by Indigenous women of my age, I began doing what I always do: I read anything and everything that might bring me to an understanding of this in-between space. This process allowed me to begin understanding what the responsibilities of my ancestral grandmother would have been at my time in the life stages and, through that, to renew my sense of our responsibilities today. As I reflect on her story, a number of key teachings stand out for me as an in-between woman: the need to renew our place in the seven generations, the role of colonial forces like land ownership in undermining root values like sharing, the relation between the shielding of ceremonies from colonial eyes and our fragile connection to cultural teachings today like the Thanksgiving Address, the role of women in providing the sustenance of food and culture to family and community, and the heaviness of taking on the responsibilities of our culture in the aftermath of colonial impacts on our communities.

During the storytelling ceremony of coming into relation with the time and teachings of my seven-generation grandmother, I felt that it was important to say that her teachings shared through the missionary were never published or given to our people – that her words were read only generations later by church members who discovered them from time to time. These teachings did not find their way to her daughter and the next seven generations, as was her intention and hope. They did not find their way to me and other in-between women who are struggling to understand our roles and responsibilities. It was the changes wrought by colonialism that impacted the strength, resilience, and identity of Indigenous women over the many generations that followed, and we now also know that these changes have damaged the sustainability of Mother Earth for all the generations to come.

Wanting to understand why I and other in-between women do not feel empowered to express the knowledge that we inherently hold, I began wondering how much of a part expectations around gender roles played in what these women did or did not say. I am struck by the words of Makere Stewart-Harawira: "I do not consciously engage in writing or speaking from a feminist position. This is not due to any deliberate decision. I simply am what I am – Indigenous woman, activist, grandmother."[9] I have come to love this quotation because it encompasses my thoughts so thoroughly that I could have written these words myself.

I have always felt that feminism is what we do as part of who we are. Yet I have always struggled to explain how I feel inside my body when someone asks my thoughts on feminism or being a feminist. Women-centred activism and advocacy exist with or without a label, for their actions speak to the elemental coexistence of a goal and action. This perspective is connected to how my ancestral grandmother brought herself into relation with the responsibilities and actions of one who would become an Elder. It is an understanding that caused me to wonder whether I should even name the space of in-between women, and it is probably also related to my difficulty with the teaching about straddling the space of the Two Row Wampum.

Although I understand that the knowledge of Indigenous women is diverse by virtue of experience, "oral history, interviews, economic processes and life histories,"[10] I still have an understanding that the majority of Indigenous women aged forty to sixty are subjected to domination in unique yet common ways. That is what I began recognizing at St Francis Xavier University. Although it has been written that these dominations "have rendered Indigenous women's knowledge invisible and politically marginal,"[11] this is for me an argument that enhances my supposition that Indigenous women are written about as being either strong and politically outspoken or invisible. In between these stories are many who possess knowledge like that shared by my ancestral grandmother but who often do not, cannot, or will not share that knowledge.

In the university's leadership program, we were all given the task of doing a project that would primarily benefit our community but could perhaps reach others as well. I chose to write a children's book about a young child working with a grandmother to garden and plant food. The focus was on the Haudenosaunee Three Sisters – corn, beans, and squash – but the book was really about connection to self, family, community, our cultural self, and the generations before and after us. The child would tell a story about helping Grandma to plant a garden in this time and place, but this story would reflect the continuity of Indigenous planting practices across the generations. I could use my knowledge to reintroduce and reinforce the concepts and cultural connections to gardening and agriculture that have long been part of my community.

I first had to survey the community to see whether this type of book was needed. So I had groups of people gather together and answer simple questions about what to include: was it a project worth pursuing, and what kind of knowledge should be imparted? The diverse groups included all ages of women, men, and children. We shared food, laughter, and stories. The project was strongly encouraged, so I was pleased to gather the information and photographs and to write the book that was eventually launched at our Farmer's Market. It was well supported by family, friends, and community, and I felt like I had made a contribution.

As I gathered information for the book, there was a recurring theme to what women of my age were saying. At issue was not necessarily what they were saying but the fact that I was not hearing what I had thought I would. There were no strong assertions of knowledge, and there was no recognition of these women in their role and place in the life stages. They often stated that they had nothing to share. Even women who gardened felt that an Elder should be consulted, not them. Who were they to have something to say? In keeping with the image of a broken, spiritless shell of a woman who shares no knowledge, we had internalized the view that we had no strength to care for ourselves, much less for our family or community.

In contrast to my ancestral grandmother, who felt a responsibility to take on the role of an Elder for her culture, these women fear that they do not have the right or privilege to do so. The evolving story of the world taking note of Indigenous women's knowledge is largely the story of Elder women, survivors of colonial violence, and more recently, young women. Although hearing their voices fills me with joy, it also furthers my sense that those of my age are in-between women.

I went back time and again to the things that I had read and reflected upon in my journal while at St Francis Xavier University and then while creating the children's book, and this process solidified for me the need to tell stories across the seven generations. I would learn more by connecting myself to my ancestors and to my descendants. I taught my children to research things at a very young age, years before the Internet. Wherever we lived, we would go to the local library for books, papers, and resource people. In one community, the only place that we had to research things was the bookmobile that came to our community every other week. Because of our interests, one librarian began bringing in an assortment of what she called "strange-topic" books. I do believe that she enjoyed it very much and felt stimulated, becoming more animated as time went by.

I have this same feeling when I research something new, and I felt it as I worked on my children's book and on these stories of my seven-generation grandmother and granddaughter. It makes me think of another journal entry that followed my time at the university:

Such fun planning the fairy party! My granddaughters are even more excited. I wonder if someday they will do things such as this. Am I being the best example of sharing stories that help with the connection to who we are culturally? Is the fairy party, which includes feeding the little people, an important piece of our story? I am hoping that there are more people willing to share information or even talk a bit about the knowledge that I know is there to be garnered. What if I am expecting too much? I kind of feel nervous.

I am struggling with the feelings that I have about being the one to do this project. I feel in between the spaces that the groups talk about. How can I work through the feeling of not having anything to say or share even though I have lots of things to say and share? Should I keep quiet? Should I proclaim that the information is someone else's? No wonder the women in my groups don't share. That feels wrong to me. (Personal journal)

My Seven-Generation Granddaughter

Reflecting on my uncertainty, I am drawn forward in time to my descendant and what she can teach about our roles and responsibilities. I am hoping that, as I move into the future, the answer will become clear. Is it my role to ensure the transmission of what I want my grandchildren and their children's children to know? I want my grandbabies to know who they are and where they come from. Would I and other in-between women feel more capable if we had some connection to the ceremonies and traditions of our ancestral grandmothers? I want my granddaughter to carry the ceremony and language of the Thanksgiving Address and to know her place in the seven generations. Is this something that I need to learn more about? Can we learn together? Perhaps the answer to both of these questions is yes.

I raise these questions through the ceremonial storytelling of my seven-generation granddaughter, who I imagine living and writing in a sustainable home while immersed in the relations of Mother Earth, who is in her full abundance once more after the passing of the storms of our time that Gae Ho Hwako talks about. I imagine her having fresh and clean water to drink, good and plentiful food to eat, and clean and toxin-free air to breathe. It is not a utopian society but one where the connection described by my ancestral grandmother has been replanted. This is a place and a time where differences are celebrated, knowledge belongs to everyone, and all *share what they need* rather than a *few owning all that they want.* Although I imagine these things, I hope for at least a world where the beauty of nature is still available to be enjoyed and to sustain life – all life.

Here is my imagined account of the future words of my seven-generation granddaughter:

> This is the first time that I will use my spirit pen, the perfect tool for this creation of epic thought on how we have renewed our culture and lifeways. When the people began to embrace the need for truthfulness and integrity in dealing with themselves, each other, and our place on E tinoha ongwesidage'dra gwe' (Mother Earth), many new tools were created that I am in awe of. The spirit pen allows our innermost thoughts to flow through it and onto the virtual paper. Thus far, I am undecided about whether I believe that our thoughts should be so readily accessible, even to ourselves. I know that in the past, the sharing of our knowledge as a people was jeopardized, and so I will let my thoughts flow. I do this for several reasons, but it was when I found an old document written by one of my ancestors that this need to add to the knowledge arose in me.
>
> It is my hope that my words and thoughts will someday be of importance to my descendants, just as the writing of my ancestor has helped me. The author of this document from 2021 is Kitty Lynn Lickers, my seven-generation grandmother. Her words overwhelm my heart and spirit. I am humbled by the connection to the past, and I intend with much decorum to express myself in a similar way in order to connect our line of knowledge and guidance from the past to the seven generations to come.

I must first give thanks in the spirit of the Ganǫhǫnyǫhk (Thanksgiving Address) for Shogwaeyadisho' (the Creator) and for the world that has been saved for all who are here. I offer condolences for the plants, medicines, birds, fish, and animals that we could not save, and I give thanks for the ones who still inhabit this earth with us. I give thanks for the knowledge from our ancestors, Elders, leaders, and Knowledge Keepers that helped us to save as much of the essence of our Mother Earth as could be saved. I offer my voice to the many who give thanks for the changes brought about by ancestral knowledge that enable us to continue to be here as we have been for so many generations. I give thanks for the people, animals, plants, and medicines that help us to continue to thrive as a united human race. I give thanks to the world leaders who help us all to have a voice in how our world is cared for. I give thanks for the ceremonies, and I acknowledge the ways of being and knowing that saved us from the extinction that we were headed for.

Without the integration of what was and now is, there would be a failure to protect everything for the seven generations to come. I give thanks for the life-sustaining waters that remain. I give thanks for the efforts of our water protectors, who keep a careful watch on the precious lifeblood of our Mother Earth, which sustains us. I give thanks to the many races of people who brought their cultures into relation with the ways of knowing and being that we carried across the generations to the time when they were most needed. I give thanks to Mother Earth for holding onto us in her most dire time of need and for waiting for us to come together to once again protect her as we should. I give thanks for all that the Creator has given and continues to give.

I now must address my seven-generation grandmother's document with a saddened heart since, despite the joy of connection that I feel at having read her words, which I treasure, I am saddened by the despair that my ancestral grandmothers, aunties, and mothers felt. Although my seven-generation grandmother does not speak directly of despair, I feel it strongly in her words of uncertainty as she tries to understand the in-between space that she and other Indigenous women found themselves in. I acknowledge the in-between space that she writes about and how it must have taken a great deal of reflection to see the colonial roots of this space in so many "isms." I also admit that she knew of no way at that time to remedy the problem of being in this space. I acknowledge the time and effort that she put into her attempts to encourage others to see that change was needed. I admire her search across the generations for the stories and ceremonies that would create understanding and perhaps offer a way forward for herself, other in-between women, and their descendants. I acknowledge that my life would be much different if the teachings of my ancestors that came from their struggles had not survived this time, and I give thanks for these teachings.

The in-between space that she writes about is the epitome of the displacement of respect for Mother Earth and for the land connections of her Indigenous peoples. I know that because of my place and responsibility as an Indigenous woman, I must continually speak about these things and must hold in high regard both Mother Earth and our place within all her relations. I feel that the writings of the past tell us of a time when the necessity of showing such esteem for Mother Earth had been forgotten. This was a time when the connections between the truth of Indigenous knowledge and what was happening in the world were not being acknowledged.

Indigenous peoples knew what needed to be done to save our Mother Earth, yet in the lands that we call home, settlers were still stuck in a culture of dominance. They had not learned to uphold sacred treaties like the Two Row Wampum by working side by side with the Indigenous Knowledge Keepers to do what had to be done for their well-being and that of the coming generations. This was a time when Indigenous people were not able to express to the world the need for all to come together to eradicate the racism, colonialism, and patriarchy that encompassed everyone. They were still deeply impacted by elitism and by the overwhelming reach of unwarranted privilege that saw settlers greedily trying to own the land rather than sharing what was given.

It was this behaviour that allowed for the near destruction of Mother Earth and for our near destruction as part of her. Settlers had to learn the importance of the knowledge that Indigenous people had carried in their stories, traditions, ceremonies, and ways of living. The most dire outcome nearly came to pass for all peoples before they bound themselves together with the intention of saving all our relations. To reconnect with the knowledge needed to renew relations, Indigenous and settler peoples of this continent had to change their ways of relating so as to become sympathetically interconnected, to foster mutual trust, and to begin striving toward the reparation of our Mother Earth.

We renewed our original value of sharing the land, a value that stretches across the seven generations and beyond. I cannot imagine a time when we were so wanton in our desire to have more that we neglected the most important tenants of who we were. To me, those tenants are to understand that we are keepers of the sacred knowledge that is shared by women. It is this same knowledge that those women described by my ancestor as falling in between felt so uncertain about lifting up.

My daughters have been taught that they have a sacred responsibility to be providers of sustenance in every way for the people – sustenance for body, mind, and spirit – as well as providers of knowledge about caring for each other and for our Mother Earth. I do not feel the agony of the "isms" that my ancestor writes of, but I also acknowledge the painful growth that occurred during that time. I am thankful that we all now share the understanding that we must work together and support our Knowledge Keepers in order to maintain the teachings and ceremonies that are most important to our survival. I know that without the group of in-between women discussed by my ancestor – women who are now held in high esteem in our time – we would still be floundering in our responsibilities.

Today, I cannot imagine living in a time when the waters are not being cared for. I cannot imagine not working side by side with everyone on Mother Earth – working in such a way that our diverse and unique cultural gifts complement each other rather than coexisting in a way that violently suppresses our Indigenous culture. As I read my ancestor's words, I cannot fathom the destruction that must have been created when our ways of knowing and being were not used respectfully by all. I realize my advanced degree in Indigenous agricultural practices is a large portion of what I share with others seeking to know how to grow food in a sustainable and cultural way. I share this knowledge and intention with my ancestral grandmother, as well as sharing her concerns. How can this knowledge not belong to everyone?

I have so many questions about the my ancestor's document, or perhaps I should call her Kitty, as it seems that everyone referred to her by this name. I am consumed by thoughts about the forces that created the situation that she describes, and I am curious to know how she found the strength to seek out answers about the in-between space that she inhabited and about women who were in the strong, reflective time of their lives and who should therefore have been the sustainers of their community and Mother Earth. What if the stories about what it means to be a strong Indigenous woman who connects across the seven generations had not been renewed by women like Kitty? I am certain that I would not be here. I believe that none of us would be here.

It is very humbling to know that in some small way my ancestors had a part in this beautiful world not only being healed but also being here for all of us. I am filled with gratitude.

Here and Now in 2021

This get together went so well! I had lots of food, and we sat outside in the shade, with kids running everywhere. It was a totally social event, and I was thrilled at the connection that everyone seemed to have with one another. I had one of the greenhouse girls write down everything on a giant piece of paper and had people add anything that they thought was missed. I posed questions but mostly let people tell stories. I believe that this is our way. I know it. I feel it. Consensus is such a foreign concept in today's way of doing things. My grandbabies took turns sitting on my lap, learning, listening, and becoming who they are in all of their fullness. I really felt connected to my family and my community tonight, as it should be and always has been. (Personal journal)

Reflecting on the story of my seven-generation granddaughter, I can see hope that suggests a way forward for myself and other in-between Indigenous women. I want to take up the responsibilities that have the potential to leave the door open for the future to unfold. I need to ensure that the storytelling ceremony that I am enacting here becomes something more than the uncertainty that stops me and others from acting with the knowledge that we hold. More women need to feel the power of their stories that spread across the generations so that they can be heard. More women need to be asked what they know and to share their knowledge – even if they feel uncomfortable doing it.

What I take from the storytelling spirit pen of my descendant is her fervour to know and share more, and thus I feel a need to share my knowledge. I receive this impression from her beautiful expression of thanksgiving, which opens me to the future in the hope of reconnecting her time with my time and our common ancestral past. In storying my in-between struggle, I also hope to give my descendants a sense of where they have come from and what they will stand for. Her story offers to me another view regarding how the changes of Mother Earth reflect her resistance to colonial changes and how these changes call us to renew our original teachings around the seven generations, sharing the land, and thanksgiving. Across the generations, we need to model for our children how we take up our cultural responsibilities so that they can be carried to our descendants.

Growing food, sharing traditions, and giving my family the things that I have learned are all part of the sustenance that positions me in a role between the generations. The research of Kim Anderson tells of women my age as having the "responsibility of ensuring sustenance for the community and caring for the young and old."[12] When I completed my storybook about a young child gardening with Grandma, I felt that I had done my "job" by fulfilling my responsibility in the life stages to provide sustenance for my community. Sustenance for me is about more than the food grown, harvested, and prepared; it is also about sustaining the soul and the physical self in all the dimensions of who we are. The way that I know the world requires me to share my knowledge.

We know this truth in our very bodies. Our place within this world is one where we need to care for the earth as though she were our own body. Those who have been in between or who are still there need to regain self-confidence and to trust themselves if they are to step forward and claim their voice in order to speak and defend their knowledge about how to care for the earth as she deserves. I recall Gae Ho Hwako's words: "A Haudenosaunee woman, a matriarch, is the voice of all that she understands and experiences: the pain, grief, life, and ceremony. But she is also someone who does not understand violence, for she knows the power of compassion, forgiveness, and love … I am woman; I am the storm that comes to cleanse our understanding of who we are. We will forever be here with E tinoha ongwesidage'dra gwe'." We need to step into the storm and know that we are one with it.

Indigenous ways of knowing and being are about the connections between all the components of our world, from the relations of the Thanksgiving Address to the seven generations to renewing our place in the life stages to the gifts of our diverse cultures. The ceremony of research described by Shawn Wilson helps me to understand why I was so transformed by this storied search for the in-between space, followed by sharing the stories in the reflective circles that preceded the writing of this book.[13] The telling of these stories became the ceremony that I needed to enact in order to replant a part of myself and, through that, to become someone who can give sustenance to the women around me, from my children and grandchildren to friends, co-workers, and the seven generations behind and before me. This ceremony has been a planting of seeds, the sustenance needed for our future.

What if I had never taken the step to pursue the leadership program at St Francis Xavier University and then a master's degree, where I thought through these stories? This question occurs to me with considerable regularity. Would I one day have become an old woman (I intend to live to be 123) and then realized that in not telling these stories, I had missed something important. I did think for a time that my master's education was a diversion from my work on the pedagogy of sustainability and of awareness of our place on Mother Earth. I was immersed in the teaching of food as medicine that can reconnect our spirit to who we are. I focused on reclaiming our culture by using food as our connecting thread. It seemed like this education journey into the in-between space was completely separate from my everyday life. But as I came to understand this research as a storytelling ceremony, I realized the deep connection between my work on the sustainability of our sustenance and the storied responsibilities of being in between the generations. It finally occurred to me, consciously, that they are not different but support each other.

There are connections that I may not have noticed in the beginning but that I now see very clearly because of the ceremony of the research. This storytelling has shown me that the strongest connection between the in-between space and my sustenance work is an understanding that sustainability is rooted in who we are – our physical, mental, emotional, spiritual, and cultural selves, which connect across the generations. For every Indigenous woman who speaks, writes, and acts with confidence in what she knows, there are legions of women in that in-between space who are not saying a word. But with these stories, I have also learned that there is sustenance in this in-between space if we can lift up our responsibilities for sustaining the communities that we are a part of.

My journey into this work continues to unfold with a group of in-between women that we call the Earth Souls. As the Earth Souls group has evolved, what began as a place for support and socially connecting around food and wellness has shifted into an instrument for actions where these women now eagerly reach out and plan new ways of interacting with the community. They are seeking and finding a voice that can contribute to the community in terms of food, gardening, and other social activities. As I listen to these women, I realize that just by planning, we are doing the things that we need to do. They are being heard, which means that they are speaking, moving, and acting. We are no longer in between but are heard and seen for the messages that we can share. This is the sustenance that we must provide in our role as Haudenosanee women.

Sustainability grows from our cultural knowledge, Indigenous languages, stories, ceremonies, and sustenance, which includes food, spirit, and all that binds us together when we recognize our place in these relations. This foundation for sustainability needs to be recognized by all women if we are to summon the strength to preserve the world. Have I reached an answer to my questions? Is there a solution? Although I wish with all my heart to say yes, I know that the glimmer of what I am seeing and vaguely exploring in these stories is only a beginning whose future depends on us taking up our place in the generations of our people on Mother Earth in a spirit of thanksgiving. This journey excites me, for exploring, examining, and reflecting will entail a great deal more ceremonial work, time, and effort. Doing these things will allow me to return to the circles of *ǫ da gaho dę:s* in order to receive and share again. So I might just have another story to tell … one day.

In between the Lines of Your Apology

Awnjibenayseekwe (Banakonda Kennedy-Kish Bell)

In the last sun of the day
Across the expanse of autumn land
I am in that moment
Before
It lowers itself to the horizon
As colours splash across a cold crisp sky
Highlighting
A full-breath communion
Of light fall
And night rise crossing

Thoughts rise out
Of the belly of me
My story
Our story
In your words
Press down on me
In between the lines of your apology

As a child
The land, sky, and water
Were bigger than me
Bigger than my parents, my siblings
My grandparents
Bigger

Sun, rain, snow
Voiced the presence of the Creator
Through
Pine, balsam, and cedar trees
Across the Superior
There is nothing like the sound
Of wind through trees
Like the sound of rolling, crashing waves

I remember
Northern roots in me
Me in the land
The land in me
Root rhythm
My breath
My heartbeat

I remember
Torment
In my father's eyes
In my heart
My struggle to honour
My father
My ancestors
The spirit

If I pull my roots
I cut out the tongues
Of my grandchildren

Your words
Press down on me
In between the lines of your apology

If I cut my roots
To survive
How do I progress

Yellow tape
And chalk-mark image
Baby sister
On concrete

I would have to stop hearing
With my heart
Lose myself
So many I have loved did
Alcohol and drugs
Medicated
Repressed
I remember
Know what has long been denied
What is still hidden
In between the lines of your apology

The wind chilled the hollow
In their bones
As they turned away
Stopped hearing the drum
Within
Stopped
Their breath

My story is rising, swelling
In my breath
In the wind and water

From the ground
Raising earth in me

So many have left us
Their echo
Their memory
Is a storm in me
A song
A lament
Raising earth in me

I have found the amethyst rock in me
Traces of copper and silver
And even gold in me
Pressed from the knots
Fibre and fire in me
In between the lines of your apology

I cannot forget the fallen, the lost
Time cannot erase them
Those ghosts
Do not go away
They rise up within me
Calling up a cry
And the spirit in me
Sister
Father
Uncles
Aunties

Beneath the soil
Listening
Through the leaves and stems and flowers
Budding then
Falling now

There is a storm in me
Crashing thunder
Lightening stabbing
Pounding rain in me
Pouring grief
Working my inner land
To let in the new
See the beauty that remains
That emerges

The rain is opening me
All the land songs
Songs of old
Are in the same wind
The wind that continues to move
The earth, the water, the seasons

Still my fists are clenched
Contracted
Against your justice
I see the clear-cut across this land
It is good you say
It makes room
For new growth
I see the clear-cut across our communities
In our families
The strangled discord

Without the shelter of old
There is no Honesty

The wind knows
It is the great and forever one
Who witnesses

Those old standing ones
Great old grandmothers
Old grandfathers
Their creaking swaying
Forever movement
They are the clear expanse
In me

Yet they are falling like rain
Old one's old words
Old beliefs
Lying with them in the soil
Of the great Superior landscape
My beloved

In those silent listening rocks
The small worn pebbles
The giant rock mountains
Who dreamed the soil
That their hands moved in
Searched in
For roots
Pathways
For seasons

Root rhythm, root melody
Forever
In the wind and water
Waves to our shores
Dancing light
On the earth

I remember
My niece and great-niece
Receiving their spirit name
And my mother asking for hers

How vivid that moment's wistful desire
Rose up
Bigger than her
And moved her

Moved us
Beyond the judgment
Shame
And internalized racism
Palpable
Sobering
Informing
Her hunger for wholeness
For self-acceptance
In that moment raw and honest
I understood
I witnessed and remembered

Growing up feeling
I was the evidence of her failure
To stay away, deny
Her own roots
A place she loved and hated
Played out passionately
With my father
Both oppressed and oppressor
Running in their veins
All those deeds
In between the lines of your apology

On the land
No running water
No electricity
How different light was back then
Telling stories
Around the kitchen table

A kerosene lamp at the centre
In my grandmother's house
Dark enough
To see the fire in the cracks
Of the wood stove that warmed us

Faces and shadows
Sounds of voices
And the crackling, spitting logs in the fire
A more potent presence of breath
We are seldom that close to each other now
As a child, I heard my grandmother breathe
My snoring uncle
The fire, the wind outside

I sat by the window
Enjoyed the first hot rays of summer
In a cold house
Jumped out of the second-floor window
Into a snow bank
Cousins and siblings
Digging out the snow
From our front door
To open it

Nature was a big presence
It was a direct, honest
Real relationship
It is much harder to be present now
A struggle not to be part of
Destroying it

I remember health, joy, and the knowing smile
In my grandmother's eyes
So I am turning
My back to the wind

It is pushing me forward
This yellow girl
Is shaking off this despair
Her sorrow
This is my giveaway

Let your apology pick it up
It belongs to you
You separate your apology
From the broken treaties
The land sales to mining and logging corporations
The flooding of our ancestors' graves
Our communities

Why is it still
English and French
A nation of two nations
Does your apology include us at all

The old voices' crackling sounds
Old songs breathing them in the wind
Their voices sounding
Rain in me
Falling into rhythm
Moves the shame in me

The grief pushing through
Into the earth
Only to rise
This old
To make new

I am the breathless river
Running to its source

A Prayer: Shkaakamigokwe

Awnjibenayseekwe (Banakonda Kennedy-Kish Bell)

"The universe cares. The earth is a conscious living being that cares. She is our First Mother."[1] The Anishinaabe expression of meaning, of purpose, of taking up our place within the wholeness of life is centrally important to the living of a Good Life.

Within the conception of Mino-Bimaadiziwin (the Good Life) is the perception of *ddaadendiziwin* (humility), a valuing and knowing of oneself as a sacred part of creation. To live in a good way is to be a good human; it is to strive for balance and harmony through engaging respect, reciprocity, and regard for all life.

"Harmony and balance are the motivational forces that move us towards healthy and co-operative co-existence … Respect is the principle that binds us together in collective well-being and in a life of quality."[2] I am lifted up by these beautiful words of Onaubinisay (James Dumont). They fill me up with gratitude and thanksgiving.

We come to value, experience, and know our First Mother, Shkaakamigokwe (Mother Earth), in the place where we draw our first breath. We take up our place with her as her children; our breath and heartbeat move within the wonder of the great mystery – this breath that we ourselves hold onto, each of us, singular and together. Here in this place, transmission unfolds, uninterrupted. In the words of Lee Maracle, "The earth and its children are subjects and not objects."[3]

The earth always engages us in her cycles, her rhythms, her songs. We sound with her as she moves her waters without and within each of us, within her seasons and our own. She is the daughter of Nokomis, the moon, and Mishomis, the sun. We are her children. From our ancestors to the present, with the dream we have for the time ahead, for those yet to come, we are history, we are new, we are on our way.

The earth's waters rise up from underground, fall from the sky, softly quenching us or full of storms of wind and movement. *Nibi* (water) moves uniquely within and over the body of our First Mother. She is *gichi zhewitaganibi* (the great salt waters), *gichi-gami* (the inland freshwater seas), and the vast bodies of water, lakes, rivers, and streams on and within her. She is in *goon* (snow), *mikwaniwun* (hail), *mikwan* (ice), *gimiwun* (rain), *animikee* (thunder), and *wawasum* (lightning). She is *bimaadiziwin* (life), moving in relationship with all – the surrounding marshes, great bushes, forests, and deserts – with reciprocity giving expression to energy, breath, and motion. She has her own spirit, purpose, and memories.

Nibi comes first in this physical life; her fundamental movement, rhythm, and song find a unique voice in each of us, within all life. Breath and water are the very energy force of spirit – the life breath and lifeblood of our First Mother, the earth. Water is in relationship, sculpting, singing, dancing, manifesting, moving with gravity and levity, expanding, and contracting at the centre and at the circumference. Her movement within, through, and on Shkaakamigokwe causes her breath, our breath. Water is life-giving and sustaining. As human beings, we are inseparable from the land. We are the land, water, and sky.

There is a great need to resist other narratives that are not our own, that distance us from our place with and on Turtle Island. As we strive to keep ourselves standing, we must reach to resee, revalue our connection, our relationship with our First Mother. She is not the colony. She does not belong to the ship; rather, the ship and the canoe are of our First Mother. Here again in Gae Ho Hwako's words, we belong to E tinoha ongwesidage'dra gwe' (Mother Earth), to her "river of life." In this part of our Mother Earth, in our place on Turtle Island, we come to know her again and again.

Before the great migration, we lived on the shores of the great salt waters in the east. The people, those ones lowered from the Sky Realm – the Anishinaabe of the Three Fires Confederacy – migrated from the eastern shores of the ocean. We are the people of Midewiwin (the Grand Medicine Society).

In every movement, every formation, Shkaakamigokwe carries Kendaaswin (the Original Instructions) for passing down teachings of respect and regard for all life. She nurtures all our relations, honouring the nature of change, causing change, always engaging in reciprocal sacred relationship. The spirit, respect for all of creation, is our ancestral inheritance, the heart bringing us into relational experience and expression, the mind coming to Anishinaabe *gikendaasowin* (knowledge), to knowing one's self as a part of the family of creation, to embodiment of the force that calls us to develop, grow, and activate Mino-Bimaadiziwin in our way of being and in our way of taking up our place in creation. In that way, the knowledge of life is ancestral, life-long, forever listening to the teachings, the inherent principles, within the wholeness of life.

I recall again Gae Ho Hwako lifting up the words of the Ganǫhǫnyǫhk (Thanksgiving Address), calling us to stand up for our place in creation. Our foundational principles – the four sacred gifts of Kindness, Honesty, Sharing, and Strength – are held in plant life, tree life, animal life, and rock life. Each is a stage, each an unfolding, one with the other, of Kind Honest Sharing, bringing one to Strength, to truth. That truth is a coming into wholeness, a way of being that we strive for in our journey, deepened and informed by living in relationship.

Megwetch Gitchi Manidoo (thank you Creator) and all my relations.

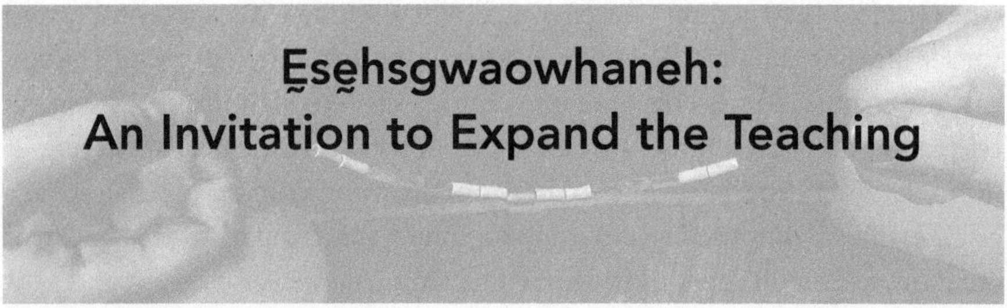

Ḛsḛhsgwaowhaneh: An Invitation to Expand the Teaching

You need to expand the teaching or story beyond what you hear and see; it is about clarity, questioning, and seeking answers.

The string is now passed to you, the reader, to "expand the teaching" in relation to your own experiences, stories, and knowledge. Is there a part of Gae Ho Hwako's teaching that really resonates with you or perhaps something from one of the responses? Begin by reflecting on that in relation to your story. In this way, you can help us to expand the circle of truth, sharing, and healing.

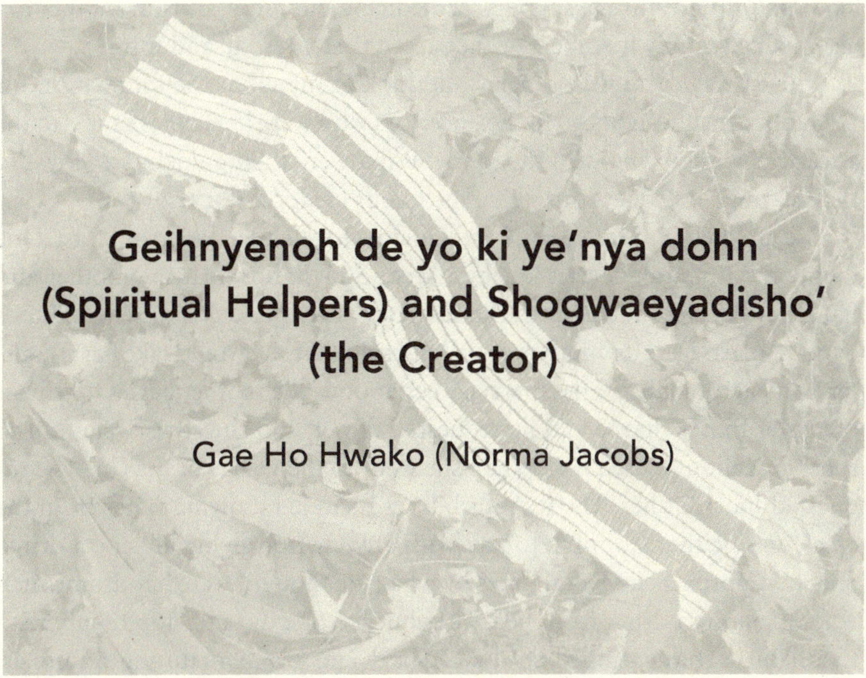

Geihnyenoh de yo ki ye'nya dohn (Spiritual Helpers) and Shogwaeyadisho' (the Creator)

Gae Ho Hwako (Norma Jacobs)

> These spiritual beings guide and support our journeys, keeping us aware of our attitudes and behaviours so that we may be safe. When we leave our places of shelter and travel away from our families, our helpers keep us safe. And when we return home, they offer a web of safety so that we might arrive at our places of shelter. We say *nya weh* (thank you) to those spiritual beings. Let it be that way in our minds!

Our E tinoha ongwesidage'dra gwe' (Mother Earth) nurtures all of life – the trees, shrubs, grasses, medicines, hanging fruits, flowers, edible plants, fresh seasonal foods, and nuts – all that gives sustenance to restore and rebuild our bodies. Life is sustained by the two-legged humans, the winged ones, and the four-legged animals, all of whom are nurtured and sustained by the water, the blood of our mother. The plants hold hands beneath her grass skirt, at times changing various colours, represented by the many florals and medicines. Every aspect of this land is healing and cleansing, and we are on this human journey to understand our relationship, interconnectedness, and *okyadaot* (friendship as a supportive medicine) not only with our mother but also with all family members of the sacred past, present, and future.

When I reflect on this journey and look at myself as the foundation for my family, my thoughts go to the ancestors who were here before me – to the ancestral women who held the canoe. What were their guidelines? How did they learn? These questions guide me to our creation story.

The families in the Sky World were invited to attend a leadership feast. One family did not attend, so it was by a second invitation that the mother and daughter decided to come. At the feast, the leader asked for the daughter's hand in marriage. Her mother agreed but said that she would take her daughter home to prepare for the marriage ceremony. The mother began to tell her daughter things that would be requested of her, and she advised her not to speak out about these tasks. When she went to the village of the chief, he requested much of her. The responsibilities included drawing water from the creek and neither stopping to talk with anyone nor giving anyone a drink. She was approached several times by what she thought were handsome men who asked for a drink from her water bucket. She did not stop to talk with them. But as she continued, she looked back and saw them turn into animals: a fox, wolf, and bear. She never questioned and carried on until she arrived back at the village of the leader, who asked whether she had encountered any incidents on the path, to which she replied that she had not.

Women in the Sky World were being controlled by the male leadership. She was told not to speak to anyone as she was drawing water from the stream. She had been deceived by the animals who had transformed from men back into animals. On another occasion, the woman was asked by the leader to make a pot of corn mush. As it splattered, she was told not to move away from it but rather to stand there and let the boiling mush splatter on her body without crying out! The chief then called for the dogs to come and lick the mush off, and the woman did as she was told. The chief and other men were creating problems in relationships. This dysfunction was *otko* (bad medicine), and it had permeated the Sky World.

Sky Woman wanted to create a new world, as change would help to birth a new beginning. It was with this intention that she fell through the hole in the sky and came to land on the back of Turtle Island. This was the beginning of a new creation. When I think of this story, I reflect on Mother Earth in spring as she gives birth with the snow melting and the rains coming with the thunder. As with Sky Woman falling onto the back of a turtle surrounded by water, we are surrounded by water when we are birthed.

No one can fully understand a story like that of Sky Woman until one actively participates in it; then we come to an understanding of the story and the teachings that it holds. There are many interpretations of this story, as people have their own experiences, ideas, and reflections that arise from the journey of their life. Stories can be very beneficial. As we share them, we can feel parts of us opening that were previously blocked by some negative action or behaviour. Our stories never blame; they only share experiences that might touch a chord in another's life. This effect allows people to learn through reflection and to take part in an opening of our hearts and minds.

Just as humans have basic needs like shelter, food, fun, and safety, E tinoha ongwesidage'dra gwe' also needs appreciation and understanding. I am reminded of a dream where I approached a group of leaders from another territory to explain my actions after doing something wrong. I began by explaining who I was and where I was from, and I acknowledged that I had overstepped my boundaries according to my nation's law. I was weak and vulnerable, and what I did was wrong. I was sorry to those I hurt. I am a human being who made a mistake, but I explained that our law also says that it is not the role of people to judge or punish others. Another force will take care of that. The people resounded with confirmation, "NYEH!"

Reflections on dreams, stories, and experiences are a huge part of our learning, for when we learn from these sources, we are able to think without pressure. Something then begins to change within. Our spiritual fires begin to ignite from being in relation with the spiritual fire of another held in that person's story. We begin to recognize our story and our dreams as valid, and through that, we become empowered by the relation of our story to those of others, including to that of Sky Woman and the creation of Turtle Island.

Our birth connects us to Sky Woman's sacred journey here from the Sky World, which started all of life. I began to learn about this connection after I had my six children, as it was only then that I began reconnecting to my culture. I missed out on all these reflective teachings until my last child, so I made sure that I was at the birth of all my grandchildren. Each time I saw them, I was reminded of Sky Woman on the back of the turtle needing help, and how a muskrat dove deep into the water to bring that soil up and help to create life as it is today. To see that muskrat coming out of the river of life, drenched with the water flowing off of it, that is how our babies are when born. They are covered with fluid as you go to grasp them, and then they cry right away to take their first gasp of air. I think of that in terms of being able to see Shogwaeyadisho' (the Creator) standing there blowing life three times into that baby as it arrives here.

I know that feeling of giving birth and how it is so painful that I thought, "God, I just can't do this anymore; when is it going to be over?" I now know that it is not about the pain but about how we take care of our bodies, nurture ourselves, and are active during our pregnancy. We have so many stories and teachings for pregnant mothers. One tells us to never stop in a doorway when you are pregnant because when the time comes for the baby to be born, it will just stand in the doorway and your labour will be extended. Our body is responding to this new baby in us, and it has its own way of expanding through the birthing time. The pain that we are going through is actually the movement of our organs in our lower body as they open the doorway to birth. It is such a beautiful idea for us to hold, that our bodies naturally open up to be able to bring this new life, rather than just thinking of all the pain that is experienced.

Like Sky Woman, I know how it feels to have to start over. From the stories of my life, I have also learned about violence, gossip, and dishonesty in my relationships with males and females. I know how it feels to be expelled from my home and needing to look for a new beginning, a new foundation with values and beliefs for my family. I had to make changes in my life so as to strengthen myself. I needed to reflect on my past so that I could see how I had arrived at this place in my life.

The stability of my children's lives was important to me. I realized that I had to learn new skills, as I did not want to rely on social assistance, so I returned to school. I struggled to remain strong and to not give up. My mother stood with me and helped with my children as I returned to school. While there, I was told by my professor, "You will fail this course," but I graduated from the course and the program to become a community counsellor. It was a two-year program, and many times I asked myself, *What am I doing here?* I endured the hardships of catching a bus every day to Toronto and back. I had to take my children to my mom so that she could provide care while I was at school, and then I had to return in the evening to pick them up, cook supper, and get ready for the next day. I did not realize the tremendous work that these things required until I graduated and someone said to me, "That was lots of work and you did it." I just felt weak!

Taking that journey was like opening a door and asking, *What direction do I walk? Where do I find help to support me in this new journey?* The old ones supported me by telling their stories, and as I listened to them, we became one, an extended family. We supported one another by finding our similarities and by building on our strengths – on love and peace. We made decisions for ourselves, we knew our identity, and we followed our ways.

Throughout this change, my ceremonies were very important, as I had been told, "When you have questions, go to the Longhouse to find your answers." I followed my instructions and attended every ceremony that I could. It is possible to be in ceremony every day. The creation story, as I understand it, has taught me that change is inevitable and good. It asks me to gather my strength, listen, watch, learn, reflect, communicate, trust new beginnings, believe in our gifts, honour self, and respect others. Our E tinoha ongwesidage'-dra gwe' is our foundation, she is accepting, welcoming, forgiving, and loving. She gave life to a negative energy and to positive energy, which exist to this day. We need both to create a balance.

Things are out of balance today because our instructions were jeopardized by colonialism, a system that wants power and control rather than the peace of friendship. We were given families to be thankful for – not just our human families but also families of plants, trees, birds, and animals – along with the *geihnyenoh de yo ki ye'nya dohn* (spiritual helpers), Shogwaeyadisho' (the Creator), and so much more. When we acknowledge them in the Ganǫhǫnyǫhk (Thanksgiving Address), they feel the appreciation and are empowered by our ceremony of gratitude to give more.

❀ ❀

We have been gifted with many teachers who continue to bring messages from the Creator about how to live according to the instructions of our ceremonies, songs, and speeches. Our ancestors teach us about the importance of boundaries, values, discipline, and honouring oneself. We are fortunate to have so many young ones emerge from the earth who take our

> culture seriously. Our stories and songs guide us to stay in balance, and if we stray, the Creator does not judge us but understands that we are on this difficult human journey. We say *nya weh* for our teachers. Let it be that way in our minds.

We are on this human journey, and it is hard. It is so easy to forget that we are spiritual beings, and we are often reminded only when we forget our boundaries and invade another's sacred space. At those times, we need to remember that we are here to love, honour, and encourage each other. We each have knowledge and stories that are to be validated through communication and walking in each other's moccasins to a place of understanding, to *ǫ da gaho dę:s* (the sacred meeting space). It was in the hopes of fostering such a relationship that *og ya:dao* (friendship) was offered through the Two Row Wampum so that we could share the river of life.

Oda:otra (friends) come in many variations. There are acquaintances, the people we work with and see every day, others who provide services, some whom we meet through activities like sports or children's programs, family relations who so influence our life, and the list goes on. *Oda:otra* are those who help without trying to help, for they stand with you through challenges and opportunities. They offer congratulations on seeing your accomplishments, assist in your dreams, offer different views on issues, share conversation about nothing and everything, laugh with you, and make time for you. As I reflect on *og ya:dao*, I recall a close and confident walk with one of my friends who listened without judgment – who supported, encouraged, and empowered me.

When I was growing up, I had a few close friends who I would meet at the corner store and with whom I would do things like dance and sing. We were like a girls' club. As we grew up, we moved away from each other and found other interests. I cannot say that we had dreams, but we were young and tried to express ourselves in relation to the rules and boundaries taught by our parents. In my teen years, my friends changed as I met new people in school. We were learning about life and became interested in the opposite sex, young males. When I think of that time as a young girl, it seems like we were always looking for a tall, dark, handsome man. Our dream then was about having a perfect life, partner, kids, home, and family. The dream was magical. These friends also changed as I grew up and took on the responsibilities of a parent, organizer, cleaner, cook, gardener, sewer, berry picker, preserver of food, and someone who in time learned the cultural responsibilities of my name, Gae Ho Hwako.

Later in life, in my mid-twenties, I remembered the importance of the *okyadaot* that had grown between myself and this particular *okya tsi* (friend) when we were young and in our girls' club. We had lost contact, and I began realizing how much I had left behind. I reflected on why I had grown angry with her so long ago. These feelings to renew our *okyadaot* arose during a time when I began healing from the violence that I had experienced as an Indigenous woman and, through that, also began learning about myself. It was in a sharing circle that I apologized to her and said how much I missed her. As we renewed our friendship, I felt a great weight lifted from my shoulders.

At this time, we saw each other in different places or at events and ceremonies, and it was then that we began having a conversation about helping people to understand our language and ceremonies. With a few other friends who supported us through this process, we developed ways of communicating to help clarify the language in our Longhouse ceremonies. During this time, we had children and grandchildren who recognized our relationship. I was so proud and happy when my friend told me that she had always been there for my daughter and granddaughter. We are *okya tsi* forever.

Time plays such a big part in our lives, in our *odaotra* (friendship). My friend was sick with disease for some time, and my thoughts and prayers were constantly with her. I prayed for a miracle so that she would get well. I kept telling her that we still had much work to do! Yet I knew our time was limited. With her loss, I have struggled with my responsibility to continue the work that we started as I educate others and share about my vision, thoughts, and dreams. When I think of her and other friends, I feel honoured to have them as gifts who have helped to support, encourage, empower, and activate my life so that I could arrive where I am today. I am grateful!

I have experienced loss over the years – some through accidents, illness, natural death, alcoholism and addictions, and suicides – but nothing compares with someone taking the life of someone you love. I experienced the loss of a most precious granddaughter through the most heinous crime: murder. At the time, I was mentoring her, and she came to workshops and classes. She was always helping by babysitting my other grandchildren or helping her brother to get ready for practice. She was active in sports, had a great sense of humour, and liked lemon pie. She loved dancing and wearing her cultural regalia. She was beautiful and loving. When she was taken from us, I thought that I would lose my mind. I did not think that I would recover. It was the most horrendous experience in my life.

From the experience of losing my granddaughter, I became a family advisor for the National Inquiry into Missing and Murdered Indigenous Women and Girls (MMIWG). I chose this work because I wanted change. I have been through the courts in regard to divorce, family support payments (or lack of), and the murder of my granddaughter. Each time, I came away disillusioned and angry. If one tells the truth in court, you lose. It is not a system based on the values of my Longhouse, as it allows violators, abusers, and murderers to go free. There is no justice! I wanted to raise awareness about the injustices experienced by our women, who are the foundation of life. I have had the opportunity to work with many organizations to share my cultural teachings across the United States and Canada, and for that I am grateful. I have met and worked with fabulous people whom I have learned from. We have touched each other's lives. I am grateful for what I have learned through the spirit of *odaotra*. Love is the greatest medicine, for that was our sacred beginning!

My grandson came into my life nineteen years ago, and he has been another huge part of my learning about acceptance, love, relationship, honouring, gratitude, communication, the importance of visiting family, and the significance of knowing family ties. He is reflective, loves to sing, and constantly wants to know about ceremonies. His first greeting is, "Good morning, Grandma. The sun is shining! What are you doing today, going to work? Did you have a grand sleep? Did you dream?" When he comes home, he asks, "How was your day?" He is concerned when I am not well and asks whether I need anything. "Did you take your medicine? Want me to rub your back? It's okay Grandma!" He is a gift who reminds me of simple things in life by the purity of his being. He honours me when we spend time with friends and says to them, "See this woman, she is an awesome woman!" Sometimes, his words overwhelm me! I feel grateful that his friendship is a huge part of my life. *Nya weh* (thank you).

In my past, I was not honoured or respected as a woman, and it has made me leery of relationships. Do not get me wrong; I still watch for that "tall, dark, handsome man," but I realize that this is a dream, not a reality. This is a human journey, not a perfect world with a perfect man, home, family, and everything. We are spiritual beings experiencing a human journey. We create balance by opening our bundles and expressing *ganigǫhi:yo* (a good mind), values, beliefs, and attitudes that we want to carry into our relationships. It is a daily task to create the harmony of *odaotra* in our lives, our communities, and on the Two Row Wampum's river of life.

As for my dream of a partner to whom I could come home and with whom I could share my thoughts, accomplishments, and work, I have realized through my healing journey that I have been honoured by the *odaotra* of many males, both from our communities and from other traditional homelands. They have heard my story and truth. I have one special long-time male friend who was there for me when I decided to leave my relationship and walk alone with my children. He realized that I needed the support of a male friend. We do not see each other often, but when we do meet and converse, it is like we have never been far from each other. Our friendship can span time and distance!

There are so many memories, stories, ceremonies, children, grandchildren, great-grandchildren, losses through death, and gains through births. The support that friends share is ongoing. It is a phone call, a chance meeting, a visit. Life changes and moves us forward, but once understood, the love of *odaotra* never changes. Love is a constant that is fundamental to creating friendships. We get angry with one another because we love them so much that it hurts us to see them being involved with things that we do not approve of, but they are on their path of learning. Acceptance is huge in our lives, something that we strive for in every activity that we are involved with. True *odaotra* is a human need.

After my granddaughter's death, I became more aware of changes to the environment. I see changes to the trees, leaves, and grass. I note the rising waters, stronger winds, and more frequent tornadoes, which even come to places that have had no experience of them before. At the same time, people seem to be more violent, to be losing control, and to be exerting the power of their positions against others. Everything is changing because there is no respect for life, unborn life, or the future; our foundation has no love, respect, or valuing of truth.

My Haudenosaunee culture has been given leadership, stories, and ceremonies for nurturing our relations with the environment, with the creation of E tinoha ongwesidage'dra gwe'. All the beings we give thanks to in the

Ganǫhǫnyǫhk work with us daily. They try to teach and share with us in the spirit of *odaotra* about caring for family. They nurture, embrace, support, and encourage us to be humble and to appreciate the time that we have with all our relations. Our Mother Earth is tired of the disrespect, hurt, and pain that are inflicted on a people the Creator honours. Our true mothers – the mothers of our nations, families, and myself – are the storm. I am the storm!

❀ ❀

> We acknowledge the great visioning for our human journey. Our original instructions for relating with each other were handed down to us by Shogwaeyadisho' (the Creator). Everything was provided for our health and well-being on this human journey, and all that is expected of us that we give thanks for all that is! So we send our greatest greetings to Shogwaeyadisho', who carries our best interests in health and wellness. We say *nya weh*. Let it be that way in our minds!

Our journey to giving birth is so close to death. Watching my daughters give life was a joy, but I was afraid at the same time. They say that we can pass on at our time of delivery. But we are also told that if a mother passes in that sacred space at her time of delivery, then she goes from here to Shogwaeyadisho'. Although we grieve, we know that her life has gone to another realm. It is a huge cause for celebration to see that and to be in that precious space where the woman is in labour, delivers her baby, has the umbilical cord cut, and then passes to Shogwaeyadisho'. The feelings are mixed at that time because there is death and life, but it also reminds us that death is always walking right here with us, just as life is.

When you are disconnected, have a loss, or are grieving, you can just rub your navel and you will start to feel reconnected with your mom, grandma, and E tinoha ongwesidage'dra gwe'. Life on Turtle Island began with a woman, life sprung from her body, and by rubbing your navel one way and then the other, you can reconnect with your ancestors and come back to this sacred place again. We spiral into the world through the navel, and rubbing it in this way connects us with this spiral. There is a lot to this teaching, as it reconnects us to the beginnings of our stories, to our life and death, and to the opening and closing of our ceremonies.

When families experience a death, there is not one person or element that is not affected. It is felt across the territories, families, clans, and nations. Time is given for the family and the deceased to comprehend the loss. Much of the responsibility is with the clan family, who have to make many arrangements. Every nation does things a little differently because of outside influences, so we try to remember the protocols in order to respect the journey that this individual travelled. We honour the number of days that they were given to experience this earth walk and to utilize their gifts for the health and well-being of themselves and of their family, clan, and nation. As I mentioned, all of our ceremonies are meant to be empowering, uplifting, and strengthening, and because of this purpose, they are held in the highest regard.

After the mourning period, the clan family also have to remember and honour the people who came forward to help without question. It is like a giveaway ceremony. This process reminds us of how closely our relationships are interwoven. It is a time of reflection for us to remember the experiences that have woven us into the dance of intimacy through ceremony, councils, medicines, songs, speeches, and other community gatherings. We remember all the good things about them! There is a lot of communication that transpires at this time; that is why I know how important communication is to everyone, whether they are alive or journeying to the spirit world.

Our original instructions for relating with each other were handed down to us from Shogwaeyadisho'. Each ceremony needs to be closed, just like the way that we close our rubbing of the navel by circling one way and then the other. If we leave a ceremony before it is over – if we do not do that closing of our navel – then we leave that spiral undone. It stays open. When we do not close up those sacred spaces for ourselves so as to wrap up what we have learned, we cannot feel complete in the experience.

Everything in this world has a spirit that connects it to everything else. When we give birth, after the umbilical cord is cut, part of it stays on the baby until it dries up, and then we bury it. We are told that if we do not bury the baby's umbilical cord, the baby will always be looking for its belly button. The baby will climb everything as soon as it starts walking – a couch, kitchen table, chairs. When children were seen doing that, the old people always used to ask, "Didn't you bury their belly button? They're looking for it." When my son's daughter was born in the month of December, he and his wife kept the belly button cord because they live up north and it was too cold to bury it.

They kept forgetting to bury it, and when I visited, she was crawling into the cupboards, on a chair, over the couch, and reaching for a shelf. I asked, "What is up there?"

"Her belly button," they said.

"You gotta get busy and bury that because she is looking for it," I said. "She wants you to take care of it."

We have to re-educate ourselves about the things that children do that are medicine for them. For females, we are to bury the umbilical cord near the house, as in our teachings, this is the woman's space. The cord of males is to be buried in the woods or a woodpile, as this is where their responsibility is found and what gives them the strength and the endurance to work hard in the forests. Men and women have different kinds of strength within them, although there is not a man who could give life because of that kind of pain.

Lacrosse is a gift from Shogwaeyadisho' to men, which is why we call it the "Creator's game." This game is claimed to be Canada's national summer sport, but it belongs to the Native people. It is our game. No one sold it. It is given to men for entertainment, for skill development, and for building the strength needed to come into their responsibilities.

Traditionally, lacrosse was played with wooden sticks, and catgut was used for the webbing. The stick was made from a hickory tree, which represents how males are to carry themselves – tall, straight, without anger, and honoured by the medicines of the tree. A lot of hard and time-consuming labour went into making these lacrosse sticks by hand, which required cutting, shaving, bending, drying, and reshaping. I have seen sticks hanging and drying, and it probably took a whole year for a stick to be completed. While they were doing this work, plenty of stories and teachings would also have been shared by the men. It was an honour for these talented men to receive the gift of giving life to these sticks.

I remember as a child going with my parents and siblings to watch my father play lacrosse. It was fun loading up the car and heading out to other Haudenosaunee communities for these games. We travelled to tournaments in Onondaga and Newtown, and their teams would come to play here at Six Nations. I used to see my dad getting ready, and I thought that the players looked funny with their strong legs and team shirts. All the families would get together after the games for a meal that the women would prepare. Lining up with our plates, we would have white beans, mashed potatoes, macaroni salad, hot dogs, hamburgers, and desserts. It was a great time.

I loved watching my dad play lacrosse! He played for the Hamilton Bengals and wore a black and orange uniform. He was a great player who could manoeuvre his way through the opposing team. My brother also played, and in those days, they used pillows and sponges as pads for protection. Some of the players had nicknames, and they would tease my dad and call him a dirty player. I always defended him and said that he was just too fast and tricky for them, and we would all have a good laugh. It was good to see that twinkle in my dad's eyes when they would tease him. He knew that they could not keep up with him. He would be running and realize that someone was going to check him from behind, so he would duck down, causing the player to topple over him, and my dad would finish his run and score! Those are such good memories.

They would win and they would lose, but it was all about having a great time and bringing families and nations together. Lacrosse today has changed so much. It has become so competitive and is now more about fighting, jealousy, bullying, and aggression. The values of the game have changed. My sons participated in lacrosse, and they were always being attacked for being Native. Others would make whooping sounds like what they saw in television shows, and they would tell our players to go home. There were always so many fights between Natives and non-Natives, and I was always afraid of my boys getting hurt. I do not think that it was ever recognized as racism, but it never felt good.

I remember that when my son played in the professional National Lacrosse League, we travelled to Philadelphia for the playoffs. We took our banners, as fans do, and people made hurtful remarks to us. My sister and I had to be escorted out of the arena by security and police, and the people kept taunting us. Our parents were with us, and as they are older, I felt afraid for their safety because the fans were like a mob. To this day, the taunting has become more aggressive. Recently, the crowd was yelling at one of the Native players that he needed to cut his braids off. This sparked a new conversation, as the two individuals spoke openly about the incident to reporters, and now the teams have cultural sensitivity training. Whether that will change anything remains to be seen.

Lacrosse is an Indigenous game that is to be utilized by men as medicine for strength, stamina, speed, accuracy, flexibility, interconnectedness, family cohesion, and fun. It is no longer about this kind of medicine, about healing, or even about fun, all of which were given to us by Shogwaeyadisho'. The wooden stick has become outdated and replaced by plastic ones that are manufactured by machines in faraway places. Some sticks have metal shafts and synthetic netting, and there is nothing natural that tells us about discipline, relationship, or values. There are still a few people who make lacrosse sticks by hand, but they cannot be used in professional or amateur lacrosse.

The rules also keep changing, which changes the whole game of lacrosse. Our game was traditionally played between Native nations, and those who were Seneca, Onondaga, Cayuga, Oneida, Tuscarora, and Mohawk played for their nations. Today, players can be bought, traded, and retraded to other teams. Players become a commodity or slave. Is that not a form of human trafficking? This practice of creating hierarchies of people – blue-collar, white-collar, poor, rich – is something that colonial settlers brought with them from the ship.

I have been asked to talk to the Liberal Party of Canada three times about the history of colonialism and our culture. Each time, I have been limited to twenty minutes, so I have educated them the best that I can in the time given by starting with the Thanksgiving Address. I then talk about all the issues around racism, resource extraction, and how people always want to dig for more – how they are never satisfied with what they have and always search for something more. I say, "I think you are looking for your belly button." They seem stunned by what I am saying, although some have come up afterward to ask me what I mean by that. From my teachings, it seems that they are looking for that navel part of the umbilical cord because no one took care to bury it, and so they are always searching, like a hungry ghost. The ceremony of their birth was not closed.

Whether it be in the game of lacrosse given to us by Shogwaeyadisho', in the ceremony for a loved one going to the spirit world, or in the burying of an umbilical cord, I am looking for value, relationship, connectedness, grounding, purpose, healing, and medicine. Everything is connected, and these are teachings about how to heal ourselves, how to listen to ourselves, how to honour ourselves, and how to create relationships. There are always interruptions that take us away from the realities of life. Our individuality has value as we come to know and work on ourselves, building on our strengths and weaknesses. The whole process is about nurturing our individual *ganigǫhi:yo* (good mind) so that we can come together to create peace, *odaotra* (friendship), harmony, and balance on the river of life.

Daneto n'agahtgwe nih. (That is all for now.)

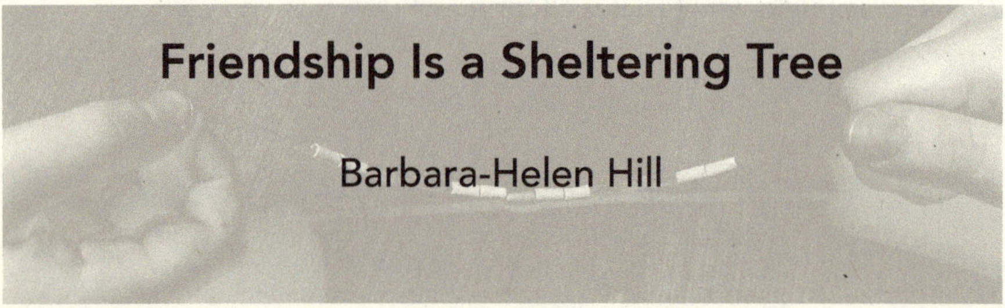

Friendship Is a Sheltering Tree

Barbara-Helen Hill

At the time of this writing, we are in lockdown because of the worldwide Covid-19 pandemic. Many countries are shutting down, and Canada is doing the same. We are not able to do all the things that we used to do. We are not travelling as much. We are not eating out at restaurants or going out to shows and sports games. For many, this isolation and slowing down seem ludicrous, unthinkable. But for others like myself, I see health returning. The air has become clearer. The waters are flowing cleaner. Animals and birds are feeling safer, I am sure.

The earth and all our relations can recover from the damage done to them. Nature knows how to heal, how to make things better for all the beings of the Ganǫhǫnyǫhk (Thanksgiving Address), including us as well. Gae Ho Hwako (Norma Jacobs) reminds us of the friendship that nature teaches us – like the trees that hold space for us, creating the air that gives us the oxygen that we need for our lives. This oxygen is given even though the greed of some humans causes them to take those trees. And with fewer trees, the air becomes more polluted, and the diseases in our lungs become more prevalent. It is so true, as Samuel Taylor Coleridge wrote in *Youth and Age* (1823), that "Friendship is a sheltering tree," a view expressed in the profound teachings shared with us by Gae Ho Hwako.

If we make friends and have friends to support us, and if we in turn support them, we are imitating the natural world, E tinoha ongwesidage'dra gwe' (Mother Earth). Gae Ho Hwako introduces us to our mother, the one who "nurtures all of life – the trees, shrubs, grasses, medicines, hanging fruits, flowers, edible plants, fresh seasonal foods, and nuts – all that gives sustenance to restore and rebuild our bodies. Life is sustained by the two-legged humans, the winged ones, and the four-legged animals, all of whom are nurtured and sustained by the water, the blood of our mother." She talks about friendships between the plants, animals, two-legged humans, and the spirits that are unseen, those I choose to call faeries, gnomes, and elves because I do not have the Mohawk language. All those connections were in place long before the invasion of the people from across the waters and the rejection of the Two Row Wampum's offer of friendship.

I was brought to tears as I read what Gae Ho Hwako wrote about the death of her very special *okya tsi* (friend), a close confidant who walked with her, listened without judgment, and supported, encouraged, and empowered her. Although it is softer and easier to say that "her friend passed away," which sounds gentler, the harsh reality is that her friend died. I know how hard it was for her. We need to understand that the connection of *og ya:dao* (friendship) is not broken with death. Their friendship did not die when her friend died. It lives on because of the love and the memories that she has of her friend. It takes a long time to grieve for anyone who passes on, but it is especially difficult when it is a special friend who dies.

When Gae Ho Hwako talks of special friends, she does not mean only humans; we can also have animal or natural friends. Some people grieve losing a dog, cat, or any other pet. We had a workhorse when I was a child, and my dad had to shoot it because it broke its leg. We all cried, especially our father. Our cousins were sad for a while when we learned that the peony bushes that our grandmother had planted were dug up and moved. We could no longer get a cutting of the plant to have in our own gardens.

I especially grieve the loss of so many sheltering trees. Where I see a living, green, special friend, many others see something that stands in the way of progress. They cut the trees to pave the land and make a parking lot, parking garage, or building site. And then there was the time that a man went along the fence line on a public road and cut a row of walnut trees. That person was an official of city council, and what he saw was an opportunity to make good money selling the trees for the walnut lumber – for expensive walnut boards. The really sad part, what made me angry, was that there was no road construction; there was no need to remove the trees along that road except for his greed.

Friendships and relationships of all kinds need to be honoured and encouraged from childhood. I did not grow up with the teachings that Gae Ho Hwako talks about. I was between the church and the Longhouse people. I came from the mixed family of a Haudenosaunee father and a British Isles mother. There were gifts from both sides, but I was not able to see that until I was much older. I never saw the British Isles side. I thought of myself as an "Indian" because I grew up on a reserve. I never saw a difference between me and the boys and girls at our school or in our neighbourhood. I was welcomed into the homes of my Indian friends. Later on, as I got older, I began to see how people were treated. It was when I went away to work that I really began to see the prejudices of the white people against the Indians.

If I could make a wish, it would be that the teachings given by Gae Ho Hwako about the Two Row Wampum and the honouring of friendships be taught all over the world no matter the language. If all children grew up into adulthood with an education for reflecting on these kinds of teachings, they would in turn share them with their children. I believe that we need something like this if we are going to reduce bullying in our schools, domestic violence in our homes, and racism on our lands. Right now, it brings tears to my eyes that there is so much negativism and violence in the world. I see and hear so many stories of abuses of all kinds, of children who are battered and abused. I want to stand up to those who do these things and ask, "What kind of world do you need us to live in?"

Truth and reconciliation can be thought of as something between the Canadian government and Native people across Canada, but really it should also be about each and every one of us. We all need to look inside and ask ourselves whether we are at peace and whether we can extend that sheltering peace to everyone we meet. That is what I have learned from Gae Ho Hwako.

After years of working away from Six Nations, I came back and was fortunate to reconnect with Gae Ho Hwako and her special friend who has since died. They were telling people about our stories, ceremonies, lessons, and teachings. Later, Gae Ho Hwako became an Elder-in-Residence at Wilfrid

Laurier University. What a blessing that must have been for the staff and students who were able to attend her classes with an open mind. Gae Ho Hwako would become a mentor to some, a friend to others, and even a grandma to a few.

But through it all, the spirit embodied by Gae Ho Hwako has never changed. I remember her telling me about unwrapping the bundle of one of the teachings for a ceremony. She explained in detail something about a ceremony that I had participated in over the years where I had lived in a marriage with a Seneca man. I had never been taught what happened in this ceremony or what it meant because I did not have the language. Gae Ho Hwako unwrapped that bundle just as gently as a breeze dancing through the summer flowers that we both enjoy, and when she was finished, she wrapped up that bundle again.

Elsewhere, I have written, "Hearing from the Creator is just as easy as listening. With no TV, radio, books, people to distract, in a quiet room we can listen to the stillness. Listening to the small voice, letting the subconscious thoughts come through. One needs to ask the smart, intellectual, self to take a vacation. It will not die. One needs opportunity to take some time to talk with the Creator and spirit guides. Then invite the smart intellectual self back. The brain can use the rest. It has worked hard to keep the body alive and well through many traumas."[1]

Reading Gae Ho Hwako's teachings about E tinoha ongwesidage'dra gwe' and the medicines, I kept thinking of the little people in our traditions that I call faeries, gnomes, and elves. I believe in them. They are there to take care of the natural world, and we should be there to help them. They are part of the myths and stories of other countries and nations as well as here. I used to listen to radio stories as a child; yep, no television until I was older. One of the stories I remember was told by Fibber Magee about his wife, Molly. She came home and started to tell him about the things that people were saying in their neighbourhood. He stopped her and said that he did not like hearing all that gossip. He told her that gossip was harmful and could hurt. She, of course, asked what he meant. And so he began,

> Once the whole country was covered with green faeries. They lived in their little houses next to the big houses where the people lived. The people invited them over and served coffee and donuts. The faeries

invited people over and served mushrooms and dew drops. One day, a man was watching a faery walk by, and he walked in front of a green bush, and the man couldn't see him anymore. He rushed home and told his wife that he had seen a faery walking and that it had disappeared right in front of his eyes. He said, "Don't tell anyone what I just told you." Well, she told her friend, and then that woman told her friend, and then she told her friend, and then she told somebody else. Pretty soon, the rumour got around that the faeries were disappearing all over the place. Finally, the rumour got so big that people said all the faeries had disappeared and there weren't any more faeries. That is why nobody can see them anymore, although the faeries are still around today.

That was from the *Fibber McGee and Molly* show in 1952. Now, I do not have that good of a memory, but I just heard it again on Sirius XM Radio as I was driving a few months back. This story of the green faeries disappearing was an example of gossip and how it took away from our beautiful natural world. Gossip is like a damaging fungus. It can travel and glom onto anything and eat away at the foundation of things. That loving world of green faeries and other elementals helping the earth is not any different from the loving relationship that can be found between people, men and women, women and women, men and men, or parents and children. Gossip, nasty innuendos, and jealousy can eat away at a friendship and other relationships.

I have written, "The Two Row Wampum Belt is a contract … our written record of the treaty between two peoples, two governments, two distinct nations … The Europeans would not interfere with ours and we would not interfere with theirs … I see the Two Row Wampum also used when describing a relationship, any relationship, not just between two governing bodies. The relationship between husband and wife, friend and neighbour, etc. It is not that I have my laws and you have yours, but we both have our own individual choices. We have our own truths, and we both follow the laws of the Creator."[2]

I see the Two Row Wampum as a contract or treaty between two nations, but it is more generally about relationships, friendships, family relations, and marriages. As Gae Ho Hwako teaches, it is not just between two governing bodies. Any friendship, any good relationship, is about respecting boundaries.

Gae Ho Hwako writes, "We have long forgotten about *ǫ da gaho dę:s* (the sacred meeting space) between the rows of the Kaswen:ta (Two Row) Wampum, where we get information and where we communicate, acknowledge, and validate what we each bring into relationship across the river of life." She says that the Two Row instructs us to travel down these waters together without interfering with the other, and she tells us that if we choose to straddle the space between the ship and the canoe, it will bring difficulties. We are taught that if we do that, there will come a time in our life when it will be difficult to maintain a clear mind about where we want to belong, especially when a big storm arises and disturbs the waters that we are journeying on. If you have one foot in the canoe and one on the ship, when the water gets rough, you will have to decide about where you stand.

I do not like attributing all the negativity in our lives to the residential schools, as there has been so much more involved. I think about the Indian Act, passed without any consultation or consent from the Native peoples. The original version of the Indian Act came into effect in 1876 under a government that believed that the Indians had no special rights as the original occupants of the land. The government thought that the original inhabitants should be eliminated as distinct peoples and assimilated as soon as possible into the mainstream of Canadian society. Because of that plan, we now have people unable to stay in the canoe, as it is all muddled up. I cannot operate strictly from a place within the traditional Longhouse and the canoe and at the same time be respectful to myself and others, as I come from a mixed family. I am a Mohawk, but like my sister tells me, I do not look like a Mohawk; I look like the Scots-Irish-English of my mother's people. Yes, we even have a clan, but it is not recognized by Indian Affairs or by the Government of Canada, and it certainly is not recognized by the people where I come from. These divisions have made it difficult to operate in our home world, or maybe I should say that we are in the world that divides and conquers, but we are not of that world.

Until I read Gae Ho Hwako's piece about *ǫ da gaho dę:s*, I had paid attention only to what was said about the two strips of purple on the white background of the Two Row Wampum and about the treaty between the canoe and ship that they represented. It was not until Gae Ho Hwako reminded me with her writing that I thought of the sacred space between those two purple strips, where we come to agree on the boundaries and the idea of noninterference that will guide our relations. This sacred space is also present between people. In other words, we can try to help and to shelter others, but there is a time when we recognize that people are on their own path, and we let go. That is part of friendship.

I have learned to do that, letting people walk their own path. For a long time, I struggled with that because I came from a background of helping or trying to help others. I was talking with Gae Ho Hwako one evening, and she asked a question. I gave her my answer, and we finished our conversation. I did not hear from her for a few months, and I did not know whether I had offended her or what was going on. I just kept living my life, and when I thought of her, I kept getting the message not to call or send a text. Some weeks later, I heard from her. She had lost her phone. We met and continued on as if we had not lost contact. Friends.

I had to keep praying for her wellness, but she had no idea that I was doing it. It was not just her I was praying for, as the space was also healing my anxiety about not being able to speak with her, to help her if she needed my help. The love that she speaks of in relation to friendship is real and true love. She tells me, "That dark and handsome man we laugh about is old and grey or bald now, and I'm too tired." The friendship and love that we focus on now are for everyone.

I truly wish that everyone in the world had been raised with these Two Row teachings that we have been given by Gae Ho Hwako. Really connecting with this spirit of friendship would do a lot to heal the world. We need to teach children about the responsibilities of being a friend, about the boundaries or the space between the two rows of purple beads, and about the sacred space between themselves and their friends and relatives. If we taught these things to each person, then we would not have to worry about how our children are going to be treated when they go out into the world of education. We would not need to make children responsible for their own safety regarding good touch and bad touch. This should not even be an issue in the world. Adults raised to know and live the boundaries and the sacred space of the Two Row Wampum would treat each other with respect and, in turn, teach this respect to children.

It was back in 1991 that I first heard about "noninterference," and I did not understand what the person was talking about. But reflecting on Gae Ho

Hwako's teaching, I have come to understand it differently. It does not mean that we throw the people away or set them out to struggle alone. Look at some of the people who have wanted to straighten out their lives, those suffering from confusion, fear, abuse, and addiction, and how they have been painted with a negative brush. The noninterference that I have come to understand from Gae Ho Hwako requires that we teach our children about good boundaries, right from wrong, and that we encourage and love them, and if they stray, we must try to lead them back to the right way. If they choose the other path, then we just have to love them and let them go. We just have to wait to welcome them back when they choose to come back on their own. When they do ask for help, we should not turn them away. We should welcome them home.

The Two Row Wampum is a guide for people, nations, and countries to be in a relationship that fosters friendship. Somewhere its messages became corrupted, changing so that men and women think that they cannot have a friendship with the opposite sex. I do believe that such a friendship is possible, but people from the outside looking in at these relationships often judge based on their own teachings and experiences. Because of the experiences in residential schools and the distortion created by the Christian churches and Canadian governments, people do not feel safe in having a true friendship. Gossip comes in and makes it feel dirty.

Gae Ho Hwako spoke of her friendship with a male after her marriage ended. She spoke of the support that the male friend gave her when her own partner was unable to honour the boundaries of their sacred space. I had a friendship with a man when I moved back to my home territory of Six Nations after being away for years. We spoke often and went to dinner occasionally. He then brought his new family here, and our friendship disappeared. I believe that there was jealousy in his marriage. Many years ago, I was taught that jealousy happens when people think that their partner is doing the same things with another person as their partner does with them. My friend and I had nothing more than a platonic friendship, which I was sad to see end.

Friendships between males and females grow stronger over time and can be very supportive to each person. Women and girls need male energy, and men and boys need female energy – the good, healthy energy. When we do not have relatives like fathers and uncles, then male friends can be important to us. Young men and boys also need the friendship of their aunties, grandmothers, and female friends. There is sacred energy in those friendships that should not be distorted with lies and gossip.

In the ceremonies in the Longhouse that Gae Ho Hwako describes, there are two sides. The speaker from one side stands and gives his oration, and the other speaker from across the floor stands and says, "This is what I heard you say. Am I hearing you correctly?" This practice was also agreed upon with the Two Row Wampum so that the people in the canoe and those on the ship could travel side by side down the river of life without either one interfering in the ways of the other. Friends need to be clear in order to maintain the spirit of this kind of friendship. Not speaking the same language can make doing that difficult. But we have the ability to speak to each other and to clarify the meaning of what we each say so that there are no misunderstandings or hard feelings. That is what Gae Ho Hwako describes as *ganigǫhi:yo* (a good mind), which is what keeps a friendship strong.

We both speak English or our idea of English, but being raised in different families, we sometimes misunderstand each other. Gae Ho Hwako and I have been friends for many years, but we have travelled different roads. When I moved back here to my community, I started to learn more from her. She reminds me often with her teachings, and it is done with love and laughter. Our friendship is like a sheltering tree.

❁ ❁

What I have found in writing this chapter is that I do not know how to describe friendship. It is a word about relationships, it is about emotions, and it is about loss. I found that I was taking friendships very seriously. Two great friends died, and I took that loss very hard. I have a few friends who are living far away, and I do not get to see them very often. The people whom I thought were friends are really just acquaintances. Friends are concerned for each other but not to the point of living each other's lives. We help each other out by listening to them when they need to talk, but they also have to listen to us; it is reciprocal. Friends are not therapists, even though we share, we listen, and we support.

Sometimes, there is a parting of the ways. We physically move somewhere else, or we recognize that we have different paths. What do I mean by different paths? Our interests change, our families change, or there are times when a partner dies or there is divorce. I have heard from one friend how things changed drastically for her when her husband died. They used to go out as a couple and attend dinners, dances, and other celebrations with couples. When her husband died, she said that these friends stopped asking her to go out with them. It finally occurred to her that she was seen as a threat to the married couples. I thought, *How sad.* They must not have been very secure in their marriages because I know that my friend and her husband had a very secure and loving marriage. She has many male friends, and her husband had female friends. But at the end of the day, they most importantly had each other.

Friends often have a common interest that brings them together, like gardening, sewing, cooking, woodworking, and arts of many kinds. Often friendships are made from attending the Longhouse, or churches, or language classes. Gae Ho Hwako had a great friend who went to the Longhouse and spoke the language, and from this common interest, they together taught about their culture, stories, and ceremonies. That friend passed away a couple of years ago. It was a great blow to her. Even though I was there for her as a friend, I cannot take that woman's place, nor should I, and Gae Ho Hwako would not want me to.

Friendships are often closer than the relationships that we have with our own sisters and brothers, our family. Friends do not intentionally hurt each other. Sometimes, we may say something that hurts the other person, but it is not intentional. Gae Ho Hwako told us of the two speakers in the Longhouse and how the second one seeks confirmation that he has correctly heard what the first one has said. This goes back and forth until all is clear between the two sides, and then they move on. I think that this is the spirit in which friendships need to operate. We must understand what is said, and if we do not understand, we must ask for clarification.

Friendship is sacred. It is something that you grow together out of commonality. A true friendship is built on caring for each other, sharing your likes and dislikes, learning together about your unique gifts, and being honest. Friendship forms a circle of love that shelters you in this life.

Teachings from Spruce: The Nature of Prisons

Giselle Dias

In the spring of 2019, I tore my Achilles tendon and was unable to go outside for a month. During that time, I began nurturing a relationship with a spruce tree just outside my window. For nine months, I had been living within fifteen feet of this tree but had never taken the time to get to know them.[1] As I took the time with Spruce, they reminded me that "we are always on the land" and in relationship with the land even when we feel disconnected because of the concrete that separates us.[2] Gae Ho Hwako (Norma Jacobs) reminds us that E tinoha ongwesidage'dra gwe' (Mother Earth)[3] "teaches us about values, boundaries, forgiveness, encouragement, patience, love, laughter, strength, and *awehaode'* (soft, kind, nurturing words)." This new learning about how I am always in relationship to land, and about what land teaches us, has led me to deepen my reflections on twenty-five years of prisoners' rights work. My kind, embracing relation with Spruce was calling me to look more closely at the relationship between prisons and the many ways that they uproot our relations with creation. Their concrete walls, bars, and surveillance systems epitomize colonial ways of being that, as Gae Ho Hwako teaches, have consistently broken the boundaries of good relations that were supposed to be honoured by adhering to the principles of the Two Row Wampum. But the way that Spruce called me to this reflection was through my friendship with Peter Collins, one of my dearest friends, who died in a federal prison in 2015.

When I began to contemplate the relationship between prisons and land, Anishinabek Elder Tina Armstrong told me that I *am* the land. My spirit is fire, my body is earth, my blood is water, and my breath is air. This knowledge shapes some of the ways that I understand the relationship between the land and prisons. When I use the word "land," I am referring to the earth, sky, sun, and moon, to wind, water, trees, and rocks, to animals, crawlers, ancestors, and all other spirit beings. In the Haudenosaunee traditions of Gae Ho Hwako, these relations are honoured in the recitation and teachings of the Ganǫhǫnyǫhk (Thanksgiving Address) that opened this book. As my relationship with creation deepens, it shapes how I think and leads me to wonder what the land under and around the prison is saying. Does the soil beneath the prison know what is happening to the people in the cages above? In some ways, these questions cannot be answered concretely, but I can draw upon the wisdom of what I am learning from teachers like Spruce and my lodge of life – my body.

My lodge of life and my spirit have encountered the penal system in many ways over the past two decades. Some moments were in confrontations with the police as I tried to hold my body strong and to find strength in my voice during protests, demonstrations, or vigils. My lodge of life has held the tension of visiting prisoners in solitary confinement and walking down long corridors with steel doors locking and slamming behind me. My lodge of life has felt the tension of assisting prisoners at parole hearings and facing the victims of their crimes. I have had parole assessments done at my home and have felt the invasiveness of parole officers asking me deeply personal questions while they attempt to interrogate my character. I have spent nights in private family visits while watching a friend die of cancer. Each of these experiences of the criminal justice system influenced my spirit in different ways. Spruce helped me to deepen my understanding of my relationship to my lodge of life, to creation, and to other people while engaged in prisoners' rights work.

Going into prisons created a disconnection from creation and from my lodge of life. This disconnection has made my healing journey from prison work long and complicated. It was my time with Spruce that taught me about connection, reciprocity, healing, and friendship. The relationship helped me to consider how the disconnection from creation affected me, how it must affect prisoners, and how it affects anyone entering a carceral institution. At the same time, Gae Ho Hwako's teaching on *geihnyenoh de yo ki ye'nya dohn* (spiritual helpers) and Shogwaeyadisho' (the Creator) explains, "Every aspect of this land is healing and cleansing, and we are on this human journey to understand our relationship, interconnectedness, and *okyadaot* (friendship as a supportive medicine)." So how do I reconcile that the land on which prisons are built can be healing? How do we heal land – *our bodies and the land* – at sites of ongoing colonial violence?

Spruce and I stayed together in this tension while I tried to reconcile my heart, mind, body, and spirit to these seeming contradictions. This tree in my front yard seemed to be soothing and healing me in the spirit of *awehaode'* as Spruce called me to ground myself and, by doing that, to open up to other understandings on my prison work. Gae Ho Hwako seems to talk about this kind of relationship with trees when she states, "If this energy [of peace and friendship] can pass between two people, it certainly can also pass between those trees and the people. The trees begin to shape how we behave – how we respect and honour one another."

Just like with Spruce, my roots travel through the earth to ground me, yet my roots also take me across oceans and land that stretch into the four directions. My ancestors travelled from India, the Seychelle Islands, Kenya, Ireland, England, and across Turtle Island to settle in Treaty 3 Territory. My maternal grandfather, who was Métis and came from Cree and Salteaux people, settled in the Red River area. My second mother, who raised me, is Oneida and Scottish. The knowledge that I share here has been informed by my family's stories, my life experiences, my relationships, and my work with prisoners. The reflections and knowledge that I am sharing have been gained through my relationships with Spruce, Peter, and others – relations that were rooted in the value of friendship.

Prisons as Sites of Disconnection

As I drive down Highway 33, I am taken by the beauty of the winding road and the view of Lake Ontario to my left. The water is calm, and the colour is a mixture of light and dark blue. The sun is shining and makes the lake sparkle. The beauty of creation is easing my churning stomach. After a twenty-minute drive from Katarokwi (Kingston), I arrive at the long driveway that will take me to the prison. Just past the sign for Correctional Service Canada (CSC) is a lush forest, and to the right is a long stretch of green lawn.

Sometimes when I drive up the small hill, there are deer eating grass. In Anishinaabe teachings, the deer represents gentleness, kindness, and reciprocity. The deer gave its life to the Anishinaabe people so that they could have food, clothing, and materials to make drums – the heartbeat of Mother Earth. When I see a deer, I think about how to be kind and gentle to myself and others. The deer makes me feel quiet, reflective, and grateful for this life. Anishinabek Elder Awnjibenayseekwe (Banakonda Kennedy-Kish Bell) speaks to the teaching of kindness within the four foundational principles of Indigenous traditional practice.[4] She describes the principle of kindness as foundational to a wholistic[5] approach that has the intention of promoting balance and harmony: "It is not possible to engage wellness without kindness; we cannot even be respectful without kindness. Nurturing kindness is a living, breathing challenge to employ. We have to see it to be able to reach for it, experience it, express it, to be able to know and understand it."[6] Kindness is rarely found within prisons. My momentary meeting with the deer grounds me and reminds me of the generosity of creation.

Driving up the lane, I get a glimpse of the prison, and my stomach lurches. I feel sick. I never know what I am going to encounter with the guards when I walk through the prison gates, and the constant surveillance is always unnerving. I am entering the panopticon, an architectural structure designed with the intention of exercising complete power and control over prisoners, who are under constant surveillance, always visible: "He is seen, but he does not see; he is the object of information, never the subject of communication."[7] Stepping into the prison, I can feel the guards' watchful gaze. I am being watched with suspicion, and I notice that my breath becomes shallow and that my anxiety starts to rise.

Awnjibenayseekwe reminds me,

Breath is life.
Breath feeds my spirit.
Take a deep breath.[8]

The air in prison is often stagnant, and the flow of air is cut off by windows and doors that do not open freely. Spruce teaches me about breath, as their medicine is used for respiratory sickness and helps to clear the lungs. In these moments, I must remember to breathe.

As I continue my drive, the barbed-wire fence comes into view, and I can see the CSC van circling the perimeter of the fence. I park in the visitors' lot, knowing that I will not be back at my car for six days. I slowly walk up to the gate with my overnight bag and wait. I hear a hollow voice over the intercom asking me what I am doing there. I explain that I am coming in for a private family visit (PFV).[9]

Buzzzzzz.

Click.

This is my cue to push open the gated door and walk in. I stand between two barbed-wire fences waiting for the door behind me to close before the second gate slides open to the left. I walk through the second gate, walk thirty feet, and open the door to the administration building. I wait for the front door to close and the second door to open. I sign the visitors' log and slide my identification under the slot of a tinted window, where I can see a distracted guard talking to someone else. I wait. She looks at me uninterestedly and takes a quick look at my identification before pushing it back under the slot and telling me to wait off to the side. As I look out the window, I can see the barbed-wire fences surrounding us.

As I retell this story now, Spruce grounds me. I look outside my front window, and there are no barbed-wire fences. There is nothing to make me feel like I am disconnected from creation.

Continuing into the bowels of the prison, I go through a series of humiliations before I am processed and allowed to visit my friend. First, they go through my bags, pull out items, and hold them up for everyone in the waiting room to see. They ask me about my medications, and they go through my toiletries. After they have done a preliminary search of my belongings, they ask me to step forward so that they can take a swab of my identification to see if there are any traces of drugs. The guard puts on rubber gloves, wipes my identification with a small piece of cloth, and puts it into the ion scanner,[10] I am holding my breath and hoping that I have washed my identification carefully enough that nothing shows up. The ion scanner is an arbitrary and unreliable test, but CSC continues to use it to determine whether someone might be bringing in drugs. I pass the test and let out my breath.

Next, I walk through the metal detector. It has not been working effectively for years, so they wave a handheld metal detector over my body to make sure that I am not bringing in any contraband.[11] Again, I pass the test.

I am asked to leave my belongings, and I wait for Peter's family to be processed in the same way. They have been doing this since Peter was incarcerated thirty-three years ago. By some miracle, we all make it through without incident and walk to the visiting area in the building next door. Here, we stand an arm's length apart.

Waiting here, the memory of the water, deer, lush forest, and fresh air disappears. All that remains in this moment is the panopticon. I become self-conscious and anxious thinking about the eyes of the people I cannot see who are watching me. This experience changes my breathing, hardens my heart, and consumes my mind. My spirit feels violated, and I am only a visitor. This entrance into the prison has disconnected me from my lodge of life and from the beauty of creation that I was experiencing before I arrived at the prison.

Ten minutes later, the drug dog appears and is instructed to sniff and circle us to make sure that we are not hiding drugs somewhere in or on our bodies. After a minute, the dog leaves and we wait until the guards and dogs have done a more thorough search of our belongings. Eventually, we are escorted to a two-bedroom trailer. The guards leave, and the trailer door shuts. I take my first deep breath in over an hour.

Over the past two decades, I have come to see that prisons continuously perpetuate conditions that separate prisoners from relationships to themselves, their families, and creation. Colonization through measures such as reserves, the Indian Act, residential schools, the Sixties Scoop, and the Millennial Scoop have disrupted Indigenous people's relationship to land. However, prisons provide a very distinct separation. Within the federal and provincial prison systems, security levels – high, medium, and low – determine how much access prisoners have to the outdoors. Due to colonialism and racism, Indigenous people are incarcerated at higher rates than non-Indigenous people and are held in prison longer,[12] which results in less access to the outdoors. The prison that I am visiting provides opportunities to go outside; however, there are prisons where people have not seen the sky or touched a blade of grass for years.

Earlier on in his sentence, Peter was in solitary confinement, and his short visits outside consisted of being in an outdoor cage. From this confined position, he describes the "yard" as "a small asphalt enclosure with high concrete walls. The sun never shines into the 'yard,' but if you look up, past the chain link fence and razor wire that spans wall to wall like a porous steel roof, you can see the sky, maybe a cloud or two, and occasionally you might even see a bird fly by."[13]

Something about Peter's description makes me think of Potawatomi scholar Robin Wall Kimmerer's reflections on "species loneliness," a term coined by philosophers to describe a state of "deep, unnamed sadness stemming from estrangement from the rest of Creation, from the loss of relationship."[14]

It is clear that prisoners suffer from loss of relationships to loved ones and their communities, but what about their relationship to creation?

Throughout Peter's years in prisons, other prisoners often brought injured or parentless birds for him to take care of, including sparrows, seagulls, killdeers, and songbirds. He spoke about the "challenge and pleasure of helping a disadvantaged bird to find the sky again" as one of the most rewarding experiences for him.[15] I know that this connection to creation renewed his spirit at some of the hardest points in his sentence. I never had the chance to tell Peter about my relationship with Spruce, but I know that he would have appreciated it. I started to learn the names of birds when they took shelter in Spruce, and Peter would have asked me to send him photographs so that he could paint them for me. He was a gifted artist and often painted scenes of animals and nature, which he hung around his prison cell.

In the poem "Four Seasons of Prison," T.A. Glaremin, a former prisoner of Prison for Women,[16] provides what Deena Rymhs describes as a "reflection on removal from the natural rhythms of day and night and the cycles of the seasons. The women experience the seasons only indirectly; the spring 'rains that echo from the concrete' are faint reminders of the innocence and renewal of these cycles once signalled (8). Winter brings the 'voices of dead sisters' (6); autumn leaves the women 'deadened to the long winter ahead' (12). Even summer, the most revitalized of all the seasons, takes on destructive dimensions that reflect the extent of the inmates' deprivation: 'When summer comes, we burn our bodies – nude in the sun – in the prison yard, / hoping to die by nature, than by our own hands' (10–11)."[17]

Changes of the seasons are such an important time in many Indigenous cultures and traditions. The seasons represent times of rebirth and renewal as well as death and dying. In nature, with death comes renewal. It is evidenced in everything around us, from dead trees with moss growing on them to the composting of fallen leaves that feed the earth. In prison, there is very little renewal, and when death comes, it is felt by everyone. Over the past ten years, Indigenous people have made up 39 per cent of all suicide attempts.[18] It makes me ask, "What is it about prisons that is particularly difficult for Indigenous people? Is it the separation from kinship and creation that is felt so deeply?"

Gae Ho Hwako reminds us that "life changes and moves us forward." It is the same with the seasons. Spending time with Spruce over the past year, I have come to see that spruce trees are subtle in their changes throughout the season. They do not change their colours in fall or lose all of their needles, although more needles fall to the ground prior to the winter season. Spruce trees' pine needles drop throughout the year and create an almost barren environment beneath their canopy. However, even in that perceived barrenness, the squirrels, birds, and crawlers seek out shelter or find food. Spring feels like the time of most obvious transformation for spruce trees, when new growth develops and their pinecones arrive in abundance.

By summer the sap has started to seep out of Spruce's trunk, and by fall I am finding pine needles stuck to my car. It can create a tense relationship with Spruce, as sap sticks to my car like glue. This seemingly small tension in my relationship with creation opens me up to see how easy it is to want to control nature for personal reasons. The sap once used as medicine is now a source of frustration to me regarding my "property." It is humbling to see how caught up I can get in this war with nature. When I hear my thoughts wanting to cut down the branches, I am surprised by my reaction. I start to feel guilty and think about the Anishinaabe teaching about all our relations. "'All my relations,' means all … [I]t's meant as recognition of the principles of harmony, unity and equality."[19] Spruce, their sap, their pine needs, and I are all related. I have no right to try to control nature. As I go deeper into this thinking, I remember hearing that the sap from spruce trees was used for canoes and that Gae Ho Hwako's name means "ancestral females holding the canoe before me." The sap that is flowing through Spruce makes me reflect on the teachings of Elders who are the glue of our culture, our connectivity to creation; that is what the sap symbolizes. The sap is strong, and every time I touch the tree to offer my thanksgiving, I smell the fragrant scent and feel the sticky residue on my hand. It always brings a smile to my face.

Connection to Creation in Prison

As I sit with Spruce, I reflect on my last visit with Peter.

I remember how the guards escorted us to the PFV trailer.[20] I can see Peter being pushed up to the trailer in his new wheelchair. His bladder cancer has progressed, and the weight loss and pain have taken a toll. I can see it in the expression on his face. We all greet him and tell him about our experiences coming into the prison. He hates that we have to go through those humiliations. Peter is tired and has to lie down. His sister and I go outside to steady our nerves after the stress of coming into the prison and seeing the deterioration in Peter's health.

It is a sunny day, and the warmth feels good on my face. I start to look around and see that we are locked in a small yard with a ten-foot fence surrounding us. Beyond this fence, there are two higher and longer barbed-wire fences surrounding the prison. My mind reorients myself to remind me where I am. It is not that I have forgotten, but the desire to get away from the guards and to get into the PFV means that I have not looked around much.

As we sit outside, we are visited by a squirrel and a chipmunk looking for food. They are not afraid of us, so it is clear that other people in the PFVs have fed them before. A sparrow flies on to the fence and then disappears quickly, followed by a songbird. I am struck by the many birds that come to the fence to say hello. I can see why Peter has painted so many birds over the years. They are so beautiful and delicate. For just a minute, their chirps and songs bring us into connection with creation, and it is easy to dismiss the barbed-wire fences. This reconnection with creation provides some relief from the tension of our entrance into the prison, and I feel my breath return more fully.

Gae Ho Hwako's words about E tinoha ongwesidage'dra gwe' come to mind: "We never go without the nurturance of her love, which is our very existence." But the healing potential of friendship is exactly what the prison and colonial institutions attempt to violently disconnect us from in a host of ways. During my visit to the prison, Peter finds no relief outside. When he is outside, he is made acutely aware of his confinement by the view of the barbed-wire fences all around. He wants this visit to happen beyond the fences, not inside them. For the duration of our visit, he goes outside only when he has to go to the healthcare unit to get his medication.

Original Instructions

When I finish writing about my time at the prison for the private family visit, I can feel the tension in my body. I go outside to the spruce tree and put my *sema* (tobacco) down. I have learned that Spruce can ground me, and in turn I pray for its well-being. I am grateful for Spruce and the calming presence they offer. Kimmerer reminds us that "cultures of gratitude must also be cultures of reciprocity."[21] As Gae Ho Hwako's Thanksgiving Address invokes, all living beings are interconnected and interdependent, and therefore we have a responsibility to be in a reciprocal relationship. Kimmerer states, "Just as all beings have a duty to me, I have a duty to them."[22] With this way of being in the world, I am acutely aware of the friendships and teachers all around me.

I recently heard Onaubinisay (James Dumont), the Eastern Door Chief of the Midewiwin Lodge, share the Anishinaabe creation story. The story tells us that humans were the last beings put on earth. People rely on everything, and nothing relies on us. Creation lived in harmony before we arrived, and it taught us what we needed to do in order to maintain this balance. Spruce has taught me that we maintain this balance through relationship, reciprocity, and thanksgiving. As Kimmerer says, "We have been given the duty to live in balance and harmony with each other and all living things. So now let us bring our minds together as one as we give greetings and thanks to each other as People. Now our minds are one."[23] Spruce has become one of my greatest teachers and has helped me to become more open to so many other teachers, including the stone people, the plant medicines, and the animal beings.

I have learned that each being in creation has its own name and song and that if you listen closely enough, you will hear it whisper to you. One day, Spruce told me that their name means, "she who provides shelter." This name was later confirmed by Mary Siisip Geniusz, an Anishinaabe writer, who tells a story of a *bineshiinh* (bird) who is seeking shelter in the winter. The *bineshiinh* has been injured and is separated from his family. Winter is coming on quickly, so the *bineshiinh* goes to several trees to seek shelter, but no tree will help. It is the spruce tree that finally offers to provide shelter, the white pine that offers to block the winds, and the cedar that offers cones for food. As a reward for the kindness of the conifers, the Creator will not allow *giiwedin* (the wind) to take their leaves, and so today the conifers are the only trees that remain full all year round.[24] I am still struck by how Spruce told me the meaning of their name and by how this meaning was later confirmed by this teaching of Geniusz.

As I sat in the prison yard, the birds were one of the only beings able to weave in and out of the barbed-wire fences, bringing their song and beauty. In the Anishinaabe creation story told by Onaubinisay, the birds carried the seeds of new life. My spirit tells me that Peter's relationship with birds and his paintings of birds brought new life into the world. Peter painted birds to tell a story of creation, friendship, and hope without using words. Despite the way that the prison isolated him from human contact, Peter's connection to creation remained strong. His paintings of wildlife covered his prison cell walls to remind him of life outside of prison. The concrete and barbed wire that surrounded him could not contain his spirit.

As I spent time with Spruce over the spring, I came to see how they sheltered and provided for so many beings, including sparrows, yellow warblers, robins, and even a northern flicker. Spruce trees can be used for lean-tos because the boughs are good protection from the elements. Sitting with Spruce, I am humbled by the gifts that they offer. I consider what it means to provide shelter or to protect, and my mind shifts to prisons. Prisons "shelter" prisoners in order to "protect" the community. Yet I do not feel safer knowing that through ongoing colonization, settlers are incarcerating more and more Indigenous people on Indigenous land and using nature for prison construction. Gae Ho Hwako shares the teachings of the Two Row Wampum and explains how the people on the ship came to our land and began taking "the nutrients from our Mother Earth by doing things like mining, oil drilling, and fracking." She speaks about how the children were taken and sent to residential schools or taken in the Sixties Scoop. Now, they are being taken by the Millennial Scoop and by prisons. She explains that this separation has "deteriorated our connection to the ways of life provided for us." This deterioration is also caused by prisons, which separate people in prison from their relationships to others and also to creation.

During my time with Spruce, I began to think about how other standing ones (or trees) are used in prison construction. This use led me to think about how other natural materials in creation are used for prison construction. I began to think about what I know about the architecture of prisons, and I started to list the materials that were used to build the prison: steel, plexiglass, bricks, concrete, insulation, glass, and drywall. I researched what each of these materials is made of and discovered that the natural components of concrete include crushed rocks. Steel is a mineral. Plexiglass has components of crude oil. Insulation contains minerals and wool. Bricks are made of clay, soil, sand, limestone, and concrete. Drywall is made of the mineral gypsum. Many of the materials used to construct prisons are rooted in creation – water, clay, sand, minerals, and soil.

In Indigenous teachings, we learn that the trees, stones, minerals, water, clay, sand, and medicines are all our relations. They are our original teachers, and now these teachers are used in the construction of prisons, court houses, police stations, parole offices, and all the institutions that have been used by colonial systems to disconnect Indigenous people from creation. Anishinaabe scholar Leanne Simpson explains that extraction from the earth is stealing: "It is taking without consent, without thought, care or even knowledge of the impacts that extraction has on the other living things in that environment."[25] Just as stones are used in the construction of prisons, I imagine the bones of our ancestors being used in the construction of all institutions. Does the intent of the construction mean anything? How does a prison differ from a hospital or a school? These are still colonial constructs. I think about building a sweat lodge and the protocols that we engage with, putting our *sema* down before we cut down the saplings and before we put them in the earth. When building our sweat lodges, we offer prayers and thanksgiving. We pray to the Creator and express our intentions to the saplings, telling them what we would like to use them for. We honour their life and offer prayers for what they offer us. The sweat lodge offers us healing. For this reason, intent certainly matters.

As I talked with Anishinaabe scholar Kathleen E. Absolon about these thoughts, she offered me a teaching that was passed down to her by Anishinaabek Elder Tina Armstrong. She told me that everything in creation is medicine and that everything in creation is meant for life. "The community is informed that our precious relations, *jihso'dak* [wild strawberry], have returned and that their presence needs acknowledgment. The community gathers, and our relations join us. We greet each other and celebrate that we still have life and that we are medicine for each other."[26] Absolon said that anything that gets abused by humans or anything that diminishes life is an abuse of our natural helpers.

My relationship with Spruce has encouraged me to learn more about natural helpers. I use the nongendered plural pronouns "they/them/their" for

Spruce because I feel constrained by the gender binary that exists in the English language, which does not fit my relationship with Spruce's spirit being. Onaubinisay offers a teaching that we relate to creation in the gender that we identify with.[27] This teaching gives me freedom to engage in relationships with the Creator, deer, or Spruce as a woman; however, my queer spirit still sits uncomfortably with the feminine-gendered pronouns "she/her." The beauty of Onaubinisay's teaching is that Indigenous people who identify as two-spirit or gender nonconforming or who identify using "they/them/their" can relate to creation through their own pronouns. Yet in spite of the inclusiveness of this teaching, it is not widely spoken about within Indigenous writing and scholarship.

There continue to be many queer, two-spirit, and nonbinary poets and writers emerging and being heard; however, bi-gendered language is still most prevalent in most Indigenous teachings and writing. For this reason, my spirit feels called by Spruce's tree roots to reach deeper within myself and to challenge the ways that I have internalized heteropatriarchy as a queer,[28] Indigenous woman and the ways that I continue to articulate values and ideas that confine and imprison me in colonial constructs. Similar to Okanagan scholar and N'silxchn land speaker Jeanette Armstrong, "I revel in the discoveries I make in constructing new ways to circumvent such invasive imperialism upon my tongue."[29] I cling to this revelling because I have felt disconnected from relationships with teachings and scholarship that render my identity invisible. However, in this moment, I feel supported by Spruce's deep roots, which ground me, and I lean on and lift up two-spirit and queer Indigenous writers who give voice to identities and sexualities that exist outside binaries.[30] Simpson's work also asks us to challenge heteronormativity and to embrace the reality that Indigenous queer and two-spirit people "also come from the land – the land that provides endless examples of queerness and diverse sexualities and genders."[31] This acknowledgment of queerness in creation makes me feel seen and connected without shame of an Indigenous identity that is so often left out of teachings because I am not a traditional life-giver. In her chapter of this book, Anishinaabe scholar Lianne C. Leddy speaks of the "problematic ways that … 'womanhood' is relegated to the role of 'motherhood,'" and when I read these words, I take a deep breath and feel relief. This conflation of womanhood and motherhood has created tension in my relationship with creation and with women's teachings.

Seeing how Spruce nurtures other life makes me feel less lonely because I know that I nurture life in similar ways. How I nurture is not about "birthing" but about being in relationship in a good way. Over time, I have learned that many Indigenous languages do not ascribe to gendered language. Instead, they rely on animacy or inanimacy when describing their relationship to spirit beings. Kimmerer describes the "grammar of animacy" within the Potawatomi language: "Rocks are animate, as are mountains and water and fire and places. Beings that are imbued with spirit, our sacred medicines, our songs, drums and even stories, are all animate."[32] Opaskwayak Cree scholar Alex Wilson explains that in the Cree language, "What is important is the relational aspect acknowledging some kind of kinship. In Cree, the land (aski) is not gendered … Same for water. It's not gendered but it has a spirit of life and it's fluid."[33] Gendered language is an outcome of settler colonialism and has seriously impacted how Indigenous knowledge is communicated and therefore how I have been able to communicate my relationship with Spruce. I honour the friends, teachers, Knowledge Keepers, and Elders who have shown me how my relationship with my queer self and with creation can be liberating.

Using "they/them/their" with Spruce can sound clumsy to many who are not used to nonbinary language, but it feels good to me. Beyond my own desire not to gender creation, I have been considering "they/them/their" in relationship to how Spruce has root systems connected to a Norway spruce, a maple tree, an elm tree, and many of the other trees in the surrounding yards. The language of "they/them/their" provides a context of a community beneath the soil whose members are helping to nourish, feed, and give life to one another. Spruce cannot exist on their own. They are dependent on other life sources and rely on "fungal connections" to "transmit signals from one tree to the next, helping the trees exchange news about insects, drought, and other dangers."[34] As Gae Ho Hwako says, "E tinoha ongwesidage'dra gwe'… connects all the roots from the plants, trees, flowers, and medicines. All the roots are interwoven so that they can supply their energy to everything." The survival of Spruce is dependent on relationships with other beings bringing in the collective nature of "they/them/their." The same can be said for the relationships that are maintained and nourished with people in prison.

Just as Spruce is in relationship with all the beings around them, so am I. The loss of these land relationships deeply impacts so much of our lives. I have learned that land holds language that is distinct to geographical regions;[35]

therefore, when a prison or courthouse or police station or detention centre is built, we lose the language that comes from this particular site and the lessons that this land has to teach us. Jeanette Armstrong, an Okanagan author and N'silxchn speaker, states that "all Indigenous peoples' languages are generated by a precise geography and arise from it. Over time and many generations of their people, it is their distinctive interaction with a precise geography which forms the way indigenous language is shaped and subsequently how the world is viewed, approached, and expressed verbally by its speakers."[36]

In addition to losing language, Indigenous people lose the medicines that come from the trees, plants, and animals that have been destroyed through the construction of these institutional sites. We lose our relationship to their teachings. Carceral and other colonial systems attempt to break all relationships among humans and creation, yet they are not *always* successful. Despite the concrete and barbed wire that cage human life, creation can still break through the cracks. Much like Spruce's root system connects them to other trees, birds, and life systems, Peter's indomitable spirit provided strength to other prisoners and reached beyond prison walls to creation and the community. His writing, artwork, and activism touched the lives of many. Stories of his life and gifts continue to travel through the wind, the trees, the soil, and the birds. Sitting now with Spruce, my grief is palpable. I am missing my friend who would have loved to sit under this spruce tree with me.

Friendship

It has been one year since I tore my Achilles tendon, and I am sitting outside with Spruce. In conversation with them, I wonder, "What was this last year about? What was it that I was supposed to learn?" Spruce whispers, "I am here with you, standing strong, deeply rooted," and I realize that Spruce has become my companion, my friend. Gae Ho Hwako shares that our spiritual helpers "guide and support our journey." Spruce is a being I can share my stories with, spend time with, reflect with. My connection to Spruce reminds me of my connection to land, to prisons, and to a friendship that carried a big spiritual fire. Gae Ho Hwako shares, "Our spiritual fires begin to ignite from being in relation with the spiritual fire of another held in that person's story." Peter was passionate about justice, strong and steady in our friendship, and caring, compassionate, and thoughtful. He cared for creation over people, and during his time in prison, he wanted to paint "different birds that visit all the different prisons across this planet, that bring with them, on the wing, the hope and promise of something other than imprisonment."[37] My friendship with Peter is deeply missed, although our spirits often meet in my dreams, and we are always happy to see one another.

My time with Spruce reminded me of my time with Peter and his family during the private family visit. I had not stopped to reflect on what it was like to be in the prison for that short time, the ways that it could take my breath away. Spruce called me to tell this story. I am reminded that sharing stories can help us in many ways, as Gae Ho Hwako relates: "As we share them, we can feel parts of us opening that were previously blocked by some negative action or behaviour. Our stories never blame; they only share experiences that might touch a chord in another's life. This effect allows people to learn through reflection and to take part in an opening of our hearts and minds."

I think that this is what the last year has been about – understanding my experiences of prison work and sharing the story of my relationship with Spruce, my prison work, and my friendship with Peter. I felt held by Spruce so that I could tell this story, the story of my friendship with Peter, which had so often revealed judgment in others.

As Gae Ho Hwako says about her experience with the court system, "Each time, I came away disillusioned and angry," and rightfully so. The criminal justice system does not work. It does not bring justice or healing to victims, and it does not bring balance and harmony back into our communities. How can it? It is a colonial system that adheres to colonial laws that have always sought to remove Indigenous people from the land, to disrupt our communities, and to commit genocide. The system is not broken: it is doing exactly what it was intended to do.[38] It breaks and severs relations and the medicines that they could offer. Despite this situation, a life-changing friendship developed between Peter and I, a friendship that called us to fight against a system intent on separating people, families, kinship ties, and relationships with creation.

There Is No Ending

In my experience of doing prison work, every attempt is made by Correctional Service Canada to keep life out of prisons. Over the years, it has been increasingly difficult to gain access to the prison, and family members, volunteers, and community workers are continually discouraged from visiting. However, the birds cannot be stopped from entering the prison, nor can the squirrels, chipmunks, and even turtles. In fact, Peter had a variety of animals that kept him company over the years. For him, this companionship kept him sane during the most difficult times.

Gae Ho Hwako remind us, "*Oda:otra* (friends) come in many variations." Spruce has taught me about the power of relationships and the interconnectedness of all life. Spruce has taught me about language, life, and the medicines that creation offers. Spruce offered me wholistic healing during a time of physical, spiritual, and emotional loss. Sitting with Spruce, I am reminded of my last night with Peter in the PFV. We heard a loon call from the lake. It is a beautiful haunting call that often tugs at my heart. This visit was the last time that I would see Peter before he died.

Sitting with Spruce while my Achilles tendon is healing, I hear Awnjibenayseekwe's teaching that "we are always on the land." I do not need to be physically touching the land for Mother Earth to be healing. I am always in connection with creation. It makes me wonder about how Indigenous people reclaim relationships to creation in prisons and other colonial institutions. I am reminded of Barbara-Helen Hill's words in the previous chapter: "The earth and all our relations can recover from the damage done to them. Nature knows how to heal, how to make things better for all the beings of the Ganǫhǫnyǫhk (Thanksgiving Address), including us as well." Her words bring me hope.

I put my *sema* down by Spruce, touch their trunk, and give thanks. As Gae Ho Hwako reminds us, "We were given families to be thankful for – not just our human families but also families of plants, trees, birds, and animals – along with the *geihnyenoh de yo ki ye'nya dohn* (spiritual helpers), Shogwaeyadisho' (the Creator), and so much more." I am grateful for Spruce, and I am grateful for my friendship with Peter.

Standing in Ancestral Waters: Acts in Naturalizing Maternal Relations

Timothy B. Leduc

Each step of the great blue heron is deliberate and slow as it stalks the edge of the reeds. A foot rises out of the water covered with a film of green algae and then slips back in with quiet grace. As the heron stops for a drink, its walk shifts into a silent repose, followed by a careful grooming of its beak between two strong reeds. Then stillness descends once more. As I place my thanks for the spirit of this silent presence in the water, I recall the *awehaode'* (soft, kind, embracing words) of Gae Ho Hwako (Norma Jacobs): "All the beings we give thanks to in the Ganǫhǫnyǫhk work with us daily. They try to teach and share with us in the spirit of *og ya:dao* [friendship] about caring for family. They nurture, embrace, support, and encourage us to be humble and to appreciate the time that we have with all our relations." Giving thanks to the heron and others of this marsh reminds us that we are part of this community that I have brought my daughter, Iona, into relation with since her birth thirteen years ago.

The long legs of the heron sink into the water as it stands on the mud that is the living matrix of our lives. These are the waters that Sky Woman fell into, and the mud below is the same substance that the small muskrat dredged from the depths to help her thrive on the turtle's back. With each inhalation of this moist humus, I recall Robin Wall Kimmerer's writing on how the "scent of Mother Earth stimulates the release of the hormone oxytocin, the same chemical that promotes bonding between mother and child."[1] What we smell here is the source of medicines that have long been appreciated in the Indigenous canoe and whose healing benefits for those suffering from inattentiveness, depression, and other mental health issues are now also increasingly being recognized by the modern ship.[2] I return to the words of Gae Ho Hwako, who tells us that we are born into this world "covered with the medicine of being in [our mother's] body … When the baby is coming, you can smell the medicine. A baby's birthing is tremendous; it is like a flower opening up."

Slowing down to breathe in the scents of the mud around us, I remember the feeling of peace and joy as we received Iona into this world. In the days that led up to and followed her birth, every aspect of our lives slowed. Socially distancing ourselves into a protective womb brought a stillness that was filled with the energy of anticipating a mysterious arrival from the waters of her mother. This source of all our lives is why Gae Ho Hwako's Haudenosaunee culture is matrilineal. Because the family follows the woman's ancestral line, behind every male chief is a clan mother, and all beings, including humans, arrive here through the flowing waters of both our mother and E tinoha ongwesidage'dra gwe' (Mother Earth). To honour those connections throughout our life, Gae Ho Hwako says that we need to "remember our journeys, stories, and songs" and that we need to "recognize that we are those sacred spiritual beings who descended from the Sky World to work on this spiritual journey."

After half a life of following my father's ancestry into more intimate relations with the canoe, it was in truly reflecting on the roots of this maternal teaching that I felt gently guided back to my daughter, wife, and French Canadien mother. I had to look at the fact that I had become focused on the Indigenous canoe because I wanted nothing to do with the French Canadien ship – its culture, spirit, and colonial legacy. Despite the renewal that I felt from relating with the land, the white pine, and the river, I was doing something very colonial in rejecting my mother's roots to the point that they were shrivelling. It is just such a turning away from our grounding that makes people prone to appropriate cultural teachings. Gae Ho Hwako's words resonate: "How long is it going to take for [those on the ship] to unravel where they have come from and why their family is here now?" This is a question that we need to untangle by reaching for the medicine in our stories, which is what I attempt in this circle of the book by reflecting on the story of my daughter, Iona, in relation to our maternal ancestors of the ship and their waters.

Being born in Canada's largest city, Toronto, can lead us to forget that we are somewhere more mysterious than is suggested by the human bustle around us. We live in "the fertile floodplains of three significant rivers" that flow into Lake Ontario[3] – waters that support two major bird-migration routes and more than 304 bird species, including the great blue heron. A half-century ago, these reeds had disappeared when the pond was encased by a concrete edge that was home to less diversity, but then an emerging conservation ethic began to reclaim and "wild" shoreline habitats. Although we may be able to see a heron and smell the mud again, the climate storms swirling around us today make it clear that more is required of us. I recall Kimmerer again, who envisions "a way that an immigrant society could become indigenous to place," even as she also recognizes that "immigrants cannot by definition" have the birthright of being Indigenous.[4] Sitting with this thought, she concludes that although they cannot be Indigenous, they still need "to throw off the mind-set of the immigrant" and become naturalized to these waters. They need "to live as if your children's future matters, to take care of the land as if our lives and the lives of all our relatives depend on it. Because they do."[5]

A few feet behind me, the presence of someone perching with a camera seems to put an exclamation mark on the challenge of naturalizing relations, for the act of photography reflects a broader pattern of relational disconnection that we participate in. We come here from our urban neighborhoods in a modern colonial spirit that positions us outside this community. Carrying the stress of school or work, we often walk these paths with our minds somewhere else. This lack of attentiveness is particularly true with the younger generation, whose members, Sherry Turkle writes, "are among the first to grow up with an expectation of continuous connection: always on, and always on them. And they are among the first to grow up not necessarily thinking of simulation as second best."[6] Distancing ourselves with cameras and other technologies that mediate our relation with these paths, we extend our uprooting tendencies, which is now due to a kind of virtual disconnect.

As Iona approached her teens, I watched our marsh relations recede from her in the wake of these virtual ways of relating, despite the expressed concerns of her parents. One day while I was talking with Anishinaabe Elder

Awnjibenayseekwe (Banakonda Kennedy-Kish Bell) about the uncertainty that I felt regarding this disconnection, she suggested that I bring my concern to the heron in a spirit of thanksgiving and see what arose. Writing about this practice, she says that when we come to sit with "our first mother," if we bring good intentions and are "seeking to experience and receive new awareness," it is possible to "deepen our experience of relatedness and our understanding of oneself in relationship with one's place in Creation."[7] In her teachings about such learning, I have often heard her draw upon the Cree thought of Willie Ermine, who writes that "other [than human] life forms manifest the creative force in the context of the knower. It is an experience in context, a subjective experience that, for the knower, becomes knowledge."[8]

Just as Gae Ho Hwako guided me to the white pine, Awnjibenayseekwe suggested that by being with heron, I would experience questions and insights arising in me; the knowledge and stories that I had brought into the relationship, the *og ya:dao* (friendship), would be transformed. This approach to knowledge is about fostering whole relations that are transformative, and thus it is vastly different from those academic critical theories that, even as they deconstruct the modern project, continue to participate in the colonial tendency to tear every relation apart. The quality of transformation in this Indigenous approach to knowledge leads me toward something much more mysterious yet grounding.

Each deliberate movement of the heron away from and back to stillness reminds me to stay present between the maddening pulls of our changing lives – to keep my feet in the mud as I struggle with being a father amidst the virtual energy that so attracts us. There is a spirit to the storm that Iona's generation has been born into, and by bringing the stories of our maternal ancestries to these waters, I hope to learn something about what it will take to naturalize modern ways.

As an author, teacher, and father, I am trying to foster a matrilineal root in our family, in our community relations, and in the story that I tell of my daughter's descent from a Scottish Canadian mother. Coming into this final circle of the book, I am guided by the words of Giselle Dias on how the "conflation of womanhood and motherhood has created tension in my relationship with creation and with women's teachings." The difficulties in translation arise again, as in many Indigenous languages, there is more changeability between the English binaries of "she" as mother and "he" as father. Saying E tinoha ongwesidage'dra gwe' rather than Mother Earth reminds me of this potential, while affirming the generative capacities of a diverse creation that is more "they" than "she."

"When our babies come here," Gae Ho Hwako teaches, "they already know their journey … and they start asking questions as they cry, gurgle, or murmur … They are asking who they are … [T]hey want to build that relationship." A similar understanding is held by Awnjibenayseekwe's Anishinaabe culture. In the words of Elder Freda MacDonald, "When you know your birth story and your birth song, you want to hear that … and you don't change it, it's THEIR story."[9] Although my focus on such teachings may seem more consistent with the book's preceding section, I offer my reflection here in relation to the *geihnyenoh de yo ki ye'nya dohn* (spiritual helpers) and Shogwaeyadisho' (the Creator) because of the colonial tendency to disconnect spirit from the medicines of this marsh and our very birth. In retelling and reflecting on our birth stories, the children that are within all of us can begin to deepen and spread their roots into a spirited creation. Although at the time of Iona's birth I was not in relation with such an ancestral teaching, I now feel that myself and my partner, Christina Lessels, were semi-consciously reaching toward this relational spirit as we wrote *The Story of Iona* (2008) and then ritually read it as she went to sleep.

❁ ❁

> On December 19, 2007 you arrived into this world, and from your first breath both your mother and father knew that Iona would be a fine and inspiring name for a girl with Scottish origins. Long before your first kicks within mommy's belly, your parents crossed the Atlantic Ocean to visit your mother's family in Scotland. Off Scotland's west coast is the Isle of Iona, and it is here that your parents first fell in love with your name and everything it means. The oldest Celtic stories say that upon islands like Iona it is possible for people to more easily speak with fairies and angels. It was this desire for spirit talk that led a man named Colum Cille to first come to this isle many, many years ago. Legends passed down to the present tell of spirits coming to talk with Colum Cille on Iona's 'hill of angels' and the 'fairy mound.'[10]

There is a stillness to the Isle of Iona even as it teems with the flight of coastal birds, including herons, although the latter I remember less from memory than from the children's stories about those Celtic shores that we read to our children. Drawing from our memories of Toronto marsh walks, I can see the lift of feet from the water and mud as the heron's wings catch air. Around this isle, the herons skip gracefully over the rippling waters of a North Atlantic bay. The grace of their S-shaped, bended neck in flight is etched in my mind, a distinctive posture that they share with other long-necked marsh birds like the crane as their wings beat 120 times per minute.[11] There is a powerful ease to the herons' movements through the air that carries my imagination with them, sending my thoughts back in time and across an ocean to the Celtic shores that inspired our daughter's name.

The story that we wrote did not begin just with Iona's birth but, for me, also with an awakening to the matrilineal pull of her mother. It has now been over two decades since we first met while doing graduate work in environmental studies, and what I recall from that time are her funky-patterned tights, army boots, and jacket, as well as her email name, Moonwomyn, which bespoke her feminist passion for all things to do with women's health. In our first years, she was a volunteer educator at Planned Parenthood and was focused on women's menstrual health, while also dabbling in natural women's health practices – the beginning of the herbs and tinctures that pervade our home. Her graduate work pushed back against the medicalization of women's bodies and the silencing of their voices, thus leading to two decades of advocacy work for better women's health policy through a broader inclusion of diverse women's voices.

I still remember the day that Christina stood up in a Faculty of Business auditorium, which was filled with aspiring Master of Business Administration students, to query a professor in corporate social sustainability on what criteria the university had used to assess Nestlé before accepting its sponsorship of a sustainability prize. She knew of the corporation's impact on women related to its promotion of formula over breastfeeding, particularly in developing countries, and we were becoming aware of Nestlé's first steps in appropriating public water in Canada to make profits at the expense of community needs. Her question descended upon the surprised professor like a revelation that seemed astounding to him, for the university clearly had not considered the sustainability ethics of accepting a poisoned gift. I came to learn much from her about feminist action, although I had begun reflecting on my role as a man years before.

During the mid-1990s, I worked in a feminist organization whose mandate was to ensure better support of women survivors of domestic violence, and I was given the task of supporting male batterer programming that would hold men accountable for their violent behaviours. This and subsequent work was focused on identifying and ensuring best practices for systemic change across sectors – such as social services, police, courts, and shelters – many of which have been shaped by the patriarchal assumptions and gender power imbalances that mark domestic violence. It was a learning experience that led me to reflect on my male tendencies toward the power (over), control, denial, and isolation that are central to this violence, as is displayed so clearly on the Power and Control Wheel, which outlines male violence.[12]

A sudden shift in the alertness of the heron to a swooping sparrow hawk draws my mind back to the marsh. In a brief moment of quiet, the heron makes a short flight into the reeds across the water. I can feel the protection of a mother, yet she has not given up the exact position of the nest. I recall Gae Ho Hwako's words: "Every woman who has lost her life has put forth a battle to protect herself and her children. She never gives up; she goes down fighting with every ounce of strength." It is estimated that 50 per cent of women in Canada have survived one violent incident (sexual or physical), that 82 per cent of the survivors of partner violence are women or girls, that globally one-third of women are survivors of violence, and that 98 per cent of sex offenders are men.[13] As of 2015, "Indigenous women made up nearly one-quarter (24%) of homicide victims in Canada," and they are "12 times more likely to be murdered or missing than any other women."[14]

Witnessing the connection between the control that characterizes male violence and colonial systems, I now view Canadian society as employing the ways of denial – minimizing and rationalizing – and isolation in its approach to Indigenous women and land. As Gae Ho Hwako's experience highlights, this violence is related to the historic vulnerability and isolation of women created by the Indian Act and by institutions like the residential schools. Those who traditionally protected and nurtured their culture came to bear the brunt of a male colonial violence focused on appropriating land as resources. The intersectional connectivity of this violence is what Gae Ho Hwako sees in the storms of E tinoha ongwesidage'dra gwe', a pattern that ecofeminists have also highlighted in a system of Western dualities – such as male/female, civilized/Indigenous, and straight/queer – that foster hierarchical and intersecting violence.[15] As a white man and a Canadien, I cannot help but to see my implicated position in all this violence, and it was from this awareness that I first wanted to be involved in change.

When I met my partner, Christina, I was just beginning to expand my education on the connection between white, male, colonial conduct and land-based violence. By the time of Iona's arrival, it was clear to us that our children would take their mother's Scottish name Lessels. Although we did not have the guidance of a cultural teaching, we seemed to be drawn by a pattern not unlike the matrilineal grounding that Gae Ho Hwako describes in relation to E tinoha ongwesidage'dra gwe'. But as the depth and breadth of her teachings display, a guiding intuition is merely a start in comparison to what a wholistic cultural tradition can offer. Everything then speaks to the gifts that we carry to the place where we have come to land on this river of life. When we have a way to reflect on who and where we are, then the earlier discussed difficulties of straddling the space of the Two Row Wampum subsides.

For Gae Ho Hwako, it all begins with the way that "our birth connects us to Sky Woman's sacred journey." She was the one who carried the plant roots and medicines from the Sky World to a Turtle Island eastward of the Isle of Iona. The words of Gae Ho Hwako resonate with an important teaching: "Sky Woman wanted to create a new world, as change would help to birth a new beginning. It was with this intention that she fell through the hole in the sky." In some tellings, a small heron called a bittern is said to have then seen what was happening as it looked up from the reeds where it was camouflaged and announced that a female was falling from above.[16] With that, a host of birds today known to inhabit wetlands flew up to catch and gently guide Sky Woman onto the back of the turtle. The origin of *og ya:dao* (friendship) on the Two Row Wampum stretches back to her fall and the support of marsh birds, the muskrat's dive for mud, and the turtle's steady support. As Kimmerer writes, it is through these sharing relations that "the original immigrant became indigenous."[17]

Although Gae Ho Hwako teaches that "our birth connects us to Sky Woman's sacred journey," she clarifies that this learning began "after I had my six children, as it was only then that I began reconnecting to my culture. I missed out on all these reflective teachings until my last child." I am reminded that the "birth story" teaching offered by Elder MacDonald is part of the guide *Supporting the Sacred Journey: From Preconception to Parenting for First Nations Families in Ontario* (2012), which aims to reconnect young Indigenous parents who have been separated from their culture but, with a new baby coming, are trying to find a way back into their home traditions. Similarly, Gae Ho Hwako offers her teachings with a hope of fostering renewal. As she clarifies, we cannot "understand a story like that of Sky Woman until one actively engages with it; then we come to an understanding of the story and the teachings that it holds." Kimmerer writes that the story of Sky Woman "endures because we too are always falling."[18] It would seem that our task is to bring ourselves into this teaching by reflecting on what this origin story might mean for us – what it means to have our fall guided into these waters.

A short ferry trip along the edge of the North Atlantic Ocean brings us to a small, majestic outcropping of rock covered in green that has long been honoured by the peoples indigenous to these waters. Long before this isle became a place of pilgrimage marked by ornately carved Celtic Christian crosses and ruins, it was understood to be a land that was home to gods and goddesses. Unlike the monolithic sky-dwelling God of the Judeo-Christian tradition or even a Greek pantheon of gods "organized into a great heavenly community," the spirits/fairies, ancestors, and divine beings of the Celts lived "underground or on the earth, often across the sea or on distant islands."[19] Our sacred pilgrimage here is to a place that has long been known to have transformative potential.

In the stories of these waters, the world came into form through a kind of spirit kin to Sky Woman, an otherworldly female known as the Cailleach Bhéara in Irish and Scottish Gaelic. It is said that she is "a gigantic presence" that covers and shapes the land, "passing through it continually in a way that … identifies her with the fertility of the natural environment and the creatures."[20] Although ever present, the Cailleach Bhéara also embodies a dynamic changeability across wide-ranging waters. This variety is represented in stories saying that she is "forever washing" her "feet and legs so as never to carry the mud from one puddle to the next." In other words, she is "not to be fixed or confined in identification with any single location, but is a shifting, dynamic, vital" reality. Whether as the Cailleach Bhéara or as E tinoha ongwesidage'dra gwe', the regenerative spirit that births life cannot be held by the violent categories of a colonial mind fixed on managing a creation of resources.

When we attend the *geihnyenoh de yo ki ye'nya dohn* (spiritual helpers) ancestral to Iona, we also hear of mythic stories where marsh birds like the heron and, more often, the crane play significant roles, just as they did in guiding Sky Woman onto the back of the turtle. Many stories depict a host of water birds as metamorphosed women who are often "linked to each other by gold or silver chains."[21] Exemplary is "Sequana, goddess of the Seine" in France, who stands on this river in a boat fashioned as a duck, which is "indicative of Sequana's aquatic identity and of the healing powers of the springwater."[22] From the deep past to the present, there have been gatherings around holy wells in Celtic lands, and people continue to offer gifts to these waters either to express thanks for their life-giving spirit or to ask for healing. Some of the oldest gifts were coins etched with "marsh-birds, such as the crane."[23] These water birds wove together the heavens and the watery underworld and thus are responsible for supporting the relation between spirit and the life given by the Cailleach Bhéara.

Following an ancient path, Christina and I also originally came to Iona in the tradition of spiritual pilgrimage as I tried to find a way to connect with my partner's ancestry. In that act, I came to remember that St Colum Cille (or Columba), whose name is so woven with this isle, also inspired my father's home parish of St Columbans and my preteen Catholic confirmation lessons at the Iona Carmelite Retreat Centre. It was in 563 CE that Colum Cille initiated the wave of Celtic Christian monks who sailed across to Iona and then to other isles on what became known as the "sea-road of the saints."[24] In contrast to much of continental Europe, his Ireland had not yet experienced as extensive a missionizing effort by external forces, and thus many Celtic traditions came into an easier braid with Christianity. As a result, Colum Cille's pilgrimage to Iona followed a route that predated Christianity, for vital to the Celts were "thin spaces" such as islands and other vital places where people could more easily attend spirit.[25]

Long before Christianity, stories tell of ceremonies led by Druids in the thin-space clearings of oak groves, which were called *nemeton*. As Celeste Ray explains, Nemetona is "a generic goddess of the grove," one who is often in relation to a close-by sacred spring or body of water.[26] It is in this context that the suffix "ona" in the name Nemetona is often found in the names of sacred waters or of an isle like Iona. Meanwhile, the name Druid arises "from two words: dru, meaning 'oak,' and wid, 'to see or to know.' Those who sang the community's stories and interpreted its laws were said 'to know the oak.'"[27] Being with an oak feels different from being with a white pine, and these trees also carry their own distinct wisdom for guiding humans. It was in this cultural spirit that we gave Iona's brother, Etienne, the middle name Dru, which we can also braid with local stories about the endangered black oak savannahs around our Toronto home.

As with sacred trees, people from across the planet have long engaged the heron and other marsh birds for teachings on how to live in a co-creative world. In Celtic tradition, these marsh birds are associated with water and the sun because they bring "together the elements of sky and water."[28] The patient purple heron of Egypt is said to carry contemplative peace connected with being reborn. Farther east in India, protective heronries have been fostered on the grounds of Hindu temples, as the status of herons "is stronger in Hindu nations than among neighbouring cultures" of South Asia,[29] where there has been extensive habitat loss. Hindu yogis are also connected with another marsh bird in their designation as *paramahamsas* (lit. "supreme wild ganders") because they participate in the "transcendent yet immanent ground of all being," which is beyond waking consciousness.[30]

Watching the heron's deliberate movements, I understand why the people of the Haudenosaunee clan that is named for this bird are said to embody "patience, intelligence, and poise."[31] I have seen these characteristics embodied by Gae Ho Hwako, whose maternal family came from the Heron Clan of the Wyandot Nation before being adopted into the Wolf Clan of the Cayuga Nation. Sometimes, I think that it is this Wyandot ancestry that has drawn me into relation with Gae Ho Hwako; or perhaps it was the patient boundary-crossing spirit of the heron, which can rise out of the *water* and and above the *land* as it flies into the *air*, where Sky Woman's descent began. Although there are diverse heron species and diverse cultural ways of relating to these patient beings, there also seems to be a common awareness of their patient, boundary-crossing spirit.

The continuation of heron's patient, boundary-crossing gift can be seen today on our home shores as the storms of E tinoha ongwesidage'dra gwe' intensify. As colonialism unfolded, Toronto's urban sprawl led to the loss of wildlife habitat, with toxic chemicals and habitat fragmentation impacting many beings.[32] These changes partook of global processes that saw eight heron species become "seriously at risk."[33] It was in recognizing this trajectory that modern society began moving toward a conservation ethic. As awareness grew about our ecological interconnectivity due to the biomagnification of industrial and nuclear pollutants following the Second World War, there was a recognition of the value of wetlands. By 1974, green spaces in Toronto had increased from a 67-hectare parcel in the mid-1950s to 3,161 hectares through the city's reacquisition of extensive tracts along Lake Ontario and rivers, with the efforts expanding throughout the 1990s and the early twenty-first century.[34] Despite the current mass extinction event, herons now have stable populations on Turtle Island of between 100,000 and 250,000. As for great blue herons, they have learned to flourish on these naturalized shores, displaying a boundary-crossing capacity that has led ornithologists to describe them as an "environmental sentinel."[35]

Whether it be the sacred heronries of India, Celtic "thin spaces," or the responsibilities of a Heron Clan, these spiritual traditions add dimensions of reverence and gratitude to conservation responses, which are often focused on human recreation and ecological services. In Celtic lands, the veneration of water continues, as people still visit holy wells and springs, such as the 3,000 found in Ireland alone. As with the wide respect for marsh birds, an appreciation of water is shared across the planet. In the words of Ray, "Zamzam at Mecca is the holiest well in Islam … Mexico has its holy water *aguajes* and Mayan *cenotes*. Water bodies, particularly wells, fountains, springs and streams, are liminal places cross-culturally and may be considered portals to other worlds … Aboriginal Australians still greet ancestors at water holes that they created in the Dreamtime. Shinto kami (spirits) dwell in Japanese springs."[36] Closer to our home, Indigenous water walks, intended to change our polluting relation with lakes, rivers, and wetlands, have an ancestral source in water ceremonies.

Something deeper than an ethic of conservation is needed if we are to renew the spirit of thanksgiving that Gae Ho Hwako carries or the veneration of sacred waters described by Ray. They commonly suggest that without cultural practices to approach the sacred, we will have only a limited relation with the water medicine. Celtic wells have particular healing qualities that are related to local medicinal plants and minerals in the water.[37] These specific medicines are on top of the positive bonding and mental health benefits discussed earlier in relation to the smell of mud and to the immersion in natural surrounds. Although you can attend close-by local wells for healing needs, people from the past to present have also gone on longer pilgrimages in search of healing for specific ailments or other spiritual needs. There are also ritual protocols for engaging the healing spirit of the wells, which can include "instructions for moving sunwise around the stations, saying set numbers of particular prayers, when to do so kneeling or standing, and when to bend one's head towards the station and kiss it, how many times a day to complete the entire circuit."[38]

All wells and springs are nodes in the Cailleach Bhéara as they flow through the land, and thus a spirit of veneration informs most people's approach to them. But Ray notes a different quality between regular visitors and those coming from farther afield. Those who have regular relations with the well describe their responsibilities in terms of ensuring that the ceremonies continue, protecting the waters from development, and being involved in cleanups and activities to ensure that the sacred place is here for future generations. Meanwhile, infrequent visitors tend to leave impromptu gifts or, when in search of healing, something like clothing related to the distressed body. As Ray explains, these differences reflect something deeper: "Those leaving worry and disease-infected votives on trees or by the well perceive a 'giving environment' in which the power of the place provides unconditionally." In contrast, regular visitors "describe themselves in more of a reciprocating relationship with the environment in which the well will answer one's needs if one fulfils obligations to respect and steward the site."[39]

Drawing all this into relation with Gae Ho Hwako's teachings, it seems that such ceremonial ways are how we foster *og ya:dao* (friendship) with sacred waters, an isle, a tree, or a heron. It is in this spirit that we often stop along this marsh to offer our thanksgiving to E tinoha ongwesidage'dra gwe'. As I reflect on this feeling of gratitude, I notice the heron lift a fish from the water and, within a few seconds, carry it to logs just beyond the reeds. Orientating the fish to its fate, the heron slowly dips its catch into the water before pointing its beak upward to let that which has been given slide down its throat. With a drink of water that has a feel of thanksgiving, the whole ceremony is bundled by a return to stillness. Something in this series of actions reminds me of Gae Ho Hwako's cycle of ceremonies from birth through a life-long journey to death. There is a dark tinge to this recognition that guides me to take a deeper look at the colonial dimensions of Iona's story.

❀❀

> As your parents walked around the Isle, just as Colum Cille did long ago, they could feel the spirit of this place in everything around them. They felt it in the old nunnery ruin known as 'An Eaglais Dhubh' [the Black Church] in the native Celtic tongue … They felt it in the beautiful and very old rock Celtic crosses. They could even feel it in the wonderful play of Iona's sheep.[40]

On each of eight logs stands a black-feathered cormorant, their stark forms contrasting with the yellowish reeds that line the shores. We could be at the bay of Iona, where cormorants and their kin gannet congregate, but the iridescent feathers of the wood ducks remind me that this telling of Iona's story is amidst our marsh community. The cormorants open me to a host of stories. One moment, I reflect on their categorization as an invasive species along Lake Ontario that is said to eat all the fish, and even though the science contests this image, they are the focus of a government-sanctioned cull.[41] This bias may be related to the Biblical myth that depicts cormorants as a ritually unclean species and a sign of apocalypse. But as I reflect on the Christian dimensions of the Isle of Iona, these cormorants also call up stories of our relation to missionaries whom many Indigenous peoples of these lands referred to as Black Coats, or Muk-a-day'-i-ko-na-yayg' in Anishinaabe, a people "obsessed with winning the Native people over to the ways of their black book."[42]

Long before I visited Iona, I spent a couple years just across the ocean on another North Atlantic isle of Turtle Island. I was there as a social worker in a northern Indigenous community and was housed in a Catholic mission. The experience highlighted for me the continuity of colonial missions, as Christian missionaries were replaced by governmental social workers focused on Indigenous child protection, an issue that Shelly Hachey and I raise in the first circle of this book. As the colonial storm swirled around this community, one also swirled to my core. On the one side, questions arose about my Canadien Catholic father's Indigenous relations, which I shared in the first circle, and on the other side, memories arose of my mother's French Catholic ancestors connected to these missions. Prominent was my memory of being asked by my great-aunt, a nun, to consider becoming a priest because I had the introspective character required for that vocation. Later, I uncovered ancestral connections to an eighteenth-century Mother Valade, who had initiated the Grey Nun missions with the Red River Métis and then with the Inuit community that I worked with,[43] but at the time, all I knew was that I could not choose that path. Yet I still found my way to a vocation that began in a mission whose focus has long been on a God who, unlike Shogwaeyadisho', has no true relation with E tinoha ongwesidage'dra gwe' or with the Cailleach Bhéara.

The sight of cormorants flying along the waters of Scotland's west coast is not uncommon, nor are the signs of apocalyptic Christian missions. I still vividly remember the short walk from the Iona pier to the ruins of An Eaglais Dhubh (the Black Church), a thirteenth-century Augustinian nunnery that for centuries was home to an order of sisters who came largely from families of the clergy and wealthy.[44] Decades before being instituted on Iona, the Augustinians had arrived in Ireland as part of a Norman wave of Roman Catholic expansion. These stone ruins partook of the unfolding conversion of how people approached sacred waters. In Ireland, the Augustinians required children to be baptized inside the church, which indicates that baptisms still predominantly occurred at outdoor holy wells. Many surviving wells "now have church walls built up against them or have churches in their immediate environs."[45] Ways of missionizing began on these North Atlantic shores before crossing the ocean to Turtle Island.

Although Colum Cille brought a different Celtic spirit to Iona centuries before the Augustinians at An Eaglais Dhubh, he also had an eye toward converting the Pictish Celts of Scotland. Stories tell of "Colum Cille purifying springs of 'demons,' and blessing and creating new wells" in direct confrontation of the Druids.[46] An appreciation of isle "thin spaces" and other Celtic practices only tempered the weaving approach taken by Colum Cille. The centuries between him and the Augustinian nunnery would bring a steady Roman Catholic pressure, and in this context, the Celtic braiding approach was for those in power a kind of stop-gap measure. In the words of Ray, "The syncretic practices that eased conversion could become obnoxious to the Church once it was more secure in a given area. The various decrees against well/spring veneration point to the longevity of indigenous traditions."[47] But even with these missionizing efforts, there was limited impact on traditional Celtic practices in these lands until the enclosure of Scottish lands in the late 1700s and then the Irish Potato Famine of 1845 to 1852. As Ray writes, "Attendance at mass was only around 30% in the 1830s, but rose to more than 90%

following the famine when devotion to official practices of the universal church ... began to supersede folk practices."[48]

It was during this period that Scots and then Irish increasingly found themselves shipped to Turtle Island, where similar disruptions were being used to displace Indigenous nations. In coming to Iona, I felt drawn into a deepening of my Celtic connection to these early colonial dynamics through a French Canadien ancestry that traversed to Turtle Island from the Celtic Brittany shores of France. Reflecting on the Breton and Scot ancestries in our family, I am reminded of John Ralston Saul saying that there is "no more eloquent illustration of the colonial mind-set than a bunch of Celts and Vikings in a distant northern territory insulting each other as *les anglais* and *the French* as if they were the descendants of the people who had subjected and ruined them."[49] The storied flight to Iona began renewing for us a maternal connection to the Cailleach Bhéara and a deep colonial uprooting.

Recalling my time sitting with the rocks of An Eaglais Dhubh, I am reminded of the story told by Alastair McIntosh about bringing Chief Sulian Stone Eagle Herney of the Mi'Kmaq Warrior Society and First Nations Environmental Network to Iona. Looking over the ruins, Celtic crosses, and restored abbey, Sulian was "rapt by the atmosphere." He exclaimed, "I never knew you people had places like this! ... If you're into all this, then how come your people destroyed our sacred sites?"[50] A day earlier, the rawness of these colonial issues had arisen after the ferry crossing from the mainland was delayed by a storm that also brought forth Sulian's anger about the Scottish role in the colonial disruption of his people through land-taking, residential schools, and related abuses. Following the airing of these truths, the next day brought a clear ferry passage to Iona, a pilgrimage that McIntosh hoped would help him and Sulian to bridge each other's spiritual vision about the kind of world that they wanted to live in.

On an isle north of Iona, McIntosh was organizing a grassroots response to a superquarry where a laird's grasping for wealth was raising the ghosts of the Scottish enclosures. After hearing about the Mi'Kmaq struggle against a superquarry project in eastern Canada, McIntosh contacted one of its leaders, Sulian, who received the call at first with silence and then with questions about what this Scottish issue had to do with his concerns. With the discussion failing, McIntosh boldly asked Sulian whether he knew where the people of his superquarry development, with "names like MacAkill and Kelly," came from.

Responding to his own question, McIntosh explained that these immigrants "came from places like the Hebrides and Ireland in the Celtic world … They got pulled like weeds from their own land and transplanted onto yours." We are "from superquarry-threatened communities," and in both cases, "they cleared the native people and now they're wanting even the rocks."[51]

Such Scottish names also surrounded my childhood Catholic school and parish experience in St Andrews West, and they can also be found in the town of Caledonia, which currently hosts real estate developments that are again violating the land of Gae Ho Hwako's Six Nations community. The same can be said of the French Canadien names of my family and their relation to historic standoffs like the one at Oka in 1990. Offering a Canadian perspective on the Scottish roots of these issues, Raymond Rogers describes being a fisher in Nova Scotia as the community-based fisheries collapsed in the 1980s: "The displacement linking my fate as a fisher to" those "who were displaced from the Scottish Highlands and Islands had its roots in industrial forces." Uprooted and poor, his ancestors "came to Canada for self-improvement," but in doing so, they fostered a settler ethos "of triumphing over the wilderness [that] erases not only Indigenous peoples but the suffering and displacement that were so much a part of this history."[52] This ongoing history plays out today in the capitalist forces aimed at expansion as Indigenous Land Back protests continue to call all of us to the task of resistance.

"Pulled like weeds." McIntosh's words return me to the difference between a weed and those medicinal plants that grow around holy wells and that are honoured in the medicine teachings of Gae Ho Hwako. It is such plant medicines that helped Kimmerer to reflect on the importance of "naturalizing" settlers to Turtle Island if we are going to approach a sustainable future. Although she talks of sacred indigenous medicines like sweetgrass and sage, she also introduces us to nonindigenous plants like the garlic mustard that sprawls across the forest just above this marsh.[53] It expands its range by poisoning the soil and spreading roots that crowd out native wildflowers. For Kimmerer, garlic mustard mirrors colonial ways, which are caught in a positive feedback loop, such that the uprooted emptiness within fosters a kind of hunger that grabs for more. Placing this sprawling greed in the context of ongoing capitalist forces, Rogers says that the settler story of "taming and making use of the wilderness" hides the potentially more transformative story "of dispossessed and displaced souls flung about by powerful forces." As he writes, it is only through reflecting on our "grief and dispossession" that "Canadians may come to more clearly see the displacement these same forces have inflicted on the First Nations who are fighting these same battles. This shared story may make us stronger."[54] Returning to Gae Ho Hwako, I know that reflecting on our enmeshment in colonial dynamics is vital if we are to engage with one another at *ǫ da gaho dę:s* (the sacred meeting space).

After hearing McIntosh describe his sense of the colonial connection between Scottish and Indigenous superquarry protests, Sulian agreed to come to Scotland. The trip to Iona was meant to initiate him into the spirit of these Isles. Amidst the rocks of the ruins of An Eaglais Dhubh burst patches of green plants capable of finding any nook to reinvigorate life by drawing from that which is seemingly dead. It is like they are acting in the spirit of the weaves etched into the rock Celtic crosses, those same stones that left Sulian "rapt." This carved "vinework," McIntosh explains, "is based on circularity, on the curve and the spiral," and it displays in beautiful etched stone "the interconnectedness of all things."[55] Although the art and worldview of the Celtic crosses stretch back to ancient times, the crosses reflect the continuation of this sensibility despite the colonial missions. I feel a personal connection to all this, one that recalls for me Gae Ho Hwako's teachings on the value of reflecting on our origin stories in relation to what they mean for us today. In McIntosh's words, "Where you come from, who you are and what your destiny proves to be are all linked within that story, which is nothing less than the story of the world's creation." From this perspective, genealogy is about more than genes; it is "about relationship and embeddedness" in the intricate vines of an unfolding origin story.[56]

Those who were "pulled like weeds" from the Celtic vinework came to spread in the surface way of a lateralized root system that will not sink into the mud of E tinoha ongwesidage'dra gwe'. There is in the stories of McIntosh, Rogers, and Ray an intimation of how a medicine becomes a weed – a being or culture uprooted by those in positions of power so as to make space for their desires. If the colonial act is to pull people up like weeds, then perhaps we need to do something similar to the ways of those who mimick the invasive garlic mustard by endlessly attempting to grab up superquarries, real estate developments, pipelines, and other resource projects. The difficulty is that when you try to pull out the roots of garlic mustard, you can disturb the ground and thus create space conducive to their further expansion. As a result, this act needs to be handled in a careful way that includes basal cutting before flowering as well as reintroducing native species like bloodroot that have the capacity to reclaim forest floors. Decolonizing and Indigenizing must occur simultaneously.

But there is something more to this intergenerational work for settlers that Kimmerer helps to highlight for us through the teaching of one other non-indigenous plant medicine. On the edge between the well-trodden paths that follow these marsh shores and the urban forest grows a delicate trail of common plantain. Often found in cracks of sidewalks and boundaries between urban and naturalized spaces, this nonindigenous plant grows in a rooted way that does not sprawl, and it offers anti-microbial medicinal properties that make it useful as a poultice for wounds. But as Kimmerer counsels, common plantain also has cultural medicine for attending to the colonial truths of our time. Indigenous peoples have brought common plantain into their healing bundles because it can heal wounds, but it does so by finding a relational niche among the land's original inhabitants rather than by taking up all the space. It is not a native plant, but Kimmerer says that it has become "naturalized" to E tinoha ongwesidage'dra gwe' – just as it was for generations in good relations with the Cailleach Bhéara.

Bending down to gently touch the wide-lobed leaves, I honour how common plantain brings its medicine while in relation with the gifts of indigenous plants like wild ginger. It naturally embodies the Two Row Wampum's *og ya:dao* (friendship) and related ethic of noninterference, thus nurturing diversity. If we truly ingested plantain's medicine, the ship's garlic mustard ways would be transformed. At the same time, the gathering climate storms are highlighting the need for just such a foundational cultural change that goes beyond tinkering. Colonial ways that want to expand endlessly need to be made small and useful to life here. In the words of Kimmerer again, "Being naturalized to place means to live as if this is the land that feeds you … Here you will give your gifts and meet your responsibilities."[57]

Acts of decolonization need to be in the service of Indigenizing for Indigenous peoples and naturalizing for those who are settlers in lands distant from ancestral waters like those of the Cailleach Bhéara. The wonder that Iona's An Eaglais Dhubh evokes in me is connected to the way that plant medicines grow from the stones of a ruined mission. A similar pattern of naturalizing disrupted relations is what I sense in McIntosh's partnering with Sulian to confront the power of colonial and capitalist systems that undermine not only people and cultures but also the sacred stones and waters that have witnessed so much. Following their trip to Iona, Sulian evoked the Mi'Kmaq's 1752 Treaty with the British in publicly declaring, "I shall take the summit of this mountain into sanctuary on behalf of all my people."[58] Together with legal actions, the resulting media around this partnership halted the superquarry, with McIntosh's isle community becoming the first in Scotland to clear out the laird and bring the land back into a community trust. A garlic mustard root system was being pruned to foster space for a naturalizing medicine.

Looking up from the plantain-lined path to the stark witnessing of the cormorants, I cannot help but see through Iona's stories something dark in institutional Christianity that has predisposed the ship to the conversion of others. But it is equally clear from McIntosh's story that this missionizing urge informs most ship institutions – from religion to how knowledge is approached in the university, capitalist expansion, the prison complex that Giselle Dias confronts in this circle of the book, and the social work profession, which Shelly Hachey reflects on in the first circle.

My journey to this point in life has continually brought me to an awareness of these debilitating invasive roots in my being as a man who was born to a French Canadien woman whom I love and on a patriarchal ship that I have to struggle with at my core. These ways invade the seemingly most mundane acts, including the virtual quality of how we now often relate with sacred waters. Watching people walk by while on their phones, it seems clear that the issue is not about holding these tools but about how we are held enthralled by screen technologies that have emerged from uprooted ways of living. As Turkle writes, digital relations "offer the illusion of companionship without the demands of friendship. Our networked life allows us to hide from each other, even as we are tethered to each other."[59] We seem to be virtually extending the experience of being "pulled like weeds," and I can feel this struggle in my bones both as a university educator concerned with land relations and as a father whose daughter is in her early teens.

Sitting with the plantain that grows along this marsh, it dawns on me that its capacity to soothe and heal colonizing ways is a gift that it shares with the still heron of this marsh and with the natural worldwide web that they patiently open us to. Their quiet, unassuming presence does not take up too much space, they find cracks in the midst of colonial developments where stone-like patience and slow living can be naturalized on driven shores, and they stand in the truth of the healing mud, just as the plantain poultice is placed on our wounds. If we have a way of coming into sustained relations with herons, cormorants, and the other birds, we can open to a boundary-crossing medicine for living in relation with the world that we long ago fell into. This is the nature of the medicine carried by the heron, the storytelling guide that has taken us to the Isle of Iona and back to our home on the shores of Turtle Island.

❁ ❁

> From the time of your parents' visit to Iona until you were born in Toronto, not far from the marshes where you visit Heron, they wanted their little girl's name to be a reminder of this world's truly magical nature. Now every time they look at little Iona, you bring a spiritual magic to their lives which makes them even happier than when they first visited that little Scottish isle.[60]

"Walking in the mountains," Gae Ho Hwako says, "I could feel the shrubs brushing away the surface pain … Drinking the herbal teas, I began cleansing and healing my insides. I prayed to the water and asked for help in reminding our women to honour and respect themselves, to know their gifts and teachings, and to raise awareness about the violence against our women!" I feel a similar release of painful disconnection as I tell the story of Iona in relation to these rocks, waters, the heron, the garlic mustard, and the common plantain. The difference is that the healing comes from within the ruins of a colonial ship rather than from a distant mountain or even sacred isle, although this difference merely highlights that the medicine of the Cailleach Bhéara and E tinoha ongwesidage'dra gwe' subsumes even our invasive virtual realities. The potential for healing is always in our midst, but we need the cultural guidance of Elders and *geihnyenoh de yo ki ye'nya dohn* (spiritual helpers) to find our way into the deep ancestry of naturalizing acts like gratitude.

At different points in our lives, we can be given an expanded sense of "who" and "where" we are through teachings and ceremonies like those discussed in this book. Such living rituals remind us that we are medicine for each other – that by naturalizing the spirit of our story, we can enhance the nourishment that we give to our relations. Reflecting on this idea, I am drawn to McIntosh's tripartite vision of inclusive community. His first point is that community must be reconnected to an Indigenous sense of local lands so that reverence can inform ecological restoration and sustainable economic practices. People need opportunities to build a human-scaled relation with their bioregion, as that can foster a stronger sense of identity and thus can generate "the responsibility necessary for upholding both the social and natural environments."[61] The land's Indigenous peoples hold the regional traditions and language for what responsibility looks like, and thus Indigenizing needs to be fostered with a recognition that there will be significant political, economic, cultural, spiritual, and land implications for settlers.

McIntosh's second point is that because we live in a time of massive global migrations that are overlapping with preceding generations of colonial uprootings, reverence for local community has to transcend racism and classism. In his words, an "inclusive sense of belonging, identity and values" needs to be fostered so that we can embody a spirit of sharing.[62] This vision is consistent with friendship treaties like the Two Row Wampum and the Dish with One Spoon, and it cannot be fulfilled without pruning political, economic, cultural, and religious ways that promote garlic mustard root systems instead of diversity. Those with ancestors from distant lands need to pick up the naturalizing spirit of plantain (or another medicine from their home shores) so that we can give our cultural gifts without trying to be "the gift" – that great colonial conceit that is always trying to justify progress by directing people into a deep forgetting of their ancestral roots and the responsibilities that they hold. We live in a world where change is always happening, but sustainable and healthy change comes from reflectively listening to our ancestors rather than being forced into a colonial ideal of progress that serves the greed of a few.

This understanding leads to McIntosh's final point, which is that community needs spiritual places, not necessarily formal religion, "where one can take rest, compose and compost our inner stuff, and become more deeply present to the aliveness of life."[63] In our age of mass global movements, such sacred spaces like the Isle of Iona and urban marshes need to serve this ancestral need in a new way. A physical flight and pilgrimage to a sacred space must increasingly hold more in common with the ancestral roots of an intentional ceremony than with the consumption of modern vacationing, ecotourism, or research. As Ray highlights in relation to the popularity of Celtic holy wells, these places are now giving people who live far from their homelands an opportunity to re-engage "with the habitus of kin-religious groups." In this sense, we do not go to Iona to consume cultural sites that are disconnected from who we are, but rather we go "to physically revisit … that habitus" of our maternal waters.[64]

But traversing great distances today must be deliberate, slow, and – due to our carbon responsibilities in a time of climate changes – rare. For our premodern ancestors, participation in a pilgrimage to a distant site may have occurred once as inspiration for their life. A rare visit to such a sacred space today needs to be in service of rooting our responsibilities in Indigenous lands and relations and in service of upholding Indigenous nations. That is what I attempt as I tell the stories of Iona through my relations with the sacred waters of a local marsh. My senses are reaching out to the birthing medicine of the mud that has long supported life on Turtle Island.

Recognizing that this insight arises from engaging with the teachings of Elders like Gae Ho Hwako and Awnjibenayseekwe, I feel called to add one vital point to McIntosh's sense of sustainable communities. Our desire for the "new" and often virtual experience needs to be rebalanced by fostering the continuation of Elder knowledge that is rooted in the wisdom of ancestral land traditions. I remember that it was Gae Ho Hwako and Awnjibenayseekwe who suggested that I go with a more conscious intention to learn from beings like a white pine or a heron. Across the ocean on the Isle of Iona, the Celtic tradition has also long upheld the elder wise woman who took on the healing role as the Cailleach Bhéara. In the words of Gearóid Ó Crualaoich, this "powerful, autonomous female agency symbolically underlies and underwrites culturally, the ritual operations and services of real human females in times of social and individual crisis."[65] Just as with Elders and traditional healers on Turtle Island today, these healers, midwives, and keeners embodied a healing knowledge that is connected to spirit, earthly medicines, and sacred waters.

We wanted to ground our children in this world by doing something with their placentas, but as we had no awareness of such teachings, we kept them in our freezer as we mulled over what to do. This all changed as I taught with Gae Ho Hwako and heard about burying the baby's umbilical cord so as to root the child in the land of this life. Reflecting on her words, I experienced a mixture of feelings as I recognized something that made sense but also wondered, with a sinking heart, what it meant that we had frozen this connection.

So many times I have returned to Gae Ho Hwako's assessment of the Liberal Party of Canada: "They are looking for that navel part of the umbilical cord because no one took care to bury it, and so they are always searching, like a hungry ghost. The ceremony of their birth was not closed." From the naming of Iona to burying a frozen placenta, our attempts to move beyond the colonial roots of our family have been semi-consciously leading us toward a matrilineal approach to living.

We did not know how little we knew and how little academics could teach us, yet this matrilineal pull brought us to the Isle of Iona and our daughter's story. Through Gae Ho Hwako's reflective guidance, we have also been given a way to reflect on the traditions of Celtic healers in relation to our maternal ancestors who chose the Catholic path of a nun. The colonization and modernization of Celtic lands led to a diminished awareness of the co-creative Cailleach Bhéara, and with that came a reduced sense of autonomous female roles for grounding spirit in land and community. It is in this sense that Celtic "Catholic devotion to the cult of the Virgin 'Mother of God' owes something of its intensity and loyal endurance to its touching on sensibilities that earlier fed on notions of the 'Mother of the Gods.'"[66] With this understanding, I can renew my sense of what my ancestors were reaching for as nuns, as well as the spirit that my wife is lifting with her work in women's health.

Supporting a naturalization of these reproductive potentials for our children is my responsibility as a father. Our *geihnyenoh de yo ki ye'nya dohn* (spiritual helpers) are within our bodies, cultures, and the land, and thus we are never simply isolated individuals. This is what I try to invoke when I connect my identity with the "they" of E tinoha ongwesidage'dra gwe', with ancestral ways of coming into relation with presences all around us. Bringing this insight within, I am a "he" as a father, and Iona has taken on "she" as my daughter, but we need to recall that we are more than that. My education in the medicines around us is that of a novice, but I am starting to learn of the spiritual mystery that cannot be contained in the sterile indoors and dualistic gulfs of our colonial languages, schools, universities, and other institutions of the ship.

Like heron, we stand rooted in the mud around us, and from this position, we must forever resist colonialism. We are called to deconstruct, destabilize, and prune the ship, starting in the place where we work and live. But that is not all, for in the living spaces that open up, we need to begin naturalizing those viable seeds from our Canadien-Celtic ancestry that can take root here in the spirit of plantain's embrace of diversity, indigeneity, and life on Mother Earth.

By reflecting on these stories of Iona, it has become clear that the *og ya:dao* (friendship) of a co-creation can happen only when we honour and support the gifts that we each bring. We need to put our feet in the waters and mud that were given to us by E tinoha ongwesidage'dra gwe' and the Cailleach Bhéara and, by doing that, renew our medicine through stories and ceremonies that remind us of our mystery. This is what I hear from others in the peace-filled circles of this book as they share their unique medicine – medicine that is not mine but that I nonetheless want to learn from.

With that, I give thanks to Gae Ho Hwako, Awnjibenayseekwe, Christina, Iona, Etienne, the relations who have shared in these circles, and all those living spirits that make our lives not only possible but also good and beautiful. And so I am brought to echo the words that conclude Gae Ho Hwako's Thanksgiving Address: "We say *nya weh* (thank you). Let it be that way in our minds! *Daneto n'agahtgwe nih* (That is all for now)."

A Prayer: Gitchi Manidoo

Awnjibenayseekwe (Banakonda Kennedy-Kish Bell)

We are in a time of great changes, and this time has spirit – the All Spirit,[1] Gitchi Manidoo, the Great Mystery, the source of all life. This life is *aanji-bimaadiziwin* (a changing life), both individually and collectively, for all of creation. I am grateful for our Kendaaswin (Original Instructions), for our prophecies, they remind us of great change in our history. They have prepared us in the past and can prepare us now to stand in the Strength of Kind Honest Sharing. Spirit remains at the centre of life.

In this great unfolding, we are praying for Shkaakamigokwe (Mother Earth), for her breath, her waters, for the life of our people, for all our relatives. We lift our voices up, across Turtle Island, with our drums, with our songs, so that we will inspire each other to reach every day to be in good relations with all our relations. We call on ourselves to recognize the spirit in all, in each and every life within creation.

In our ceremonies, we recognize the heart, which is the expression of the spirit at the centre. Here, the drum travels as sound, as energy, touches us in the way that the heart touches and surrounds us with love. In this way, the drum is the voice of the Creator. We experience our own ancestors in the sounding of the drum and the rhythm of our own heartbeat.

I have heard that sounding reverberating in between and within the words shared in the circles of this book, *Q da gaho dę:s:*. In this way, I have felt the presence of the spirit of this work.

I recognize the mind, which holds the thoughts of the spirit as the centre of our life and all life; the mind emanates from the heart, from the spirit. We lift up our shakers, our rattles, to honour the seed thoughts of the Creator, shaking awake the beautiful sacred teachings of life, doing so in the way that we were given, that our ancestors held onto for us. Here, we feel the presence of our ancestors standing with us. I recall the words of Gae Ho Hwako (Norma Jacobs): "When I reflect on this journey and look at myself as the foundation for my family, my thoughts go to the ancestors who were here before me – to the ancestral women who held the canoe. What were their guidelines? How did they learn? These questions guide me to our creation story."

We honour and express our gratitude for this beautiful life, for the gift of Kind Honest Sharing and the Strength that comes from carrying and employing these gifts in our everyday lives. Together, we pray in this way, which comes to us from our ancestors, knowing they were thinking about us, perhaps standing at a crossroads similar to the one we stand at now. In this moment, in this time, we too must think about that life, those lives that are on their way here. In this way, we ourselves are on the road to being "good ancestors."[2]

We must pray within our breath, our heart, and our mind as we speak up for our First Mother, for our children, and for their children. Our thanksgiving prayer awakens us to the sacred teachings of life.

As we pray in our own way, the Thanksgiving Address remains a beautiful blueprint with which to start each day. Reaching for reciprocity, balance, and harmony in our communities and between communities re-engages us in lifting up the All Spirit that resides within all life – in all creation.[3]

We ask for the guidance that is so urgently needed to stop spending our grandchildren's future, to respect and honour the gift of our life, the gift of all life. We *are* "all related"; we *are* connected and interdependent.

Let us lift up in song an ancient saying of our people: "Treat the earth well. It was not given to you by your parents; it was loaned to you by your children. We do not inherit the earth from our ancestors; we borrow it from our children."

Megwetch Gitchi Manidoo (thank you Creator) and all my relations.

Ḛsḛhsgwaowhaneh: An Invitation to Expand the Teaching

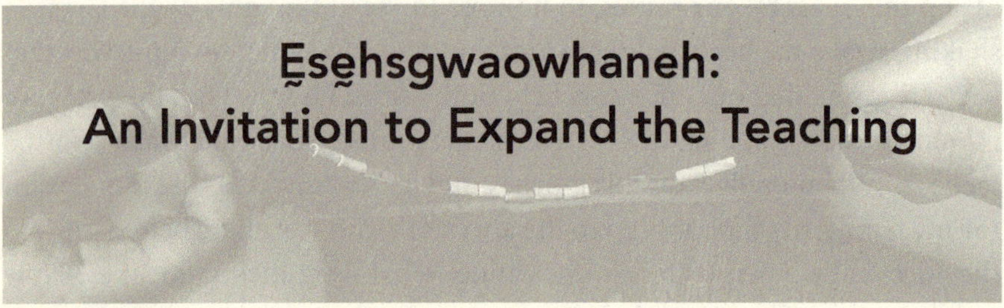

> You need to expand the teaching or story beyond what you hear and see; it is about clarity, questioning, and seeking answers.

The string is now passed to you, the reader, to “expand the teaching” in relation to your own experiences, stories, and knowledge. Is there a part of Gae Ho Hwako’s teaching that really resonates with you or perhaps something from one of the responses? Begin by reflecting on that in relation to your story. In this way, you can help us to expand the circle of truth, sharing, and healing.

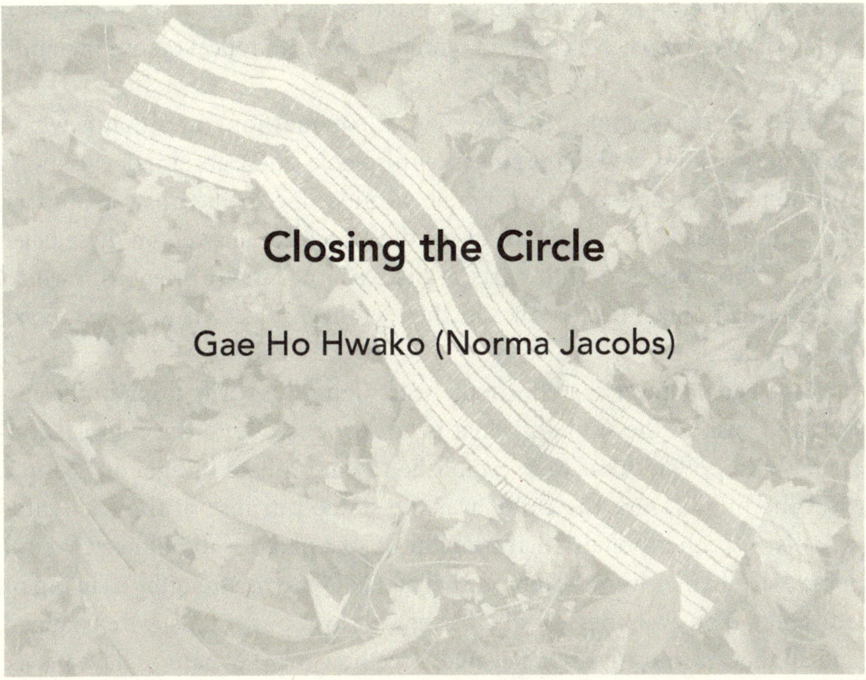

Closing the Circle

Gae Ho Hwako (Norma Jacobs)

To come to the sacred meeting space of this book, *Ǫ da gaho dę:s:*, so as to reflect on and share our journeys, all we need are simple ways of connecting who we are to values like love, peace, and friendship. People come into our lives as we connect, share, and then go our separate ways. There are many good memories and some not so good ones. But through all of these experiences, all that we take with us are our memories and learnings about skills, strengths, behaviours, and values. We need all of this in order to live a balanced life.

Many questions arise in the reflections of this book about people's origins. As Ongwehowe (lit. "original beings"), we know who we are, where we came from, and where our journey is taking us. Yet it is a huge endeavour for any of us to undergo the journey of reflection – to question our existence, our purpose, the gifts that we bring, the meaning of our names, and what has created the changes that we are experiencing. There are questions of what, when, how, and why; the list can go on and on. As I reflect on what others have shared in the circles of this book, I see that we all carry our own stories with their many different avenues, colours, scenery, environments, seasons, regalia, songs, and ceremonies. They show us that there are many veins in our bodies and roots in a tree, each a constant reminder for us to reflect on our own purpose here.

There are many who seek answers to these questions, and that is what I see in the stories shared in the circles of this book. These are simple questions, and there are people who can possibly guide one to the answers, but we must never be given the answers. I see the search for answers in these pages as the authors connect with parts of the teachings that I offer from what I have learned and reflected on and then as they reflect on what my words mean to them.

Some people never even begin the search; they just drift along in the current and bask in the sunlight. That is no surprise due to the colonial constructs and policies that were established to annihilate Indigenous people. "Kill the Indian, save the child" was the stated purpose of the residential schools and other policies that brought us to a place of disconnect! We became fearful and severed from our beliefs that gave us strength for living on our lands. The awareness of our truths was lost, our minds were changed, and all that was positive was negated. I see how these dynamics have played out in the diverse stories gathered here, and thus we see how we all struggle with this negation of our gifts by this ongoing colonialism. Is it any wonder that some have forgotten to search for their stories or to consider what a happy fulfilling life is about. Have we lost sight of even this question?

The ancestors and old ones whom I often reflect on were wise beyond their years! They had a relationship with all of creation. They listened, watched, experimented, thought in depth, and learned. I remember the old ones sitting down after a meal and getting out their pipes. Smoking while rocking in their chairs, they would reminisce about the day's activities, chuckling and laughing out loud at a youngster who did not listen to instructions. Youth had to do things the hard way before finally learning. As I remember, the old ones knew how to listen to creation. They had a conversation for reflecting on their relation to others. They could communicate without using real words, for through their feelings, a nod, or a warm embrace, they could wrap one another with their good medicine. Their ability to understand and to fully embrace each other's essence is the purpose of a ceremony like the Ganǫhǫnyǫhk (Thanksgiving Address), and it seems to me that renewing this ability would be so beneficial in our time!

We engage in all the relations given to us by E tinoha ongwesidage'dra gwe' (Mother Earth) through the daily ceremony of the Ganǫhǫnyǫhk. Where do these thoughts of connection come from? Are they in the air, water, land, strawberry, and our friendships? This simple daily ceremony brings me into relationships that help me to reflect on how I will relate. It is like the cycles of sunrise and sunset: it is something that we can just do in a way that feels natural. As with the sun, we do not need to be in a longhouse or a sweat lodge to do this ceremony. Anyone can do it, and in that sense, the circles of this book are a simple ceremony that you, the reader, have been invited to participate in.

We are a people of integrity, which is what I see shared in our ceremonies and the medicines of the surrounding environment of E tinoha ongwesidage'dra gwe'. I have used my mind to go beyond what I hear and see as I interact with our many stories, always trying to find answers to the struggles that we face. I had to go through the rigid mindset so as to ponder and visually see our behaviours and attitudes and so as to look at our foundations of truth. There are negative and positive energies in this life that I have come to understand by going back to our story about the birth of the twins, the grandsons of Sky Woman, who after falling to this earth walk gave life to a daughter who birthed these twins. We are also star people with the same struggles as the twins. Our ancestors return to the Sky World and light up the night sky. They show themselves in our sustenance, and we honour them with ceremonies at certain times of the year.

Our original mother travelled through the air and water to the earth, and by doing that, she gave us the fire of life. These stories and teachings always provided me with guidance for seeing deeper into ceremony, language, or dreams as I took this journey into the ways of my ancestors. I never asked to be invited to participate in conferences or gatherings, but all of a sudden, I was off to faraway places to share what I know about land, culture, language, treaties, history, peace, and healing. I have been honoured to be in the company of gracious people who want to follow the white roots of peace and to live a life of friendship. On the way, I was gifted with tobacco, songs, and ceremonies that helped to foster and create relationships. These medicines were offered to assist me with my development.

I recall a recurring dream that I have of a great woman who offers me a medicine bundle. Dressed in a long, fringed, white buckskin dress, she hands me this bundle as I sit in a van with my mother and father at a train station. As we pull away, she reaches out to present me with the bundle, which I go to grab. I then wake up with my hand reaching out. When I sit with this recurring dream, I have many thoughts. Maybe the gift that I am reaching for is still to come. Have I received its medicines and not understood their value? Did I already receive it and look inside? Maybe I think that I am unworthy of this bundle gifted by a spirit woman who is so magnificent. Maybe the dream is telling me to honour myself, that I am the gift, that I have been so busy looking for answers outside of myself that I have forgotten to look within.

When I was a child, we would capture grasshoppers in a glass jar that had nail holes in the lid so that they could breathe. It was funny for us as young children to watch the grasshoppers jump up and hit the top of the jar, for it is in their nature to jump. But because the grasshoppers were in this limited environment, they began to learn that if they did not jump so high, they would stop getting hurt. So in time, the grasshoppers lowered their jumps. After a while, our feelings about the grasshoppers led us to free them from the jar, but when we opened the lid, the grasshoppers were reluctant to leave. They had become accustomed to the jar and wanted to stay. Perhaps they would no longer be able to use their gift of jumping and would perish outside the jar.

When I think of these grasshoppers in the jar, I think of our people who have experienced the residential schools, incarceration in jails, and the scooping by child welfare, and I think of those who are being schooled in police academies, the military, the universities, and the schools of the ship. Many will say that these are beautiful experiences, but they have been conditioned to live in a controlled environment that they cannot escape. Since the arrival of the ship, Indigenous people have not experienced trust or inclusion. Rather than being valued, we have been objectified, becoming prisoners in our own lands through all the injustices of the Canadian government and the many processes of *genocide*. I am reminded of how, when difficult things happen in our communities, we voice our concerns but often have no action to resolve the issues.

We speak the English language while being disconnected from our language and culture, from our own gifts, like the grasshoppers that could no longer jump as high. Although we have learned much from initiatives such as the Truth and Reconciliation Commission of Canada (TRC) and the National Inquiry into Missing and Murdered Indigenous Women and Girls (MMIWG), we also need to be aware of the trickery in this English language that many of us now speak. It holds the mindset and values of the ship. Monetary compensation for past harm cannot replace the break in our connection to the cultural knowledge held in the Indigenous languages of our ancestors. As we take up our right to relearn our language, the mental abuses of trying to fit into a colonial system and language is at the forefront of our minds like a scar.

I grow tired of all that contributes to the imbalances and lack of wellness in our human existence here on E tinoha ongwesidage'dra gwe'. Since the time of contact, Indigenous peoples have been trying to share their knowledge of those values that can nurture a good and healthy relationship with the natural world and with each other. Our ancestors welcomed the immigrants from across the water, housed them, fed them, and taught them about living off the land. The immigrants suffered from diseases like scurvy, but our ancestors nursed them back to health. They displayed care and respect by helping people to survive in an unknown environment. It was a simple but rewarding life.

Through ceremony and the teachings of our wampum belts, I have heard from our ancestors about the mistreatments and the degradations of our people. My father would say that when the newcomers arrived, they asked whether they could have some land, and it was agreed that they could have some the size of a deer hide. The newcomers then cut the deer hide into strips, laid it end to end, and began extending themselves over the land more than the size of the deer hide. The law said that use of the land could be only plough deep because it was for planting sustenance for families during the winter months. Now, people drill into the earth and extract many different types of materials. These are like a person's organs and nutrients, for they give Mother Earth her life and sustain the health of her children.

Indigenous people have the responsibility to honour and celebrate our relation with E tinoha ongwesidage'dra gwe'. All of creation has a responsibility to us and we to all of creation; reciprocity is an honouring of relationships that keeps the cycle of life in balance. Today, people also dig into sacred sites and disrupt the burial grounds of our ancestors. These soils are being disrupted, and in our teachings, this activity is related to the new illnesses that we now experience, all in the name of progress and development. Pollutants are being dumped into the water from industriual sites, sewage plants, abandoned army sites, mining and fracking operations, oil fields, and gas wells. The owners are ordered to clean up, but they never do. Any person with common sense knows that processed chemicals can take thousands of years, perhaps forever, to break down. There is no accountability or respect.

I recall another dream. I was taken up a great dark mountain among other mountains, and below it was a great, clear, blue lake where one could see into the water. An elder woman invited me to that place and took me to a cabin in the mountains. As we arrived and the moonlight shone through the huge window, I told myself that this was someone else's dream. The woman then said, "Come with me. I want to show you something." We walked out to the side of the mountain as it glistened in the moonlight. She told me to "hang on tight, as we are going for a fast ride." I hung onto the mountain and heard it break away as we began our journey into the lake. At a certain point, we arrived, and she said, "That is far enough." We stayed only a moment before she instructed me again to "hold on tight as we return to the shore." When we arrived, I heard the mountain reattach itself, and we returned to the cabin, which I now noticed had a big circle on the floor.

My dream came true about a year later when I was given the opportunity to travel to Guatemala to share our teachings on the white roots of peace with elder Indigenous women from across the Americas. There, I saw pyramids, mountains, and the lake, and I also felt the presence of spirits as I witnessed prayers and ceremony. I experienced an intense and thorough thanksgiving that honoured the life-giving elements with sacred offerings of medicines. The elders were older but had no problem standing up after completing the prayers, as their limbs were still flexible. I witnessed people preparing bread in the early hours of the morning and, as we travelled, others planting or harvesting food in the fields. There was no heavy machinery, only the bare necessities, as well as trucks loaded up with produce to be exported to other countries and cities so that people could enjoy the fruits of these hard-working people filled with love for their crops.

I was amazed and struck by the powers exuding from the sacred fire. I heard no complaints, only laughter, amidst the singing and dancing of the little children and adults as we feasted together on abundant meals of corn mush, chicken, and, of course, coffee. It was refreshing to see this simple and fulfilling life filled with happiness, even though the people also struggled with colonial oppression. They were trying to reclaim and instill the importance of the Mayan language and culture, and their communities lacked many services that could be provided by their government. Despite these challenges, what I experienced was a people who were sustaining their ways. I am not sure how far removed their culture is from their original Mayan ways of living, but I felt peace and love of the land.

It seemed all so familiar to me, but it was not until the journey home that I realized that I had been to this place in my dream. They even gifted me with a black obsidian rock that was the mountain that I had clutched onto when travelling with the spiritual woman in my dream. It was a powerful experience that I will be forever grateful for!

What I have learned from reflecting on all these gifts is that the healing of being in ceremony can start with a very simple act and the good intention of gratitude. I remember sitting in a homemade sauna with a person who was very knowledgeable about our culture. He was gentle, kind, and curious about simple things like stories. I recall him sitting in our circle, laughing, sharing about health, having fun, or simply lying on the rooftop to watch the stars or the rising moon. As he handed me cedar boards, nails, and tools, we worked together to build the sauna so that I could contribute to this project that we could both enjoy. There was a nice wood-burning stove with homemade, chicken-wire saddle bags, which hung down the sides of the stove and were filled with rocks to be heated. The design was ingenious. We were excited to celebrate the project's completion, so we prepared ourselves to enter the sauna, which had been warming for an hour.

Sitting and listening to the crackling of the wood and to the medicine sizzling when thrown on the hot rocks, we could feel the sweat pouring from our bodies. The cleansing that I felt was one of the most amazing experiences of my life. With the shadows dancing on the walls, we prepared to share our stories and memories. They were so incredibly beautiful – stories about life with birds and animals that brought teachings for the people through the communication of their songs and courting dances. These words wrapped around me like a beautifully coloured robe. It was the embodiment of the loving and comforting embrace of Shogwaeyadisho' (the Creator).

When the door opened and the coolness of the night met the hot steam from the sauna, they melded into one energy and swirled around the room before exiting the door. As the door was closed once more, another teaching emerged about how people have so much to learn about love. It sounds easy to say, but in that moment, it was clear that we need to be dedicated to reflecting on the immensity and the depth of our alignment with love. Love creates a basket of interwoven legacies, values, beliefs, accountability, and responsibility. I will never forget how honoured I was to have this experience, and I will never forget to revisit what I learned in those moments of that simple, good-intentioned ceremony!

These experiences carry forward the simplicity of ceremony, healing, and stories that connect us to the excitement of life. We are so much in need of each other, and these connections are what colonialism destroys. Many of us have lost the fullness of our connection to the value of our lives – to the gift that is our place on the Two Row Wampum's river of life. It is a difficult task to move forward and to trust our truth. We need to bring our cultural values forward, as they are our ethics for living. Through ceremony, story, and reflection, our values can create cohesion in our relationships by giving us strength to believe in one another. It is in this way that we may become complementary to all our relations so that this wheel of life can once more turn in balance and harmony.

Daneto! (That is all!)

Acknowledgments

Gae Ho Hwako (Norma Jacobs)

I acknowledge my parents, Oliver and Cassie Jacobs, and the Creator for giving me the opportunity to participate in this earth walk. It has truly been a gift! I have been given the opportunity to listen, to see, and to hear the stories and songs. I have been given a sacred responsibility not only to myself but also to my family of siblings, the elder ones, my children, grandchildren, and great-grandchildren, and Mother Earth.

I acknowledge the many people who entered my life at the most pivotal moments in my journey: Agnes Williams, Fleeta Hill, Snookie Sundown, and Winnie Thomas of the Seneca Nation; Betty Isaacs/Jacobs, "Gram," and Alice Papineau of the Onondaga Nation; Jake Thomas of the Cayuga Nation; Reg Henry of the Seneca Nation; Edward Stevens, Clayton Logan, and Tom Porter of the Mohawk Nation; Simon Decoteau and Bob Brown of the Oneida Nation; and many other Ongwehowe nations of the West, East, North, and South. There were also many from the Indigenous Women's Network who introduced me to the numerous matters that confront Ongwehowe peoples. Their teachings, stories, songs, lodgings, culture, creation stories, and sustenance were medicine for me.

These people seem to have fashioned me from the clay put on the potter's wheel. Their hands held me, and their arms embraced me. They filled me with an unquenchable thirst for unconditional love, compassion, and acceptance as I welcomed and celebrated the many gifts of knowledge. They helped me to find balance. Our stories and prayers intertwined and pierced the sky. We became of one mind as we sought our truths and reminisced about the laws of the land. We worked to bring forward the truths of the Ongwehowe. Many of these wise knowledgeable people have continued their journeys back to the Creator, but their stories and teachings live in our sharing. We will always be connected in ceremony!

I acknowledge my first-born granddaughter, Tashina Cheyenne Vaughn, and her unborn son, "Tucker." Both their lives were taken without a choice, and they helped me to raise my voice and take a stand against violence, especially violence against women and children! I am also thankful to my grandson Shoshonee, who, with all of his challenges, continues to teach me every day to be thankful and to welcome the morning. He says, "Another beautiful day for my beautiful grandma," and with these words, he reminds me of the importance of family, kinship, and most of all ceremonies.

To Charlie Patton, I am thankful for the beautiful ceremony of condolence that he gave while on the Journey of the Peacemaker. I felt like a baby being held and cradled ever so gently as I experienced the tremendous, horrific losses of our people over time. It was powerful. I felt peace!

I acknowledge this great Turtle Island, the foundation of our life, identity, calling, families, clans, and nations, as well as a great teacher about the obligation to be reciprocal. To all my parts, to my body, mind, and heart, my physical, mental, and spiritual self, I give thanks.

Finally, to all the writers who, by honouring their relationships, contributed to the teachings of this book, I say *nya weh* for the experiences and reflections that you shared. I have learned, reflected, and cried tears of sadness for those who have suffered, and I have come to know about the true existence of our people. We are proud, and we continue to learn about and to confront the injustices done to our Turtle Island and to our Mother Earth, whom we hold sacred!

Glossary of Indigenous Terms

Preamble

Most of the Indigenous terms included in this glossary come from the Cayuga teachings of Gae Ho Hwako (Norma Jacobs) and thus are Cayuga. Their spelling arises from Norma's oral practice and is not based on the emerging standardization of spelling, which is related to the textual nature of colonial languages like English. As she discusses in her teachings, oral Indigenous language is deeply rooted in one's wholistic experiences of Longhouse ceremony, of land, and of spirit, and thus both her spellings and translations arise from these experiences.

There are also comparable Mohawk words used by other contributors in the book that have different spellings of a minor or major nature, and in some of these cases, we have included the term below and when possible have indicated the comparable Cayuga term used by Gae Ho Hwako. Finally, three of the contributors draw upon Anishinaabe culture and language, which have their own words with related stories and translations for various concepts, and in these cases, the associations with the Cayuga terms are indicated both in the text and here in this glossary.

It also needs to be stated once more that there are no direct one-word translations from Indigenous languages to English for the various reasons discussed in the teachings and responses of this book. Consequently, we provide here a basic sense of what these words mean through quotations or paraphrasings of the book's content, and we indicate the page numbers for those places in the book where a more detailed sensibility is offered. We hope that this glossary will help the reader to come into relation with the languages that teach us so much in the circles of this book, *Ǫ da gaho dę:s:*.

Indigenous term (culture)	Meaning
aanji-bimaadiziwin (Anishinaabe)	a changing life
Akwesasne (Mohawk)	lit. "place of partridges"
animikee (Anishinaabe)	thunder
Anishinaabekwe (Anishinaabe)	Anishinaabe woman
awehaode' (Cayuga)	soft, kind, embracing words
bimaadiziwin (Anishinaabe)	life
bineshiinh (Anishinaabe)	bird
Daneto n'agahtgwe nih (Cayuga)	That is all for now
E'dehka gakwa se dwa ja (Cayuga)	Our Eldest Brother the Sun
ęsęhsgwaowhaneh (Cayuga)	You need to "expand the teaching" or story beyond what you hear and see; it is about clarity, questioning, and seeking answers. What does this mean to you? How do we use that in our life? How do we understand that?
E tinoha ongwesidage'dra gwe' (Cayuga)	Our Mother Earth
Etisoht sohekawhnidat (Cayuga)	Our Grandmother the Moon
ga di nyo (Cayuga)	game animals
Gae Ho Hwako (Cayuga)	The Ongwehowe name of Norma Jacobs. It means "ancestral females holding the canoe before me," and it positions her in an ancestral line of great women of the Wolf Clan in the Cayuga

	Nation of the Great Haudenosaunee Confederacy.
ganigǫhi:yo (Cayuga)	a good mind
Ganǫhǫnyǫhk (Cayuga)	Thanksgiving Address (lit. "Words before All Else")
Gayensra'go:wa (Cayuga)	Great Law
ge' gyo kwa (Cayuga)	the people
geihnyenoh de yo ki ye'nya dohn (Cayuga)	spiritual helpers
gichi-gami (Anishinaabe)	the inland freshwater seas
gichi zhewitaganibi (Anishinaabe)	the great salt waters
giiwedin (Anishinaabe)	wind – known in Cayuga as *se deyowawe'nyeh*
gikendaasowin (Anishinaabe)	knowledge
gimiwun (Anishinaabe)	rain
Gitchi Manidoo (Anishinaabe)	the Great Mystery, All Spirit, or Creator – known in Cayuga as Shogwaeyadisho'
goon (Anishinaabe)	snow
Haudenosaunee (Cayuga)	People of the Longhouse
jihso'dak (Cayuga)	wild strawberry
Kaniatarowanenneh (Mohawk)	Saint Lawrence River
Kanonhses (Mohawk)	Longhouse
Kanonhseshne (Mohawk)	both the physical longhouse buildings and the Longhouse tradition
Kanyen'keha (Mohawk)	the Mohawk language
Kanyen'kehaka (Mohawk)	Mohawk Nation
Karihwi:yo (Mohawk)	Code of Handsome Lake
ka'satstenhsera (Mohawk)	empowerment
Kaswen:ta Wampum (Cayuga)	Two Row Wampum
Katarokwi (Anishinaabe)	the original name for the place where the city of Kingston, Ontario, is currently located
Kayanere'kowa (Mohawk)	Great Law of Peace

Kendaaswin (Anishinaabe)	Original Instructions
Kentyohkwa, Sewatahonhsi:yohst (Mohawk)	A Call to Listen Closely
maamoyaawendamow (Anishinaabe)	gratitude
megwetch (Anishinaabe)	thank you
Midewiwin (Anishinaabe)	Grand Medicine Society
mikwan (Anishinaabe)	ice
mikwaniwun (Anishinaabe)	hail
Mino-Bimaadiziwin (Anishinaabe)	the Good Life
Muk-a-day'-i-ko-na-yayg' (Anishinaabe)	Black Coats
Naadowewe-gichigami (Anishinaabe)	Lake Huron
nibi (Anishinaabe)	water
nya weh (Cayuga)	thank you
nyá:wen yethishot'okón:'a (Mohawk)	thank you to the ancestors
ǫ da gaho dę:s (Cayuga)	The sacred meeting space where we can communicate with one another and be really clear about who we are in our relationships. As our conversation evolves, we come to a real understanding of what the other means. This is what we refer to as *ganigǫhi:yo* (a good mind), which is needed to come to *ǫ da gaho dę:s*. This sacred space is where the ship and the canoe originally agreed upon the Two Row Wampum, and today it is the place to which we must return in order to talk about the impacts that we have experienced because of its violation.
odaotra (Cayuga)	friendship
oda:otra (Cayuga)	friends
odehadonih (Cayuga)	forests
og ya:dao (Cayuga)	friendship

Ohén:ton Karihwatéhkwen (Mohawk)	Thanksgiving Address (lit. "Words before All Else")
ojihde so:a (Cayuga)	birds
o jihso'dasha (Cayuga)	stars
okyadaot (Cayuga)	friendship as a supportive medicine
okya tsi (Cayuga)	friend
onekdangyogwe (Cayuga)	waters
onkwawenna (Mohawk)	our original languages
Onkwehón:we (Mohawk)	lit. "original beings"
onkwehonwe'néha (Mohawk)	the ways of being of the original people
Ongwehowe (Cayuga)	lit. "original beings"
onohgwatrah so:a (Cayuga)	our medicines
Ohswe:ken (Mohawk)	Six Nations of the Grand River Territory
otko (Cayuga)	bad medicine
Ouse (Anishinaabe)	Grand River, described in the original Haldimand Grant
se deyowawe'nyeh (Cayuga)	winds
sema (Anishinaabe)	tobacco
sgeno (Cayuga)	You are saying hello and that are you well. You are asking, "Are you in the good mind? Do you carry the Great Peace brought to us by the Peacemaker and Ayenwatha?"
Shkaakamigokwe (Anishinaabe)	Our Mother Earth – known in Cayuga as E tinoha ongwesidage' dra gwe'
Shogwaeyadisho' (Cayuga)	the Creator (lit. "the one who created our bodies")
Shonkwaya'tihson (Mohawk)	the Creator (lit. "he finished our bodies") – known in Cayuga as Shogwaeyadisho'
ska'nikonhra (Mohawk)	one mind, body, and soul

skowanaht (Mohawk)	It is everyone's responsibility to take in the information, knowledge, or teaching and to grow it in order to take it further – known in Cayuga as *ęsęhsgwaowhaneh* (expand the teaching)
Tekeni Teyoha:te (Mohawk)	Two Row Wampum
tikkanaagan (Anishinaabe)	cradle board, in which a baby is carried
Tsi Sniahne (Mohawk)	the place where the Racquette and Saint Regis Rivers join the Saint Lawrence River (lit. "a confluence of rivers")
tsi tyotáhsawe tsi yonhwentsiá:te (Mohawk)	when the earth began
wawasum (Anishinaabe)	lightning
wayaniyohnta (Cayuga)	hanging fruits
Yonkwaskare:wake (Mohawk)	Bear Clan
Zhaashkoonh (Anishinaabe)	Muskrat

Suggested Further Reading

Gae Ho Hwako and Awnjibenayseekwe have compiled a short selection of suggested further reading or listening that offers Elder and academic perspectives on the teachings found in this book. The items are organized primarily in relation to the Haudenosaunee and the Anishinaabe. You can also look to the bibliography for other sources.

Haudenosaunee Elder Teachings

Lyons, Oren. "Preamble." In *Basic Call to Consciousness*, ed. Akwesasne Notes, 13–25. Summertown, TN: Native Voices, 2005.

Porter, Tom (Sakokweniónkwas). *And Grandma Said … : Iroquois Teachings as Passed Down through the Oral Tradition*. Bloomington, IN: Xlibris Corporation, 2008.

Thomas, Jacob, with Terry Boyle. *Teachings from the Longhouse*. 1994. Reprint, Toronto: Stoddart, 2013.

Wall, Steve. *To Become a Human Being: The Message of Tadodaho Chief Leon Shenandoah*. Newbury Port, MA: Hampton Roads, 2002.

Haudenosaunee Academic Teachings

Hill, Susan M. *The Clay We Are Made Of: Haudenousanee Land Tenure on the Grand River*. Winnipeg: University of Manitoba Press, 2017.

Martin-Hill, Dawn. *As Snow before the Summer Sun: Our Relationship to the Natural Environment, a Resource Guide*. Brantford: ON: Woodland Cultural Centre, 1992.

Mohawk, John. *Thinking in Indian: A John Mohawk Reader*. Ed. José Barreiro. Golden, CO: Fulcrum, 2010.

Monture, Rick. *We Share Our Matters: Two Centuries of Writing and Resistance at Six Nations of the Grand River*. Winnipeg: University of Manitoba Press, 2014.

Rice, Brian. *The Rotinonshonni: A Traditional Iroquoian History through the Eyes of Teharonhia:wako and Sawiskera*. Syracuse, NY: Syracuse University Press, 2013.

Simpson, Audra. *Mohawk Interruptus: Political Life across the Borders of Settler States*. Durham, NC: Duke University Press, 2014.

Anishinaabe/Indigenous Elder Teachings

Benton-Banai, Edward. *The Mishomis Book: The Voice of the Ojibway*. Minneapolis: University of Minnesota Press, 2010.

Dumont, James (Onaubinisay). "Onaubinisay at the 2018 World Parliament of Religions." YouTube, 26 November 2018. https://www.youtube.com/watch?v=AB-Fi31klTs.

Ermine, Willie. "Aboriginal Epistemology." In *First Nation Education in Canada: The Circle Unfolds*, ed. Marie Battiste and Jean Barman, 101–11. Vancouver: UBC Press, 2000.

Johnston, Basil. *Ojibway Heritage*. Toronto: McLelland and Stewart, 1976.

Kennedy-Kish Bell, Banakonda. "Indigenous Wholistic Well-Being and Healing." In *Holistic Healing: Theories, Practice and Social Change*, ed. Peter A. Dunn, 252–67. Toronto: Canadian Scholars' Press, 2019.

Anishinaabe/Indigenous Academic Teachings

Absolon, Kathleen E. (Minogiizhigokwe). *Kaandossiwin: How We Come to Know*. Black Point, NS: Fernwood, 2011.

Anderson, Kim. *Life Stages and Native Women: Memory, Teachings, and Story Medicine.* Winnipeg: University of Manitoba Press, 2011.

Hill, Gus. *Indigenous Healing: Voices of Elders and Healers*. Vernon, BC: JCharlton, 2021.

Kimmerer, Robin Wall. *Braiding Sweetgrass: Indigenous Wisdom, Scientific Knowledge and the Teachings of Plants*. Minneapolis, MN: Milkweed, 2013.

Maracle, Lee. *I Am Woman: A Native Perspective on Sociology and Feminism.* 2nd ed. Vancouver: Press Gang, 2003.

Simpson, Leanne. *Dancing on Our Turtle's Back: Stories of Nishnaabeg Re-Creation, Resurgence and a New Emergence.* Winnipeg: Arbeiter Ring, 2011.

Turner, Dale. *This Is Not a Peace Pipe: Towards a Critical Indigenous Philosophy*. Toronto: University of Toronto Press, 2006.

Notes

Ganǫhǫnyǫhk (Thanksgiving Address, or "Words before All Else")

1 The Thanksgiving Address represented here in writing is first and foremost an oral prayer that follows this structural form but often with nuances and stories related to the speaker, audience, and time of sharing. This characteristic can be seen in the following teachings of Gae Ho Hwako (Norma Jacobs) as she unwraps various insights about the spirit of the Thanksgiving Address by drawing on her life experiences. The basic form outlined here is also part of a collective article on the mass extinction crisis published in the journal *Social and Cultural Geography* (see Theriault et al., "Living Protocols"), although the one in this book is longer and is given other dimensions by the teachings of Gae Ho Hwako and by the responses of circle participants that follow. Both that publication and this book began with circle gatherings centred by an oral sharing of the Thanksgiving Address (lit. "Words before All Else"), and thus its written form here follows Haudenosaunee protocol.

Kentyohkwa, Sewatahonhsi:yohst! (A Call to Listen Closely!)

1 This is a commonly used phrase to refer to culturally appropriate behaviour. It tells us that it aligns with the protocols and practices of *onkwehonwe'néha* (the ways of being of the original people).

2 Daniels, "Invisible Work."

3 This phrase is in reference to a prophecy shared by a tiny, yet powerful, Peruvian healer. Her nation tells us that the only people to survive into the next world will be those with hearts of honey and that the only human practices to continue will be those actions infused by great love, compassion, and integrity.

Ęsęhsgwaowhaneh: An Invitation to Expand the Teaching

1 I acknowledge the Centre for Teaching Innovation and Excellence at Wilfrid Laurier University for the original educational research grant that began these discussions with Norma Jacobs and eventually led to the vision for this book and its educational intent. In particular, we recognize the support of Shirley Hall and Joe Beer.

2 Thomas, with Boyle, *Teachings from the Longhouse*, 16.

3 Ibid., 17.

4 Truth and Reconciliation Commission of Canada, *Honouring the Truth*, 252.

5 Thomas, with Boyle, *Teachings from the Longhouse*, 131.

6 Truth and Reconciliation Commission of Canada, *Honouring the Truth*, 3.

7 M'Gonigle and Starke, *Planet U*, 33.

8 Battiste, *Decolonizing Education*, 24–5.

9 Thomas, with Boyle, *Teachings from the Longhouse*, 135.

10 Quoted in Foster, "Jacob Ezra Thomas," 160.

Maamoyaawendamow (Gratitude)

1 Teaching of Onaubinisay (James Dumont).

2 Ibid.

3 Ibid.

4 Deloria Jr, *C.G. Jung and the Sioux Traditions*, 187.

Awehaode Communication: Journeying with Norma

1 Mohawk, *Iroquois Creation Story*, xi–xii.

2 A. Simpson, *Mohawk Interruptus*, 375.

3 Ibid.

4 Smith, *Decolonizing Methodologies*; Wilson, *Research Is Ceremony*.

5 Mohawk, *Thinking in Indian*, 5.
6 Wilson, *Research Is Ceremony*, 12.
7 TallBear, "Standing with and Speaking as Faith."
8 Akwesasne Mohawk Council, "Kaswentha."
9 Wilson, *Research Is Ceremony*, 22.
10 Senator Murray Sinclair, personal communication with author, 2018.
11 Mihesuah and Wilson, *Indigenizing the Academy*, 2.
12 McCarthy, *In Divided Unity*, 44.
13 Hornberger, ed., *Can Schools Save?*, 2. See also Tehota'kerá:tonh, *Pathways to Creating*, 19.
14 Runningwater, "Exploring Ethnic Fraud," 212.
15 Haudenosaunee Confederacy, "People of the Haudenosaunee," 5–6.
16 Blaisdell, ed., *Great Speeches by Native Americans*, 15.
17 Turner, *This Is Not a Peace Pipe*.
18 Shiva, "Reductionism and Regeneration," 22.
19 Merchant, *Death of Nature*, xxi.
20 See Tehota'kerá:tonh and Owennatékha, "Root-Word Method."
21 L. Simpson, "Anticolonial Strategies," 378.

Learning to Trust the Current: My Journey down the River of Life

1 Blackstock, "Occasional Evil of Angels," 30.
2 Morrison et al., "Permanency through Wabanaki Eyes," 103.
3 de Finney and di Tomasso, "Creating Places of Belonging," 63.
4 Parliament of Canada, *Sessional Papers … 1887*, 37.
5 Quoted in Truth and Reconciliation Commission of Canada, *Honouring the Truth*, 3.
6 Kennedy-Kish Bell et al., *Case Critical*, 193.
7 Absolon, *Kaandossiwin*, 19.
8 Kennedy-Kish Bell et al., *Case Critical*, 267.
9 Awnjibenayseekwe (Banakonda Kennedy-Kish Bell), personal communication with author, 2019.
10 D.M. Hill, "Traditional Medicine," 36.
11 Kennedy-Kish Bell, "Indigenous Wholistic Well-Being," 265–6.
12 Hart, "Anti-Colonial Indigenous Social Work."
13 Simard, "Culturally Restorative."

14 Ibid., 44.
15 Ibid., 46.

Unravelling Our Roots: Wholistic Paths in Two Row Education

1 Quoted in Foster, "Jacob Ezra Thomas," 164–7.
2 Thomas, with Boyle, *Teachings from the Longhouse*, 131–2.
3 Ibid., 132–3.
4 Jen Green, *Magic and Mystery of Trees*, 38–9.
5 Wohlleben, *Hidden Life of Trees*, 10.
6 Trigger, *Children of Aataentsic*; Robertson, *Walking into Wilderness*.
7 Sagard, *Sagard's Long Journey*, 171.
8 Thomas, with Boyle, *Teachings from the Longhouse*, 137.
9 Sagard, *Sagard's Long Journey*, 160–1.
10 Quoted in Moogk, *La Nouvelle France*, 45–6.
11 Podruchny, *Making the Voyageur World*, 72.
12 Champlain, quoted in Robertson, *Walking into Wilderness*, 58.
13 Champlain, quoted in ibid., 28.
14 Quoted in Foster, "Jacob Ezra Thomas," 160.
15 Quoted in ibid., 151, 160.
16 See Leduc, *Climate, Culture, Change*; and Leduc, *Canadian Climate of Mind*.
17 Dickason, "From 'One Nation' in the Northeast," 19.
18 Bonaparte, "History of Akwesasne."
19 Ibid.
20 Ibid.
21 Bonaparte, *Lily among Thorns*, 161–2.
22 Quoted in Havard, *Great Peace of Montreal*, 137.
23 Robertson, *Walking into Wilderness*, 62–3.
24 Bouchard, *Great Law*, 19.
25 Thomas, with Boyle, *Teachings from the Longhouse*, 17.
26 Quoted in Kelsay, *Joseph Brant, 1743–1807*, 363.
27 Quoted in C.M. Johnston, "Rousseaux St John, John Baptist."
28 Kelsay, *Joseph Brant*, 371.
29 Ibid., 538.
30 Senior, *From Royal Township*, 20.
31 Bonaparte, "History of Akwesasne," 10.

32 CDSBEO Indigenous Education Program, "Treaty and Land Claim Information."
33 Monture, *We Share Our Matters*, 30.
34 Quoted in Kelsay, *Joseph Brant*, 652.
35 Quoted in ibid., 426.
36 Ibid., 87. See also Woodworth and Leduc, "We Are Renewable."
37 Elbourne, "Broken Alliance," 506.
38 Quoted in Truth and Reconciliation Commission of Canada, *Honouring the Truth*, 2–3.
39 Quoted in ibid., 105.
40 Blackstock, "Occasional Evil of Angels," 29.
41 Truth and Reconciliation Commission of Canada, *Honouring the Truth*, 3.
42 Ibid., 59.
43 Franklin, *Real World of Technology*.
44 Quoted in Kelsay, *Joseph Brant*, 652. I also want to acknowledge that I worked through some of the ideas around Joseph Brant, residential schools, and land-based social work education that I discuss here in a different context in a publication with the *Journal of Social Work Education*. See Leduc, "'Let Us Continue.'"
45 Truth and Reconciliation Commission of Canada, *Honouring the Truth*, 252.
46 Benton-Banai, *Mishomis Book*, 110.
47 Jen Green, *Magic and Mystery of Trees*, 36–7.
48 Blackstock, "Occasional Evil of Angels."
49 The role of land in healing is discussed in more detail in my reflection in the final circle of this book.
50 Leduc, *Climate, Culture, Change*; Leduc, *Canadian Climate of Mind*.
51 Franklin, *Real World of Technology*, 19.
52 Mohawk, *Utopian Legacies*, 11–13.
53 Truth and Reconciliation Commission of Canada, *Honouring the Truth*, 3.
54 Thomas, with Boyle, *Teachings from the Longhouse*, 137.
55 Truth and Reconciliation Commission of Canada, *Honouring the Truth*, 17.
56 Foster, "Jacob Ezra Thomas," 159.
57 Thomas, with Boyle, *Teachings from the Longhouse*, 135.
58 Foster, "Jacob Ezra Thomas," 159.
59 Ibid., 151.
60 Ibid., 159.
61 Thomas, with Boyle, *Teachings from the Longhouse*, 145.

62 Bouchard, *Great Law*, 27.
63 Thomas, with Boyle, *Teachings from the Longhouse*, 144.
64 Powell, trans., *Meditations on the Tarot*, 223.
65 Thomas, with Boyle, *Teachings from the Longhouse*, 135.

A Prayer: Two Road

1 Hill, "Two Row History."
2 Neihardt, *Black Elk Speaks*, 115.

Teaching Them to Dance: Reclaiming Indigenous Parenting

1 Johnston, *Ojibway Heritage*, 13–17.
2 Absolon and Willett, "Putting Ourselves Forward."
3 Anderson, *Recognition of Being*, 171–3.
4 LaRocque, "Métis and Feminist," 63. See also Snyder, Napoleon, and Borrows, "Gender and Violence," 611. This discussion in the context of Indigenous feminisms is also present in several chapters of Nickel and Fehr, eds, *In Good Relation*.
5 For example, see Lavell-Harvard and Lavell, eds, *"Until Our Hearts Are on the Ground"*; Lavell-Harvard and Anderson, eds, *Mothers of the Nations*; and Neufeld and Cidro, eds, *Indigenous Experiences of Pregnancy and Birth*.
6 Simpson, "Birthing an Indigenous Resurgence," 32.
7 Simpson, *Dancing on Our Turtle's Back*, 66.
8 I have written about this experience in detail. See Leddy, "Mum with the Dark Hair."
9 Ibid.
10 Ibid.
11 Lippert and Engel, "Great Lakes in Ojibwe."
12 Simpson, *Dancing on Our Turtle's Back*, 148–9.

Haudenosaunee Women in between the Generations

1 Anderson, *Life Stages and Native Women*; Wilson, *Research Is Ceremony*; Smith, *Decolonizing Methodologies*; Kermoal and Altamirano-Jiménez, eds, *Living on the Land*; Sams, *13 Original Clan Mothers*; Chacaby, with Plummer, *Two-Spirit*

Journey; Kimmerer, *Braiding Sweetgrass.*

2 National Inquiry into Missing and Murdered Indigenous Women and Girls (MMIWG), *Interim Report*; Bourgeois, *Warrior Women*; Hunter, "Violence That Indigenous Women Face"; Dean, *Remembering Vancouver's Disappeared Women.*

3 Maracle, *I Am Woman*, 40.

4 Wilson, *Research Is Ceremony*, 175.

5 Friedan, *Feminine Mystique*, 15.

6 Anderson, *Life Stages and Native Women.*

7 Wilson, *Research Is Ceremony*, 13.

8 Spittal, ed., *Iroquois Women*, 85.

9 Stewart-Harawira, "Practising Indigenous Feminism," 125.

10 Altamirano-Jiménez and Kermoal, "Introduction," 5.

11 Ibid.

12 Anderson, *Life Stages and Native Women*, 97.

13 Wilson, *Research Is Ceremony.*

A Prayer: Shkaakamigokwe

1 Dumont, "Onaubinisay at the 2018 World Parliament."

2 Teachings of Onaubinisay (James Dumont) and personal communication with author.

3 Maracle, *Celia's Song*, 4.

Friendship Is a Sheltering Tree

1 Hill, *Shaking the Rattle*, 130.

2 Ibid., 54.

Teachings from Spruce: The Nature of Prisons

1 As explained more fully later in the chapter, I use the language of "they/them/their" to avoid gender binaries.

2 Teaching of Awnjibenayseekwe (Banakonda Kennedy-Kish Bell).

3 Although Cayuga is not my traditional language, I use words here that Gae Ho Hwako (Norma Jacobs) lifts up throughout the book.

4 Kennedy-Kish Bell et al., *Case Critical*, 4, 6.

5 I am engaging Kathy Absolon's spelling of "wholistic" versus "holistic" to represent a wholeness that is "complete, balanced and circular." See Absolon, "Indigenous Wholistic Theory," 75.

6 Kennedy-Kish Bell et al., *Case Critical*, 6.

7 Foucault, *Discipline and Punish*, 200.

8 Awnjibenayseekwe (Banakonda Kennedy-Kish Bell), personal communication with author, 2017–20.

9 Private family visits are offered, under certain conditions, in federal prisons across Canada. It is an opportunity for families to spend time with their loved ones in a "home-like" atmosphere.

10 The ion scanner is used as a drug-screening test to see whether you have traces of drugs on you. It has been proven to be an ineffective method of screening, yet it is still used by CSC, with serious consequences for prisoners and their families.

11 Contraband includess anything that the prison administration deems to be "illegal," or not allowed into prisons.

12 Zinger, *Office of the Correctional Investigator*, 61–2.

13 Collins, *Living without Human Contact*, 2.

14 Kimmerer, *Braiding Sweetgrass*, 208–9.

15 Collins, *Free Inside*, 129.

16 Prison for Women closed in 2000.

17 Rymhs, *From the Iron House*, 69.

18 Zinger, *Office of the Correctional Investigator*, 65.

19 Wagamese, "To say All My Relations."

20 The PFV quarters are similar to a two-bedroom trailer with its own kitchen and washroom.

21 Kimmerer, *Braiding Sweetgrass*, 115.

22 Ibid.

23 Ibid., 107. Kimmerer explains that "the actual wording of the Thanksgiving Address varies with the speaker. This cited text is the widely published version of John Stokes and Kanawahientun."

24 Geniusz, *Plants Have So Much*, 77–80.

25 Simpson, *As We Have Always Done*, 79.

26 Kathleen E. Absolon, personal communication with author, 13 May 2019.

27 I have heard this teaching from many different people, all of whom refer back to Onaubinisay.

28 I do not identify as two-spirit.

29 Armstrong, "Land Speaking," 155.

30 Driskill et al., eds, *Queer Indigenous Studies*; Driskill et al., eds, *Sovereign Erotics*; Barker, *Critically Sovereign*.

31 Simpson, *As We Have Always Done*, 122.

32 Kimmerer, *Braiding Sweetgrass*, 55–6.

33 Quoted in Women's Earth Alliance and Native Youth Sexual Health Network, *Violence on the Land*, 5.

34 Wohlleben, *Hidden Life of Trees*, 10.

35 Armstrong, "Land Speaking."

36 Ibid., 144.

37 Collins, *Free Inside*, 129.

38 Ware, Rusza, and Dias, "It Can't Be Fixed."

Standing in Ancestral Waters: Acts in Naturalizing Maternal Relations

1 Kimmerer, *Braiding Sweetgrass*, 236.

2 Capaldi et al., "Flourishing in Nature"; Williams, "This Is Your Brain."

3 Grady, *Toronto the Wild*, 5.

4 Kimmerer, *Braiding Sweetgrass*, 213.

5 Ibid., 214–15.

6 Turkle, *Alone Together*, 16–17.

7 Kennedy-Kish Bell, "Indigenous Wholistic Well-Being," 261.

8 Ermine, "Aboriginal Epistemology," 104.

9 Quoted in Best Start Resource Centre, *Supporting the Sacred Journey*, 28.

10 Lessels and Leduc, *Story of Iona*.

11 Kushlan and Hancock, *Herons*, 8, 12.

12 On the Power and Control Wheel, see https://www.theduluthmodel.org/wheels/understanding-power-control-wheel/.

13 Baskin, *Strong Helpers' Teachings*, 159–60.

14 National Inquiry into Missing and Murdered Indigenous Women and Girls (MMIWG), *Interim Report*, 7–8.

15 Shiva, *Monocultures of the Mind*; Plumwood, *Feminism and the Mastery of Nature*.

16 Some of the material related to the heron is drawn from a journal article that I published in *Social and Cultural Geography* but have reworked in this different context. See Leduc, "Falling with Heron."
17 Kimmerer, *Braiding Sweetgrass*, 8–9.
18 Ibid.
19 Dillon and Chadwick, *Celtic Realms*, 143.
20 Ó Crualaoich, *Book of the Cailleach*, 90.
21 M. Green, *Animals in Celtic Life and Myth*, 174.
22 Ibid., 212–13.
23 Ibid., 160.
24 Marsden, *Sea-Road of the Saints*, 48, 45.
25 See Leduc, *Canadian Climate of Mind*, 119–21.
26 Ray, *Origins of Ireland's Holy Wells*, 40.
27 Logan, *Oak*, 86.
28 M. Green, *Animals in Celtic Life and Myth*, 212–13.
29 Kushlan and Hancock, *Herons*, 60–1.
30 Campbell, *Flight of the Wild Gander*, 168.
31 Bouchard, *Great Law*.
32 Roots, Chant, and Heidenreich, *Special Places*, 221.
33 Kushlan and Hancock, *Herons*, 62.
34 Roots, Chant, and Heidenreich, *Special Places*, 236.
35 Kushlan and Hancock, *Herons*, 56–8, 85.
36 Ray, *Origins of Ireland's Holy Wells*, 1.
37 Ibid.
38 Ibid., 100–1.
39 Ray, "Paying the Rounds," 426.
40 Lessels and Leduc, *Story of Iona*.
41 Ruiter, "Killing Cormorants."
42 Benton-Banai, *Mishomis Book*, 106.
43 Leduc, *Climate, Culture, Change*.
44 de Watteville, *Isle of Iona*.
45 Ray, *Origins of Ireland's Holy Wells*, 91.
46 Ibid., 81.
47 Ibid., 86.
48 Ray, "Paying the Rounds," 423.
49 Saul, *Reflections of a Siamese Twin*, 84.

50 Quoted in McIntosh, *Soil and Soul*, 229–30.
51 Ibid., 198.
52 Rogers, *Rough and Plenty*, 8.
53 Kimmerer, *Braiding Sweetgrass*.
54 Rogers, *Rough and Plenty*, 14.
55 McIntosh, *Soil and Soul*, 42.
56 Ibid., 45–6.
57 Kimmerer, *Braiding Sweetgrass*, 214–15.
58 Quoted in McIntosh, *Soil and Soul*, 241.
59 Turkle, *Alone Together*, 1.
60 Lessels and Leduc, *Story of Iona*.
61 McIntosh, *Soil and Soul*, 269.
62 Ibid, 280.
63 Ibid.
64 Ray, "Paying the Rounds," 428.
65 Ó Crualaoich, *Book of the Cailleach*, 95.
66 Ibid., 30.

A Prayer: Gitchi Manidoo

1 These are the words that Elder Onaubinisay (Jim Dumont) uses when talking about Gitchi Manidoo.
2 I acknowledge that this concept of being "good ancestors" arises from many discussions with Dr Gus Hill. See also his book *Indigenous Healing: Voices of Elders and Healers* (2021).
3 Teaching of Onaubinisay (Jim Dumont).

Bibliography

Absolon, Kathleen E. (Minogiizhigokwe). "Indigenous Wholistic Theory: A Knowledge Set for Practice." *First Peoples Child and Family Review* 5, no. 2 (2010): 74–87.

– *Kaandossiwin: How We Come to Know*. Black Point, NS: Fernwood, 2011.

Absolon, Kathleen E. (Minogiizhigokwe), and Cam Willett. "Putting Ourselves Forward: Location in Aboriginal Research." In *Research as Resistance: Critical, Indigenous, and Anti-Oppressive Approaches*, ed. Leslie Brown and Susan Strega, 97–126. Toronto: Canadian Scholars' Press, 2005.

Akwesasne Mohawk Council. "The Kaswentha (Two Row Wampum)." Accessed 5 December 2017. http://www.akwesasne.ca/node/118.

Altamirano-Jiménez, Isabel, and Nathalie Kermoal. "Introduction: Indigenous Women and Knowledge." In *Living on the Land: Indigenous Women's Understanding of Place*, ed. Nathalie Kermoal and Isabel Altamirano-Jiménez, 3–18. Edmonton: Athabasca University Press, 2016.

Anderson, Kim. *Life Stages and Native Women: Memory, Teachings, and Story Medicine*. Winnipeg: University of Manitoba Press, 2011.

– *A Recognition of Being: Reconstructing Native Womanhood*. Toronto: Sumach, 2000.

Armstrong, Jeanette. "Land Speaking." In *Read, Listen, Tell: Indigenous Stories from Turtle Island*, ed. Sophie McCall, Deanna Reder, David Gaertner, and Gabrielle L'Hirondelle-Hill, 141–55. Waterloo, ON: Wilfrid Laurier University Press, 2017.

Baskin, Cyndy, *Strong Helpers' Teachings: The Value of Indigenous Knowledges in the Helping Professions*. Toronto: Canadian Scholars' Press, 2011.

Battiste, Marie. *Decolonizing Education: Nourishing the Learning Spirit*. Saskatoon: Purich, 2013.

Barker, Joanne. *Critically Sovereign: Indigenous Gender, Sexuality and Feminist Studies*. Durham, NC: Duke University Press, 2017.

Benton-Banai, Edward. *The Mishomis Book: The Voice of the Ojibway*. Minneapolis: University of Minnesota Press, 2010.

Best Start Resource Centre. *Supporting the Sacred Journey: From Preconception to Parenting for First Nations Families in Ontario*. Toronto: Best Start Resource Centre, 2012. https://resources.beststart.org/product/e31a-preconception-to-parenting-first-nations-ontario-manual/.

Blackstock, Cindy. "The Occasional Evil of Angels: Learning from the Experiences of Aboriginal Peoples and Social Work." *First Peoples Child and Family Review* 4, no. 1 (2009): 28–37.

Blaisdell, Bob, ed. *Great Speeches by Native Americans*. Mineola, NY: Dover, 2000.

Bonaparte, Darren. "The History of Akwesasne from Pre-Contact to Modern Times." http://www.wampumchronicles.com/history.html.

– *A Lily among Thorns: The Mohawk Repatriation of Kateri Tekahkwi:tha*. Akwesasne: Akwesasne Mohawk Territory, 2009.

Bouchard, David. *The Great Law: Kayaneren'kó:wa*. North Vancouver: More Than Words, 2014. https://expydoc.com/doc/3457851/the-great-law—-david-bouchard.

Bourgeois, Robyn Sanderson. "Warrior Women: Indigenous Women's Anti-Violence Engagement with the Canadian State." PhD diss., University of Toronto, 2014.

Campbell, Joseph, *The Flight of the Wild Gander: Explorations in the Mythological Dimension*. New York: Harper Perennial, 1990.

Capaldi, Colin A., Holli-Anne Passmore, Elizabeth Nisbet, John Micheal Zelenski, and Raelyne L. Dopko. "Flourishing in Nature: A Review of the Benefits of Connecting with Nature and Its Application as a Wellbeing Intervention." *International Journal of Wellbeing* 5, no. 4 (2015): 1–16.

CDSBEO Indigenous Education Program. "Treaty and Land Claim Information." https://indigenoused.cdsbeo.on.ca/for-educators/treaty-and-land-claim-information/.

Chacaby, Ma-Nee, with Mary Louis Plummer. *A Two-Spirit Journey: The Autobiog-*

raphy of a Lesbian Ojibwa-Cree Elder. Winnipeg: University of Manitoba Press, 2016.

Collins, Peter. *Free Inside: The Life and Work of Peter Collins*. Toronto: Ad Astra Comix, 2018.

– *Living without Human Contact*. Kingston, ON: Bound & Gagged, 2012.

Daniels, Arlene Kaplan. "Invisible Work." *Social Problems* 34, no. 5 (1987): 403–15.

Dean, Amber. *Remembering Vancouver's Disappeared Women: Settler Colonialism and the Difficulty of Inheritance*. Toronto: University of Toronto Press, 2016.

de Finney, Sandrina, and Lara di Tomasso. "Creating Places of Belonging: Expanding Notions of Permanency with Indigenous Youth in Care." *First Peoples Child and Family Review* 10, no. 1 (2015): 63–85.

Deloria, Vine, Jr. *C.G. Jung and the Sioux Traditions: Dreams, Visions, Nature, and the Primitive*. New Orleans, LA: Spring Journal Books, 2016.

de Watteville, Alastair, *The Isle of Iona: Sacred, Spectacular, Living*. Hampshire, UK: Romsey Fine Art, 1999.

Dickason, Olive Patricia. "From 'One Nation' in the Northeast to 'New Nation' in the Northwest: A Look at the Emergence of the Métis." In *The New Peoples: Being and Becoming Métis in North America*, ed. Jacqueline Peterson and Jennifer S.H. Brown, 19–36. Winnipeg: University of Manitoba Press, 1985.

Dillon, Myles, and Nora Chadwick. *The Celtic Realms: The History and the Culture of the Celtic Peoples from Pre-History to the Norman Invasion*. Northfield, NJ: Castle Books, 2006.

Driskill, Qwo-Li, Chris Finley, Brian Joseph Gilley, and Scott Lauria Morgensen, eds. *Queer Indigenous Studies: Critical Interventions in Theory, Politics, and Literature*. Tucson: University of Arizona Press, 2011.

Driskill Qwo-Li, Daniel Heath Justice, Deborah Miranda, and Lisa Tatonetti, eds. *Sovereign Erotics: A Collection of Two-Spirit Literature*. Tucson: University of Arizona Press, 2011.

Dumont, James (Onaubinisay). "Onaubinisay at the 2018 World Parliament of Religions." YouTube, 26 November 2018. https://www.youtube.com/watch?v=AB-Fi31klTs.

Elbourne, Elizabeth. "Broken Alliance: Debating Six Nations' Land Claims in 1822." *Cultural and Social History* 9, no. 4 (2012): 497–525.

Ermine, Willie. "Aboriginal Epistemology." In *First Nation Education in Canada: The Circle Unfolds*, ed. Marie Battiste and Jean Barman, 101–11. Vancouver: UBC Press, 2000.

Foster, Michael K. "Jacob Ezra Thomas: Educator and Conservator of Iroquois Culture." In Jacob Thomas, with Terry Boyle, *Teachings from the Longhouse*, 150–80. 1994. Reprint, Toronto: Stoddart, 2013.

Foucault, Michel. *Discipline and Punish: The Birth of the Prison*. 2nd ed. New York: Vintage Books, 1995.

Franklin, Ursula M. *The Real World of Technology*. 2nd ed. Toronto: Anansi, 1999.

Friedan, Betty. *The Feminine Mystique*. New York: Norton, 1963.

Geniusz, Mary Siisip. *Plants Have So Much to Give Us, All We Have to Do Is Ask: Anishinaabe Botanical Teachings*. Minneapolis: University of Minnesota Press, 2015.

Grady, Wayne. *Toronto the Wild: Field Notes of an Urban Naturalist*. Toronto: MacFarlane Walter and Ross, 1995.

Green, Jen. *The Magic and Mystery of Trees*. New York: DK Publishing, 2019.

Green, Joyce, ed. *Making Space for Indigenous Feminism*. Black Point, NS: Fernwood, 2007.

Green, Miranda. *Animals in Celtic Life and Myth*. New York: Routledge, 1992.

Hart, Michael Anthony (Kaskitémahikan). "Anti-Colonial Indigenous Social Work: Reflections on an Aboriginal Approach." In *Wícihitowin: Aboriginal Social Work in Canada*, ed. Raven Sinclair (Ótiskewápíwskew), Michael Anthony Hart (Kaskitémahikan), and Gord Bruyere (Amawaajibitang), 25–41. Black Point, NS: Fernwood, 2009.

Haudenosaunee Confederacy. "People of the Haudenosaunee: Confederacy Response to the Federal Framework Legislation." Press release, 15 March 2019. https://www.haudenosauneeconfederacy.com/2019/05/response-to-the-federal-framework-legislation/.

Havard, Gilles. *The Great Peace of Montreal: French-Native Diplomacy in the Seventeenth Century*. Montreal and Kingston: McGill-Queen's University Press, 2001.

Hill, Barbara-Helen. *Shaking the Rattle: Healing the Trauma of Colonization*. Penticton, BC: Theytus Books, 1995.

Hill, Dawn Martin. "Traditional Medicine and Restoration of Wellness Strategies." *International Journal of Indigenous Health* 5, no. 1 (2009): 26–42.

Hill, Gus. *Indigenous Healing: Voices of Elders and Healers*. Vernon, BC: JCharlton, 2021.

Hill, Rick. "Two Row History." 2013. http://honorthetworow.org/learn-more/history/.

Hornberger, Nancy H., ed. *Can Schools Save Indigenous Languages? Policy and Practice on Four Continents*. Hampshire, UK: Palgrave Macmillan, 2008.

Hunter, Anna. "The Violence That Indigenous Women Face." *Canadian Dimension*, 3 March 2005. https://canadiandimension.com/articles/view/the-violence-that-indigenous-women-face-anna-hunter.

Johnston, Basil. *Ojibway Heritage*. Toronto: McLelland and Stewart, 1976.

Johnston, Charles M. "Rousseaux St John, John Baptist." In *Dictionary of Canadian Biography*. http://www.biographi.ca/en/bio/rousseaux_st_john_john_baptist_5E.html.

Kelsay, Isabel Thompson. *Joseph Brant, 1743–1807: Man of Two Worlds*. Syracuse, NY: Syracuse University Press, 1984.

Kennedy-Kish Bell, Banakonda. "Indigenous Wholistic Well-Being and Healing." In *Holistic Healing: Theories, Practice and Social Change*, ed. Peter A. Dunn, 252–67. Toronto: Canadian Scholars' Press, 2019.

Kennedy-Kish Bell, Banakonda, Raven Sinclair, Ben Carniol, and Donna Baines. *Case Critical: Social Services and Social Justice in Canada*. 7th ed. Toronto: Between the Lines, 2017.

Kermoal, Nathalie, and Isabel Altamirano-Jiménez, eds. *Living on the Land: Indigenous Women's Understanding of Place*. Edmonton: Athabasca University Press, 2016.

Kimmerer, Robin Wall. *Braiding Sweetgrass: Indigenous Wisdom, Scientific Knowledge and the Teachings of Plants*. Minneapolis, MN: Milkweed, 2013.

Kushlan, James A., and James Hancock. *The Herons*. Oxford: Oxford University Press, 2004.

LaRocque, Emma. "Métis and Feminist: Ethical Reflections on Feminism, Human Rights, and Decolonization." In *Making Space for Indigenous Feminism*, ed. Joyce Green, 53–71. Black Point, NS: Fernwood, 2007.

Lavell-Harvard, Dawn Memee, and Kim Anderson, eds. *Mothers of the Nations: Indigenous Mothering as Global Resistance, Reclaiming and Recovery*. Bradford, ON: Demeter, 2014.

Lavell-Harvard, Dawn Memee, and Jeannette Corbiere Lavell, eds. *"Until Our Hearts Are on the Ground": Aboriginal Mothering, Oppression, Resistance and Rebirth*. Bradford, ON: Demeter, 2006.

Leddy, Lianne C. "The Mum with the Dark Hair: Indigenous Motherhood and the NICU." In *Writing Mothers: Narrative Acts of Care, Redemption, and Transformation*, ed. Betty Ann Martin and Michelann Parr, 65–77. Bradford, ON: Demeter, 2020.

Leduc, Timothy B. *A Canadian Climate of Mind: Passages from Fur to Energy and Beyond*. Montreal and Kingston: McGill-Queen's University Press, 2016.

– *Climate, Culture, Change: Inuit and Western Dialogues with a Warming North*. Ottawa: University of Ottawa Press, 2010.

– "Falling with Heron: Kaswen:ta Teachings on Our Roughening Waters." *Social and Cultural Geography* 21, no. 7 (2020): 925–39.

– "'Let Us Continue Free as the Air': Reconciling Social Work Education to Indigenous Lands." *Journal of Social Work Education* 54, no. 3 (2018): 412–25.

Lessels, Christina, and Timothy B. Leduc. *The Story of Iona*. Self-published, 2008.

Lippert, Charles, and Jordan Engel. "The Great Lakes in Ojibwe." *The Decolonial Atlas*, 1 December 2014. https://decolonialatlas.wordpress.com/2014/12/01/the-great-lakes-in-ojibwe/.

Logan, William Bryant. *Oak: The Frame of Civilization*. New York: Norton, 2005.

Maracle, Lee. *Celia's Song*. Toronto: Cormorant Books, 2014.

– *I Am Woman: A Native Perspective on Sociology and Feminism*. 2nd ed. Vancouver: Press Gang, 2003.

Marsden, John. *Sea-Road of the Saints: Celtic Holy Men in the Hebrides*. Edinburgh: Floris Books, 1995.

M'Gonigle, Michael, and Justine Starke. *Planet U: Sustaining the World, Reinventing the University*. Gabriola Island, BC: New Society, 2006.

McCarthy, Theresa. *In Divided Unity: Haudenosaunee Reclamation at Grand River*. Tucson: University of Arizona Press, 2016.

McIntosh, Alastair. *Soil and Soul: People versus Corporate Power*. London: Aurum, 2001.

Merchant, Carolyn. *The Death of Nature: Women, Ecology and the Scientific Revolution*. New York: Harper and Row, 1980.

Mihesuah, Devon Abbott, and Angela Cavender Wilson. "Introduction." In *Indigenizing the Academy: Transforming Scholarship and Empowering Communities*, ed. Devon Abbott Mihesuah and Angela Cavender Wilson, 1–15. Lincoln: University of Nebraska Press, 2004.

Mohawk, John. *Iroquois Creation Story: John Arthur Gibson and J.N.B. Hewitt's Myth of the Earth Grasper*. Buffalo, NY: Mohawk Publications, 2005.

– *Thinking in Indian: A John Mohawk Reader*. Ed. José Barreiro. Golden, CO: Fulcrum, 2010.

– *Utopian Legacies: A History of Conquest and Oppression in the Western World*. Santa Fe, NM: Clear Light, 1999.

Monture, Rick. *We Share Our Matters: Two Centuries of Writing and Resistance at Six Nations of the Grand River*. Winnipeg: University of Manitoba Press, 2014.

Moogk, Peter N. *La Nouvelle France: The Making of French Canada – A Cultural History*. East Lansing: Michigan State University Press, 2000.

Morrison, Carolyn, Kathleen Fox, Terry Cross, and Roger Paul. "Permanency through Wabanaki Eyes: A Narrative Perspective from 'The People Who Live Where the Sun Rises.'" *Child Welfare* 89, no. 1 (2010): 103–23.

National Inquiry into Missing and Murdered Indigenous Women and Girls (MMIWG). *Interim Report: Our Women and Girls Are Sacred*. Ottawa: Government of Canada, 2017. http://www.mmiwg-ffada.ca/files/ni-mmiwg-interim-report-en.pdf.

Neihardt, John G. *Black Elk Speaks*. Lincoln: University of Nebraska Press, 1968.

Neufeld, Hannah Tait, and Jaime Cidro, eds. *Indigenous Experiences of Pregnancy and Birth*. Bradford, ON: Demeter, 2017.

Nickel, Sarah, and Amanda Fehr, eds. *In Good Relation: History, Gender, and Kinship in Indigenous Feminisms*. Winnipeg: University of Manitoba Press, 2020.

Ó Crualaoich, Gearóid. *The Book of the Cailleach: Stories of the Wise-Woman Healer*. Cork, Ireland: Cork University Press, 2003.

Parliament of Canada. *Sessional Papers of the Dominion of Canada: Volume 16, First Session of the Sixth Parliament, Session 1887*. Ottawa: MacLean, Roger & Co., 1887. https://www.canadiana.ca/view/oocihm.9_08052_20_16/2?r=0&s=1.

Pewewardy, Cornel D. "So You Think You Hired an 'Indian' Faculty Member? The Ethnic Fraud Paradox in Higher Education." In *Indigenizing the Academy: Transforming Scholarship and Empowering Communities*, ed. Devon Abbott Mihesuah and Angela Cavender Wilson, 200–17. Lincoln: University of Nebraska Press, 2004.

Plumwood, Val. *Feminism and the Mastery of Nature*. New York: Routledge, 1993.

Podruchny, Carolyn. *Making the Voyageur World: Travelers and Traders in the North American Fur Trade*. Toronto: University of Toronto Press, 2006.

Powell, Robert, trans. *Meditations on the Tarot: A Journey into Christian Hermeticism*. New York: J.P. Tarcher/Putnam, 2002.

Ray, Celeste. *The Origins of Ireland's Holy Wells*. Oxford: Archaeopress, 2014.

– "Paying the Rounds at Ireland's Holy Wells." *Anthropos* 110, no. 2 (2015): 415–32.

Robertson, Heather. *Walking into Wilderness: The Toronto Carrying Place and Nine Mile Portage*. Winnipeg: Heartland, 2010.

Rogers, Raymond A. *Rough and Plenty: A Memoir*. Waterloo, ON: Wilfrid Laurier University Press, 2020.

Roots, Betty Ida, Donald A. Chant, and Conrad E. Heidenreich. *Special Places: The Changing Ecosystems of the Toronto Region*. Vancouver: UBC Press, 1999.

Ruiter, Zach. "Killing Cormorants: Is Ontario's Feathered Pariah about to Be Culled out of Existence?" NOW, 24 March 2019. https://nowtoronto.com/news/cormorants-doug-ford-hunting-ontario.

Runningwater, Niles Bird. "Exploring Ethnic Fraud: An Analysis of Verification Policies for American Indians in Higher Education." MA thesis, University of Texas at Austin, 1996.

Rymhs, Deena. *From the Iron House: Imprisonment in First Nations Writing*. Waterloo, ON: Wilfrid Laurier University Press, 2008.

Sagard, Gabriel. *Sagard's Long Journey to the Country of the Hurons*. New York: Greenwood, 1968.

Sams, Jamie. *The 13 Original Clan Mothers: Your Sacred Path to Discovering the Gifts, Talents, and Abilities of the Feminine through the Ancient Teachings of the Sisterhood*. New York: Harper Collins, 1994.

Saul, John Ralston. *Reflections of a Siamese Twin: Canada at the End of the Twentieth Century*. Toronto: Viking, 1997.

Senior, Elinor Kyte. *From Royal Township to Industrial City: Cornwall 1784–1984*. Belleville, ON: Mika, 1983.

Shiva, Vandana. *Monocultures of the Mind: Perspectives on Biodiversity and Biotechnology*. London and New York: Zed Books, 1993.

– "Reductionism and Regeneration: A Crisis in Science." In Maria Mies and Vandana Shiva, *Ecofeminism*, 22–35. London and New York: Zed Books, 2014.

Simard, Estelle. "Culturally Restorative Child Welfare Practice – A Special Emphasis on Cultural Attachment Theory." *First People Child and Family Review* 4, no. 2 (2009): 44–61.

Simpson, Audra. *Mohawk Interruptus: Political Life across the Borders of Settler States*. Durham, NC: Duke University Press, 2014.

Simpson, Leanne. "Anticolonial Strategies for the Recovery and Maintenance of Indigenous Knowledge." *American Indian Quarterly* 28, nos 3–4 (2004): 373–84.

– *As We Have Always Done: Indigenous Freedom through Radical Resistance*. Minneapolis: University of Minnesota Press, 2017.

– "Birthing an Indigenous Resurgence: Decolonizing Our Pregnancy and Birthing Ceremonies." In *"Until Our Hearts Are on the Ground": Aboriginal Mothering,*

Oppression, Resistance and Rebirth, ed. Dawn Memee Lavell-Harvard and Jeannette Corbiere Lavell, 25–33. Bradford, ON: Demeter, 2006.

– *Dancing on Our Turtle's Back: Stories of Nishnaabeg Re-Creation, Resurgence and a New Emergence*. Winnipeg: Arbeiter Ring, 2011.

Smith, Linda Tuhiwai. *Decolonizing Methodologies: Research and Indigenous Peoples*. London and New York: Zed Books; Dunedin, New Zealand: University of Otago Press, 1999.

Snyder, Emily, Val Napoleon, and John Borrows. "Gender and Violence: Drawing on Indigenous Legal Resources." *UBC Law Review* 48, no. 2 (2015): 593–654.

Spittal, William Guy, ed. *Iroquois Women: An Anthology*. Ohsweken, ON: Iroqurafts, 1990.

Stewart-Harawira, Makere. "Practising Indigenous Feminism: Resistance to Imperialism." In *Making Space for Indigenous Feminism*, ed. Joyce Green, 124–37. Black Point, NS: Fernwood, 2007.

TallBear, Kim. "Standing with and Speaking as Faith: A Feminist-Indigenous Approach to Inquiry." Journal of Research Practice 10, no. 2, art. N17 (2014). http://jrp.icaap.org/index.php/jrp/article/view/405/371.

Tehota'kerá:tonh (Jeremy Green). *Pathways to Creating Onkwehonwehnéha Speakers at Six Nations of the Grand River Territory*. Six Nations of the Grand River Territory: Six Nations Polytechnic, 2017.

Tehota'kerá:tonh (Jeremy Green) and Owennatékha (Brian Maracle). "The Root-Word Method for Building Proficient Second-Language Speakers of Polysynthetic Languages: Onkwawén:na Kentyókhwa Adult Mohawk Language Immersion Program." In *The Routledge Handbook of Language Revitalization*, ed. Leanne Hinton, Leena Huss, and Gerald Roche, 146–55. New York: Routledge, 2018.

Theriault, Noah, Timothy B. Leduc, Audra Mitchell, June Mary Rubis, and Norma Jacobs (Gae Ho Hwako). "Living Protocols: Remaking Worlds in the Face of Extinction." *Social and Cultural Geography* 21, no. 7 (2020): 893–908.

Thomas, Jacob, with Terry Boyle. *Teachings from the Longhouse*. 1994. Reprint, Toronto: Stoddart, 2013.

Trigger, Bruce. *The Children of Aataentsic: A History of the Huron People to 1660*. Montreal and Kingston: McGill-Queen's University Press, 1987.

Truth and Reconciliation Commission of Canada. *Honouring the Truth, Reconciling for the Future: Summary of the Final Report*. Ottawa: Government of Canada, 2015. https://publications.gc.ca/site/eng/9.800288/publication.html.

Turkle, Sherry. *Alone Together: Why We Expect More from Technology and Less from Each Other*. New York: Basic Books, 2011.

Turner, Dale. *This Is Not a Peace Pipe: Towards a Critical Indigenous Philosophy*. Toronto: University of Toronto Press, 2006.

Wagamese, Richard. "To Say All My Relations …" http://misiwenirelations.ca/.

Ware, Syrus, Joan Rusza, and Giselle Dias. "It Can't Be Fixed Because It's Not Broken: Racism and Disability in the Prison Industrial Complex." In *Disability Incarcerated: Imprisonment and Disability in the United States and Canada*, ed. Liat Ben-Moshe, Chris Chapman, and Allison C. Carey, 163–84. New York: Palgrave Macmillan, 2014.

Williams, Florence. "This Is Your Brain on Nature." *National Geographic*. https://www.nationalgeographic.com/magazine/article/call-to-wild.

Wilson, Shawn. *Research Is Ceremony: Indigenous Research Methods*. Black Point, NS: Fernwood, 2008.

Wohlleben, Peter. *The Hidden Life of Trees: What They Feel, How They Communicate*. Vancouver: Greystone Books, 2015.

Women's Earth Alliance and Native Youth Sexual Health Network. *Violence on the Land, Violence on Our Bodies: Building an Indigenous Response to Environmental Violence*. http://landbodydefense.org/uploads/files/VLVBReportToolkit2016.pdf.

Woodworth, William (Raweno:kwas), and Timothy B. Leduc. "We Are Renewable: Reconciling Peaceful Relations between First Nations and Canada Requires Burying the Weapons of the Past." *Alternatives Journal* 42, no. 1 (2016): 26–9.

Zinger, Ivan. *Office of the Correctional Investigator: Annual Report, 2017–2018*. Ottawa: Office of the Correctional Investigator, 2018. https://www.oci-bec.gc.ca/cnt/rpt/index-eng.aspx.

Contributors

GISELLE DIAS is queer, disabled, and mixed-race, a Métis community organizer, an activist, and a scholar. Her ancestors, including her grandparents, travelled to Ontario from India, the Seychelle Islands, England, Ireland, and across Turtle Island. She is in her third year of the doctoral program at Wilfrid Laurier University in the Faculty of Social Work, Indigenous Field of Study, and is the program coordinator at the Centre for Indigegogy. Giselle has worked in the field of prisoners' rights, penal abolition, and transformative justice for twenty-five years.

SHELLY HACHEY is a Haudenosaunee/Oneida woman of the Turtle Clan from Six Nations of the Grand River Territory. She holds a bachelor of social work and a master of social work, both completed in the Indigenous Field of Study program at Wilfrid Laurier University. Shelly currently works as a child and family well-being policy analyst for Six Nations Social Services and is passionate about being part of changing current systems of oppression toward her people. A mother of four beautiful children, she is also a spouse, an auntie, a friend, and a daughter.

BARBARA-HELEN HILL, who is of Haudenosaunee/Iroquois and British Isles heritage, was born at Six Nations of the Grand River Territory. Helen, as she is called, received her master's degree in American studies from SUNY at Buffalo and is a storyteller both in her fabric arts and in the books and poetry that she writes. Her work draws on stories that she has heard from generations past. Helen is the author of *Shaking the Rattle: Healing the Trauma of Colonization* (1995), republished through Amazon in 2017.

GAE HO HWAKO (NORMA JACOBS) is of the Wolf Clan in the Cayuga Nation of the Great Haudenosaunee Confederacy. Gae Ho Hwako is her Onkwehón:we name. It means "ancestral females holding the canoe before me," and it positions her in an ancestral line of great women of the Wolf Clan. She has been given the responsibilities in the canoe of empowering herself, family, community, nation, and the Confederacy. Her mother told her that it was important to know the cultural ways of the Cayuga so that she would be able to help explain them to people, and it is these experiences and responsibilities that she holds as a Longhouse Faith Keeper, an advisor to the National Inquiry into Missing and Murdered Indigenous Women and Girls (MMIWG), and an Elder who has taught at universities, colleges, and other institutions.

AWNJIBENAYSEEKWE (BANAKONDA KENNEDY-KISH BELL) is an Elder, cultural advisor, traditional practitioner, teacher, author, poet, and artist who honours, respects and feels gratitude for her teachers, family, and community. She is an educator who has designed Indigenous-informed curriculum and content that reflects her commitment to the value of Indigenous teachings, concepts, lifeways, and practices. She is a co-author of the seventh edition of *Case Critical: Social Services and Social Justice in Canada* (2017), written with Raven Sinclair, Ben Carniol, and Donna Baines.

LIANNE C. LEDDY is a member of Serpent River First Nation and an associate professor of Indigenous studies at Wilfrid Laurier University. Her research is focused on questions of land, gender, and Indigenous methodologies. Leddy's work has appeared in the journals *Canadian Historical Review*, *Oral History Forum*, and *Herizons* and in several edited collections.

TIMOTHY B. LEDUC is an associate professor at Wilfrid Laurier University and the author of three books, including *Climate, Culture, Change: Inuit and Western Dialogues with a Warming North* (2010) and *A Canadian Climate of Mind: Passages from Fur to Energy and Beyond* (2016). His work is rooted in his French Canadien ancestral relations with Indigenous nations along the great Saint Lawrence River. He is a committed partner and the father of two children, who inspire his writing in this book.

KITTY LYNN LICKERS is the community food animator at Six Nations of the Grand River Territory. Kitty shares food and knowledge while teaching classes in and out of her community. She has recently contributed to the edited collection *Recipes for Reciprocity: The Regenerative Way from Seed to Table* (2021) and has published journal articles on community food. Kitty believes that gardens grow community.

KAWENNAKON (BONNIE WHITLOW) was born into the Kanyen'kehaka (Mohawk Nation) and the Yonkwaskare:wake (Bear Clan) of the Ohswe:ken (Six Nations of the Grand River Territory). She is the single mom of a beautiful young man named Rawennahatyes. Kawennakon has spent decades not only reconnecting to her cultural legacy and ancestral practices but also creating similar opportunities for others.

Index